Encyclopedia of Slide Layouts

Inspiration for Visual Communication

Andrew V. Abela, Ph.D.
and
Paul J. Radich

Published by Soproveitto Press
Great Falls, VA

THE ENCYCLOPEDIA OF SLIDE LAYOUTS:
Inspiration for Visual Communication

Library of Congress Control Number: 2014913880
ISBN 978-0-9960013-8-0

For additional copies of this book,
visit www.ExtremePresentation.com

The encyclopedia of slide layouts: inspiration for visual communication / Andrew V. Abela, Ph. D and Paul J. Radich

1. Business presentations. 2. Business communication.
3. Visual communication. 4. Slide layouts I. Title

Design by Marja Walker

ACKNOWLEDGEMENTS

This book would not have been conceived if not for all the engaged participants in our workshops, who after using the Slide Chooser™ said: "This is a great tool, but it would be really helpful to have real world examples of these layouts, that have been used successfully." To all of you—the people from the following organizations—thank you for joining us on a mission to change the world, one presentation at a time:

AARP
A+E Networks
Abbott
Agilent Technologies
American Express ~ Interactive
American Family Insurance
American Funds ~ Cap Group
Baxter International
BP plc
Brown Forman (Jack Daniel's)
Burger King
CEB - The Corporate Executive Board
CMI Market Research
Cogeco Cable - Canada
Colgate-Palmolive Company
CRC - Corporate Researchers Conference
Dell Inc.
Deloitte
E.&J. Gallo Winery
eBay ~ PayPal
Ericsson
Expedia, Inc.
Exxon-Mobil
Fiserv, Inc.
HJ Heinz
Hensel Phelps Construction
Infinitive
Iron Mountain
JP Morgan Chase
Jones Lang LaSalle
Kimberly-Clark Corporation
Kraft
Marriott International
Microsoft Corporation
Motorola
Navy Federal Credit Union
NeighborCare ~ Omnicare
The Nielsen Company
Novartis
Pfizer
PMRG - The Pharmaceutical Market Research Group
Royal Bank of Canada
Sam's Club ~ Wal-Mart
SCIP - Strategic and Competitive Intelligence ProfessionalsStarbucks
State Farm Insurance
True Value Hardware
US Census Bureau
US GSA - General Services Administration
US OMB - Office of Management and Budget
US White House - Performance Improvement Council
UnitedHealth Group
Visa, Inc.
Volkswagen ~ Audi
WW Grainger
Wm. Wrigley Jr. Co. ~ Mars
World Kitchen
Xerox

This book has been a labor of love from the beginning. What strange kind of person is in love with slides? Well, it is not the slides that we love, but the clarity of communication and the unity of purpose that arises from a well-designed slide which inspires our passion. That passion is shared by the many people who devoted their time and energy to bring this work to life, and most especially those who provided the slides that are featured in this *Encyclopedia*. Therefore our deepest gratitude is extended to Scott Christofferson, Eric Braun, and Erin O'Donnell at the Corporate Executive Board, Randy Krum of Infonewt, Irina Dobrova at Infographer, Kris Ellis of SmartDraw, and numerous other contributors. Our warm thanks also go out to Rob Headrick for his graphic design work, Marja Walker for design and layout work, Sophia Mason for editing, Theresa Abela for her research efforts, and Kathy Otey for her invaluable help constructing the various drafts of this work.

Introduction: Harness the Power of Visual Communication

Despite numerous presentation books and training workshops, "death by PowerPoint" continues to ravage business meetings, classrooms, and training sessions. The problem at the root of death by PowerPoint is simple: too many bullet-list slides. Research has shown that projecting a slide whose main feature is a list of bullets—while speaking at the same time—is less effective than speaking *without any visuals at all*. This is because viewers try to read and listen at the same time, and end up doing neither particularly well (a fact noted in the first book in the Extreme Presentation™ series, *Advanced Presentations by Design*). So should we no longer use any slides at all? No, because other research indicates that overall, visuals do strengthen communication. The real question, then, is: *What kinds of visuals work best?*

In our workshops with executives and their teams around the globe, participants develop their presentations by following the 10-step Extreme Presentation™ method (see facing page). But even before we work on the art of visual storytelling (steps 7 and 8 on the facing page), participants first work through six key planning steps: they make sure they know the communication preferences of their audience, their own objectives for the presentation, their audience's challenge or business problem, the presenter's solution to that problem, what evidence they have to support their solution, what stories or cases they can use to illustrate or enrich their key points, and what the overall narrative sequence will be for the presentation. Then, and only then, do we talk about visual design. (Implicitly, you too will likely benefit from addressing each of these areas before proceeding to the visual design phase of your presentation; if you need help with any of these steps, look at the "Design a Presentation" section of our website, www.ExtremePresentation.com.)

We begin our discussion about visual design by emphasizing the key point that the kind of slide layout that will be most effective depends on the purpose of your presentation: in particular, are you trying to inform and entertain a large audience, or are you trying to educate or persuade a smaller audience?

Advanced Presentations by Design developed the idea of using different presentation styles for different purposes, and proposed that "death by PowerPoint" occurs when different styles are muddled on

The Extreme Presentation™ Method

Ten Steps to Presentation Impact

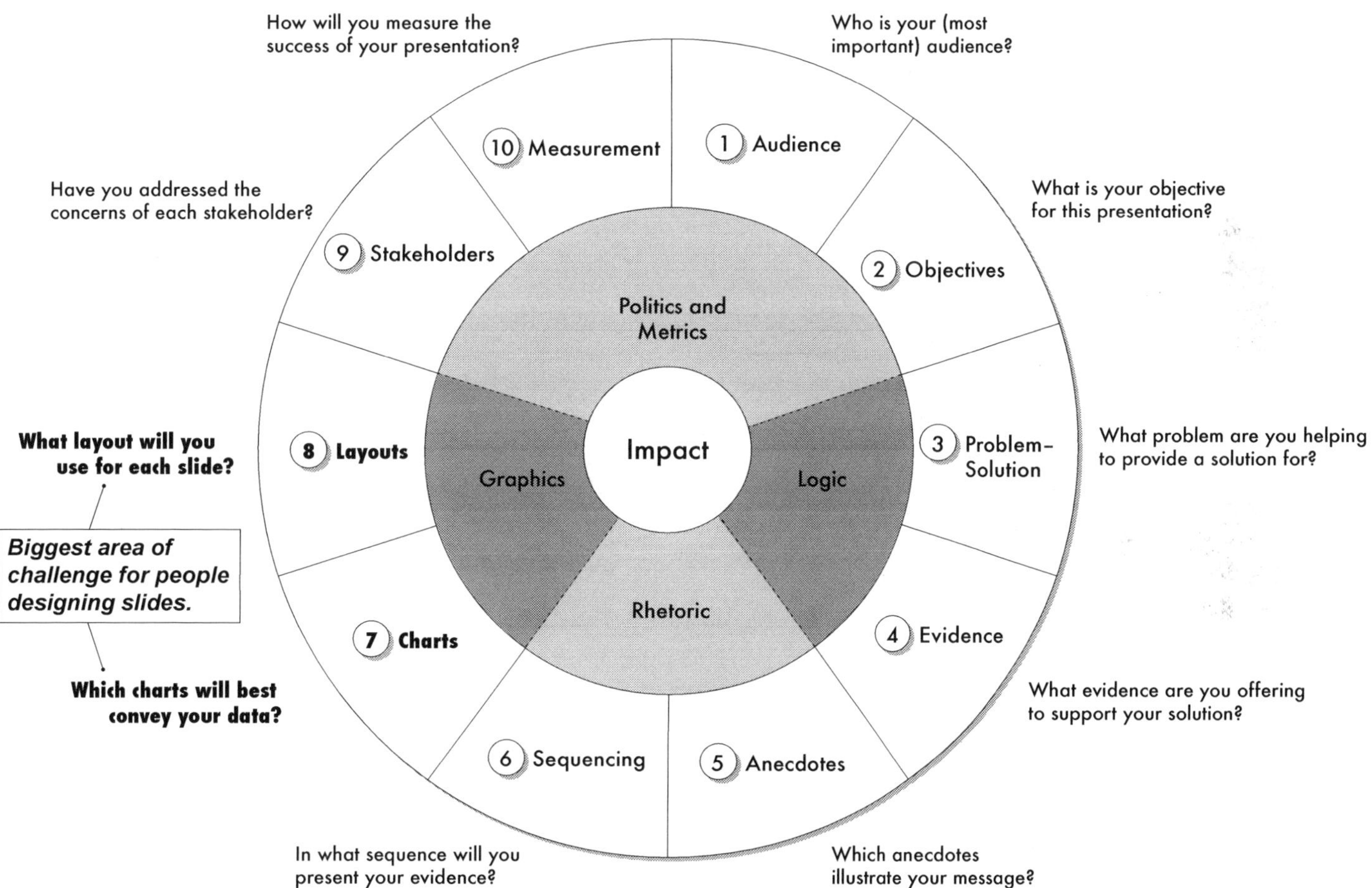

the same slide. The two paradigmatic styles are Ballroom style, which consists of projected slides with attractive pictures and very few words, and Conference Room style, which uses printed or electronically distributed slides with lots of graphics and text, while always passing the "squint test." A slide passes the squint test if its main point is reasonably apparent even when the viewer squints at it, making the text illegible. If a slide passes the squint test, that indicates that viewers will be able to grasp its central idea quickly, without feeling a need to read all the text on the slide at once (see facing page for details).

Well-designed Ballroom style slides do not contain much text and therefore do not suffer from the problem of "death by PowerPoint." They can be very effective for communicating big ideas. But research suggests that if you want to do something more than just convey ideas—if you want to *persuade* your audience to *do something* with your ideas—then you need to ensure that your communication contains all (and only) the relevant details, minimizes distractions, and fosters interactivity. Ballroom style slides do none of these things particularly well. They can't convey much detail because of the small number of words on each slide, and the images on them can be distracting. Also, a projected presentation doesn't tend to foster much interaction. You can add an "Any questions?" slide at the end, but the audience can't really engage in discussion about the material on the slides without the presenter having to do cumbersome clicking back and forth through the presentation—and there's not much detail on each slide in any case.

By contrast, a Conference Room style presentation is a great vehicle for providing details, avoiding distraction, and fostering interactivity. The key to this type of presentation is printing or digitally distributing the slides rather than projecting them. Printing allows higher resolution, and consequently smaller fonts (9 to 12 point instead of 24). The space taken up by fonts increases geometrically as the font size increases, so using a 12 point font allows you to fit not twice but four times the amount of text allowed by a 24 point font, and a 9 point font fits almost nine times as much text as 24 point.

The following page contrasts the Ballroom style and the Conference Room style, based on the purpose of your presentation. The key point: pick which style is more relevant for your goals, and then follow the design principles of that style.

Different Presentation Situations Call for Different Styles

Because the two styles have different purposes…

…each style has its own design principles.

	Ballroom Style	Conference Room Style
	To inform or entertain large audiences	To persuade or educate smaller audiences
		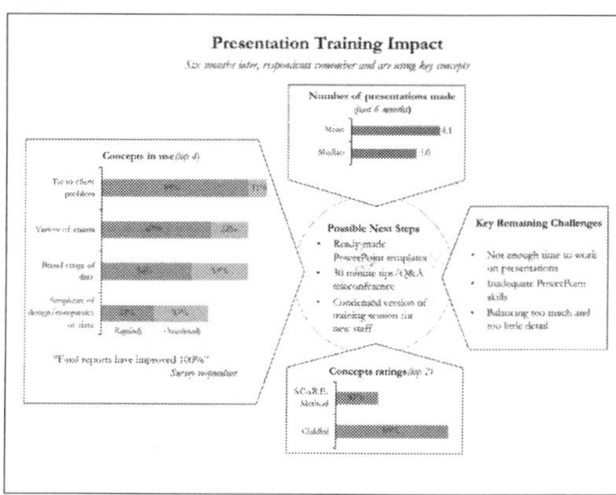
	1. Rich, relevant visuals 2. Projected, not printed 3. Minimal text	1. Extensive, relevant detail 2. Printed or distributed electronically, not projected 3. Each page passes the squint test
Typical Information Flow	Primarily one-way (speaker to audience)	Two-way (interactive and collaborative)
Audience Size	Larger: ~50 to thousands	Smaller: 1 to ~50
Visual Metaphor	Video documentary	Blueprint or architectural drawing
Use of Color, Sound, Animation	Extensive but appropriate (i.e., reinforces main message, rather than distracts from it)	Some color, for emphasis, or none at all
Delivery Technology	Projected—using attractive images and graphics, animation, video, zooming (e.g., PowerPoint 2013 magnifying glass feature; Prezi), etc.	Distributed—paper or device
Use of Text	Minimal (ideally just titles and labels). Use diagrams, illustrations, and photos instead.	Extensive, but well laid out on page
Minimum Type Size	24 point	9 point
Delivery Speed	1 slide per 1–5 minutes of presentation	1–10 pages per hour of presentation

But doesn't all this text return us to the problem of trying to read and listen at the same time—the problem of death by PowerPoint? This is where the squint test comes in. When a slide passes the squint test, viewers can tell what the slide is about and, therefore, they do not feel the need to start reading everything on the slide—they are more willing simply to follow along on the slide while listening to the presenter. What you're aiming for (to paraphrase Edward Tufte*) is simplicity of design and complexity of detail: a design that passes the squint test is simple and immediately comprehensible by the audience, and it organizes the complex details on the page that are necessary for you to achieve your communication goals (see facing page for an example). The layout of the slide is one of the most powerful—yet most underutilized—communication tools you have at your fingertips. When the very layout of the slide reinforces and communicates the main message of the slide, then you are harnessing the power of visual storytelling.

The minimalist design of Conference Room style slides also reduces distraction, and they are designed to be distributed to the audience, either as paper copies, or as electronic copies with the audience following along on their own laptops or tablets. Because the projector remains switched off and each person has his or her own copy of the presentation, this tends to encourage interaction and enables the audience to engage with your content—and with you—in a much more powerful way. Research shows that the greatest form of persuasion is *self-persuasion*—and Conference Room style fosters this by enabling your audience to focus on the details and interact with your content—ultimately making it their own.

Now we know generally what kind of slide is needed to maximize presentation success. So why the *Encyclopedia of Slide Layouts*? When we teach Conference Room style in our workshops, the single most frequent request we get is, "Can we see more examples of effective Conference Room style presentations?" Hence this book, with over 130 Conference Room style slides—each one used successfully in the real world and culled from our search through thousands of excellent slide layouts from leading consultancies as well as companies that practice the Extreme Presentation method—all of which pass the squint test, and all organized by type of layout design.

* *The Visual Display of Quantitative Information, 2nd ed.* (Cheshire, Connecticut: Graphics Press, 2001).

Anatomy of a "Conference Room" Style Presentation

Use a Conference Room style presentation when you are trying to persuade or educate a small group—e.g., seeking approval for an initiative, selling a product, service, or idea, or pitching a new venture or investment.

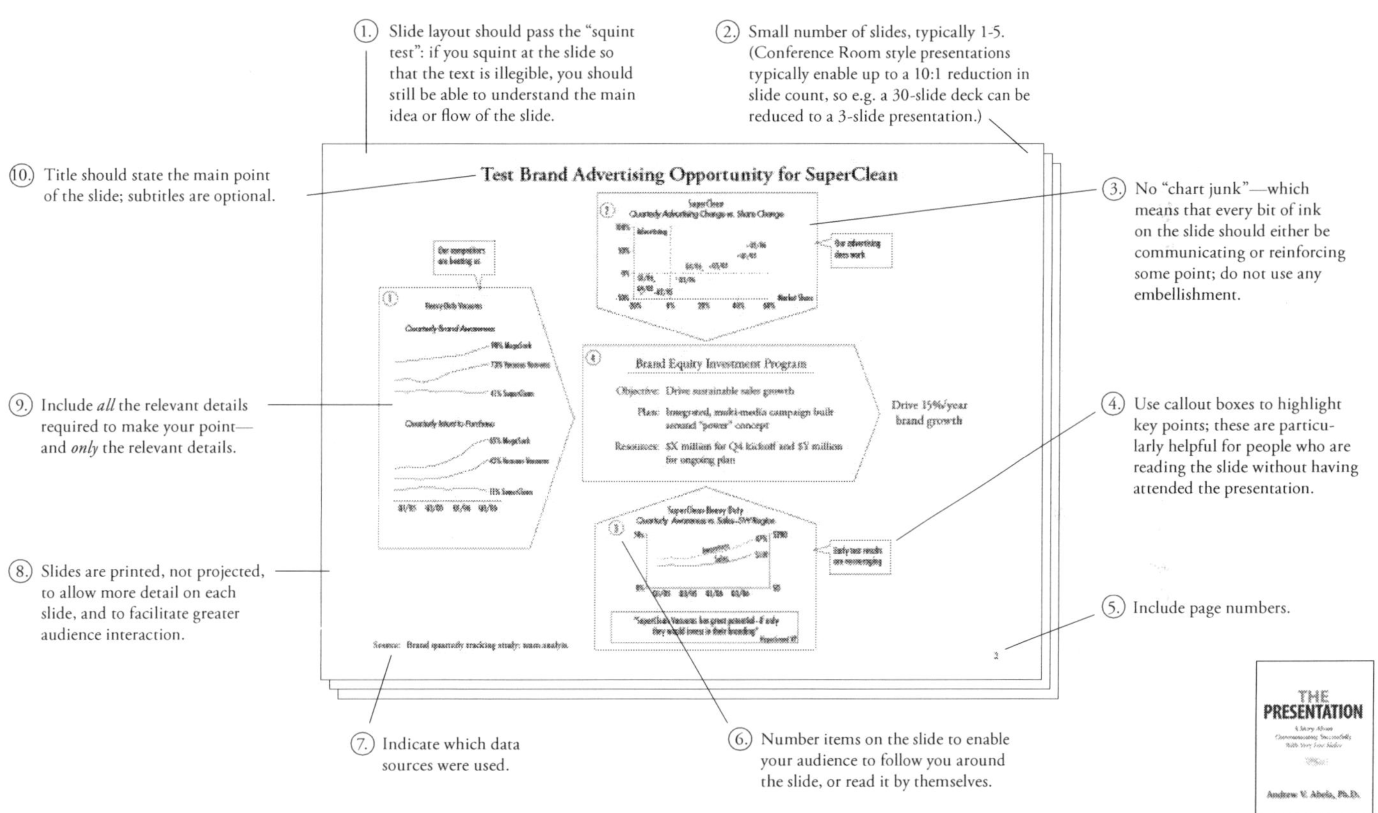

Read *The Presentation: A Story About Communicating Successfully With Very Few Slides.* Available on Amazon.com for US $7.50.

For more information on how to design a Conference Room style presentation, visit www.ExtremePresentation.com/Design and read Dr. Abela's books *Advanced Presentations by Design* and *The Presentation.*

How to Use This Book

To use the book, turn to the Slide Chooser™—the visual Table of Contents on pages x and xi—for ideas on which layout designs could be suitable for your presentation; then turn to the appropriate chapters to review the relevant examples (see also the alphabetical Table of Contents on page xii). If you are looking for guidance on how to use these slides, check out our website, and our blog at ExtremePresentation.typepad.com to learn "Practical Ways to Harness the Power of Visual Communication."

If you create any slides that you are particularly proud of, we'd like to see them. Please send them to us (with any confidential information disguised or removed, and with your written permission to use them "as is" or with modification). If we include your submission in the 2nd edition of this book, we'll send you a copy when it comes out. We invite you to join us on our mission: to change the world, one presentation at a time.

Happy presenting!

Andrew V. Abela and Paul Radich

How to Use the Slide Chooser™ on the Following Pages

On the following two-page spread, you will find the Slide Chooser™—the graphical table of contents for this book. After you have determined the main point or message of a slide, you can start at the center of the Slide Chooser™, on page xi—with the question "What is the main point of the slide?" If your slide is trying to explain something—how a process works, why something happened, who is responsible, etc.—then follow the line to the left, to page x, and follow the appropriate path to discover which layouts will be most helpful. On the other hand, if your slide is trying to recommend something—what decision we should make, how to get there from here, why your proposal will achieve certain results, etc.—then follow the line to the right as it branches out, and find layouts that will be relevant.

Each layout has a page number near it so you can find the chapter with the related examples. Each slide example comes from a real presentation that was used successfully. To highlight why each of the layouts works well, we have added a brief commentary on the left-hand page facing each slide. If you find additional slides that communicate extremely well, or if you find additional layout types that pass the squint test, please send them our way—with your permission, we would be happy to share them with the community, either online or in the 2nd edition of this book.

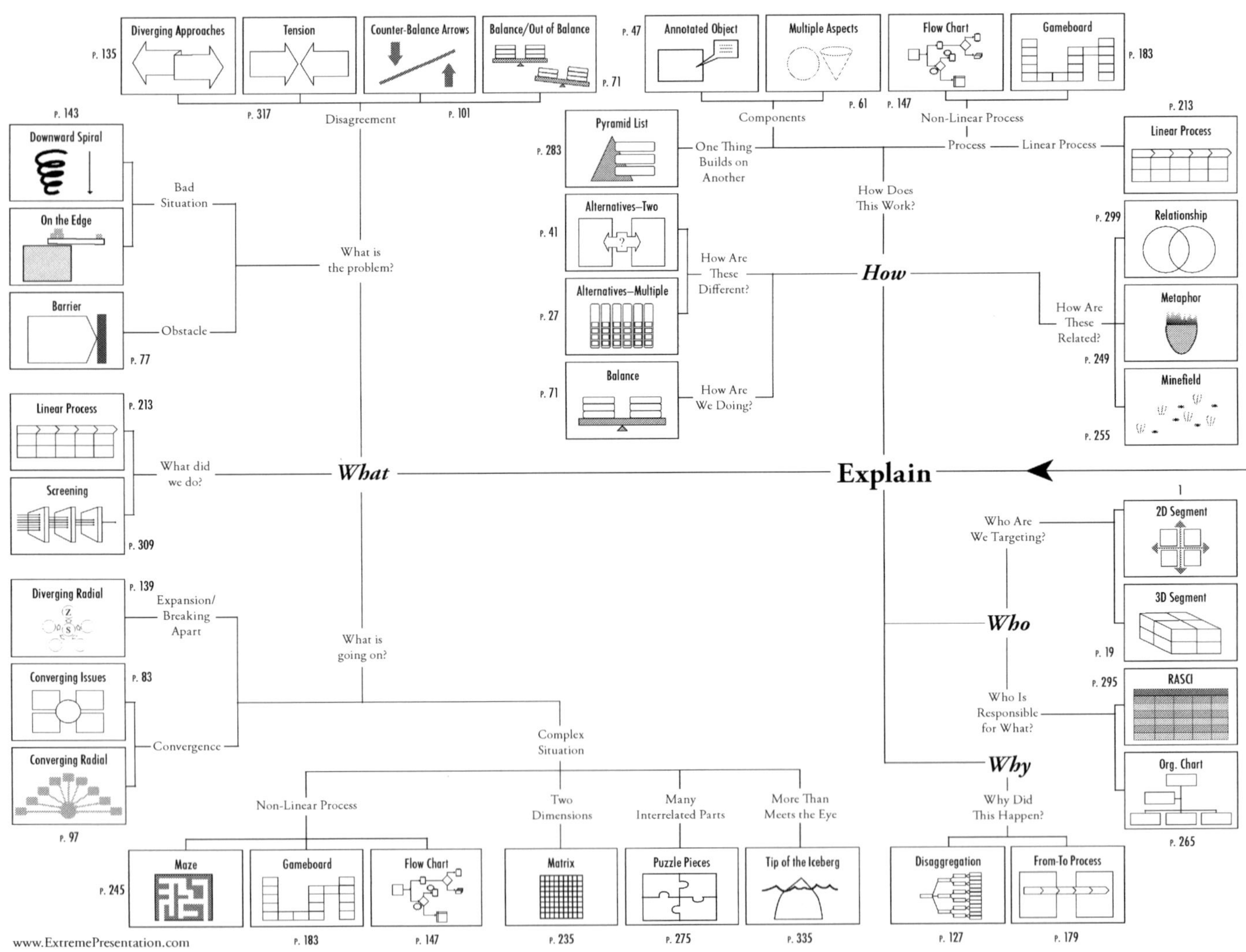
Explain
What
How
Who
Why
What is the problem?
Disagreement
Diverging Approaches
P. 135
Tension
P. 317
Counter-Balance Arrows
P. 101
Balance/Out of Balance
P. 71
Bad Situation
Downward Spiral
P. 143
On the Edge
Obstacle
Barrier
P. 77
What did we do?
Linear Process
P. 213
Screening
P. 309
What is going on?
Expansion/ Breaking Apart
Diverging Radial
P. 139
Convergence
Converging Issues
P. 83
Converging Radial
P. 97
Complex Situation
Non-Linear Process
Maze
P. 245
Gameboard
P. 183
Flow Chart
P. 147
Two Dimensions
Matrix
P. 235
Many Interrelated Parts
Puzzle Pieces
P. 275
More Than Meets the Eye
Tip of the Iceberg
P. 335
How Does This Work?
Components
Annotated Object
P. 47
Multiple Aspects
P. 61
Non-Linear Process
Flow Chart
P. 147
Gameboard
P. 183
Process
Linear Process
Linear Process
P. 213
One Thing Builds on Another
Pyramid List
P. 283
How Are These Different?
Alternatives–Two
P. 41
Alternatives–Multiple
P. 27
How Are We Doing?
Balance
P. 71
How Are These Related?
Relationship
P. 299
Metaphor
P. 249
Minefield
P. 255
Who Are We Targeting?
2D Segment
1
3D Segment
P. 19
Who Is Responsible for What?
RASCI
P. 295
Org. Chart
P. 265
Why Did This Happen?
Disaggregation
P. 127
From-To Process
P. 179
www.ExtremePresentation.com

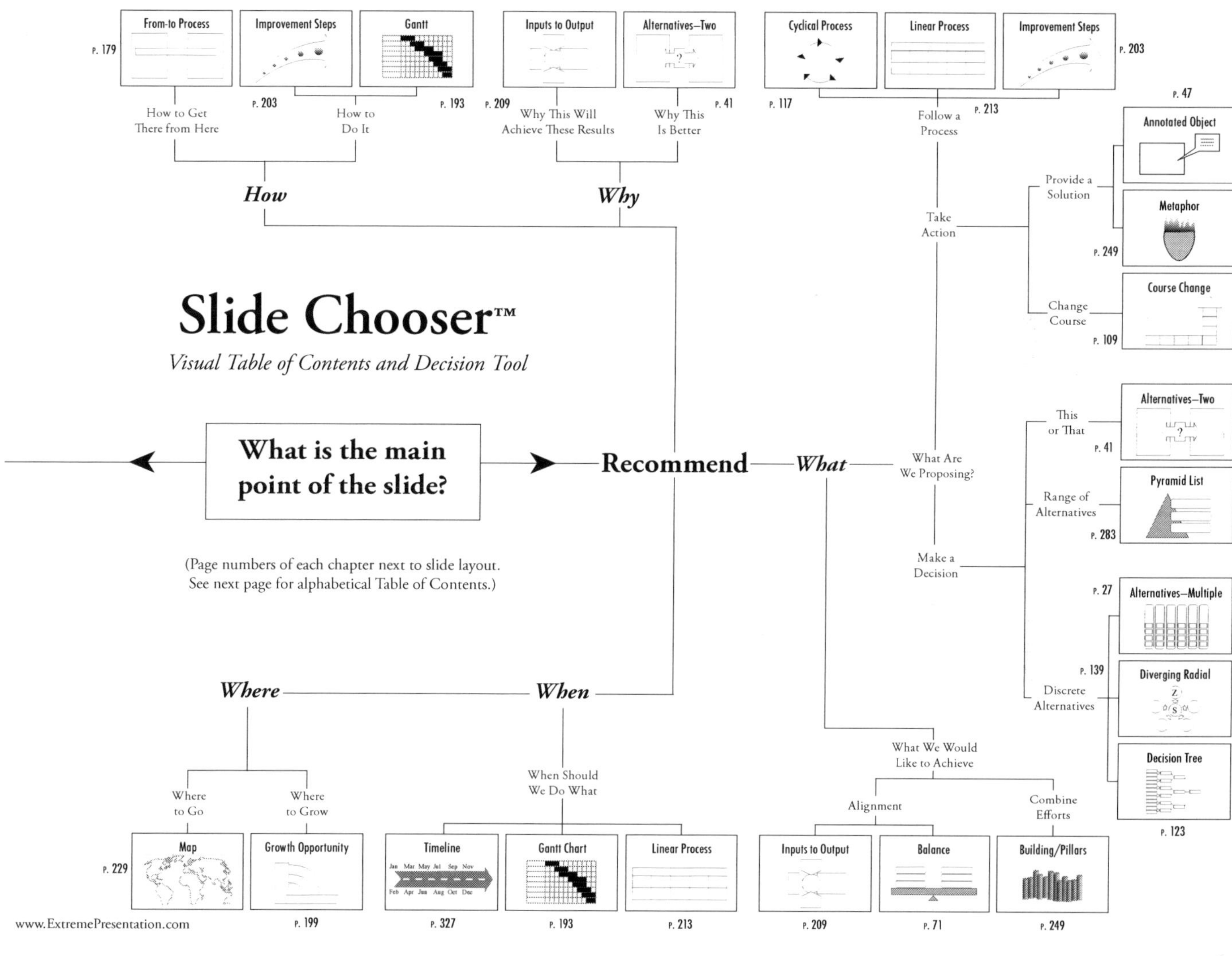
From-to Process
P. 179
Improvement Steps
P. 203
Gantt
P. 193
How to Get
There from Here
How to
Do It
How
Inputs to Output
P. 209
Alternatives–Two
P. 41
Why This Will
Achieve These Results
Why This
Is Better
Why
Cyclical Process
P. 117
Linear Process
P. 213
Improvement Steps
P. 203
Follow a
Process
Annotated Object
P. 47
Metaphor
P. 249
Provide a
Solution
Take
Action
Course Change
P. 109
Change
Course
Slide Chooser™
Visual Table of Contents and Decision Tool
What is the main
point of the slide?
Recommend
What
What Are
We Proposing?
Alternatives–Two
This
or That
P. 41
Pyramid List
Range of
Alternatives
P. 283
Make a
Decision
(Page numbers of each chapter next to slide layout.
See next page for alphabetical Table of Contents.)
Alternatives–Multiple
P. 27
Diverging Radial
P. 139
Discrete
Alternatives
Decision Tree
P. 123
Where
When
Where
to Go
Where
to Grow
When Should
We Do What
What We Would
Like to Achieve
Alignment
Combine
Efforts
Map
P. 229
Growth Opportunity
P. 199
Timeline
P. 327
Gantt Chart
P. 193
Linear Process
P. 213
Inputs to Output
P. 209
Balance
P. 71
Building/Pillars
P. 249
www.ExtremePresentation.com

TABLE OF CONTENTS

CHAPTER 1: "2D SEGMENT" LAYOUT

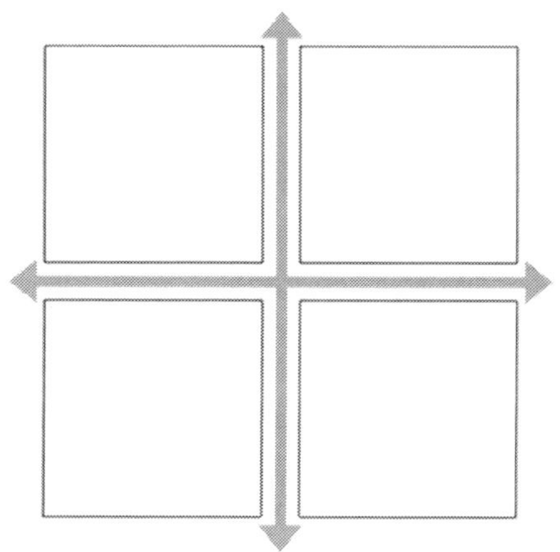

The 2D Segment layout illustrates a complex issue by drawing it out along two dimensions, which helps the audience distinguish between two distinct aspects of the issue. In a simple but common usage of the layout, each axis is divided into "high" and "low"; and the intersection of the high and low values results in a 2x2 grid. As we shall see, further complexity can be illustrated by dividing each axis into more than two values, resulting in more than four segments.

How to draw the "2D Segment" Layout

PowerFrameworks

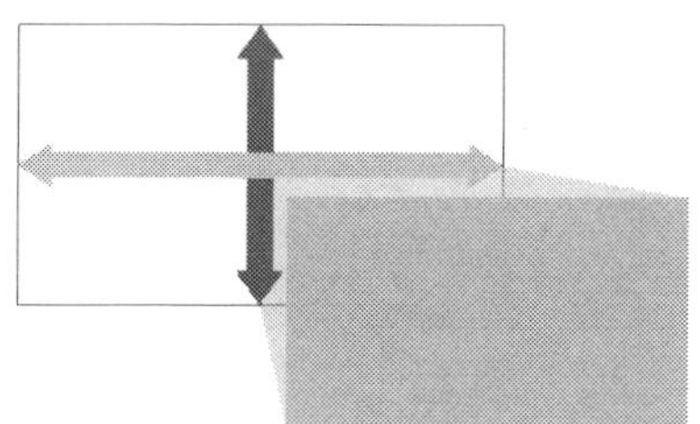

www.PowerFrameworks.com
Keyword Search "RE027","RE027-re027_matrices-Matrix"

SmartArt

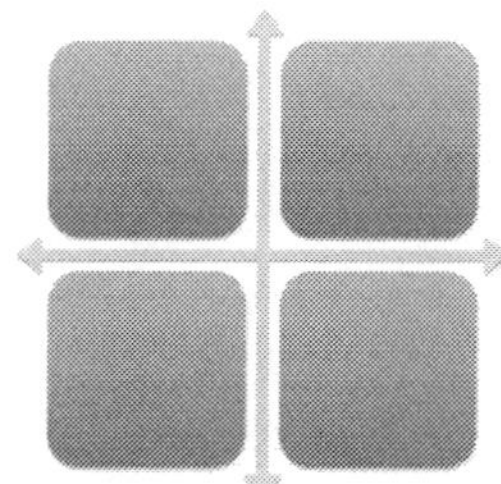

PowerPoint SmartArt
Matrix, Grid Matrix

Slide: "The Bottom Line: Lack of Focus"

In this standard version of the 2D Segment layout, each axis is divided into two sections, and the resulting intersection of values yields four segments. Here the vertical axis of Effectiveness is divided into higher- and lower-performing banks, and the horizontal axis of Efficiency is divided in the same way. The 2x2 grid holds the actual percentages of institutions falling into each segment, and each segment's text label offers a somewhat humorous description of the institutions in that group: "Incomparable" for the banks that are highly efficient and effective, and "Inanimate" for the banks that are neither. The gray shading draws the audience's attention to the three suboptimal segments, which represent over 75% of all respondents.

Board view—The result of a traditional deposit-gathering approach is disturbing: more than 3 in 4 institutions are ineffective, inefficient or both at growing deposits. Without a substantial re-think of deposit gathering, much of the industry will soon be unable to remain competitive.

THE BOTTOM LINE: LACK OF FOCUS

Distribution[1] of Institutions by Efficiency and Effectiveness on Demand Deposit

Percentage of All Institutions, Global, 2005

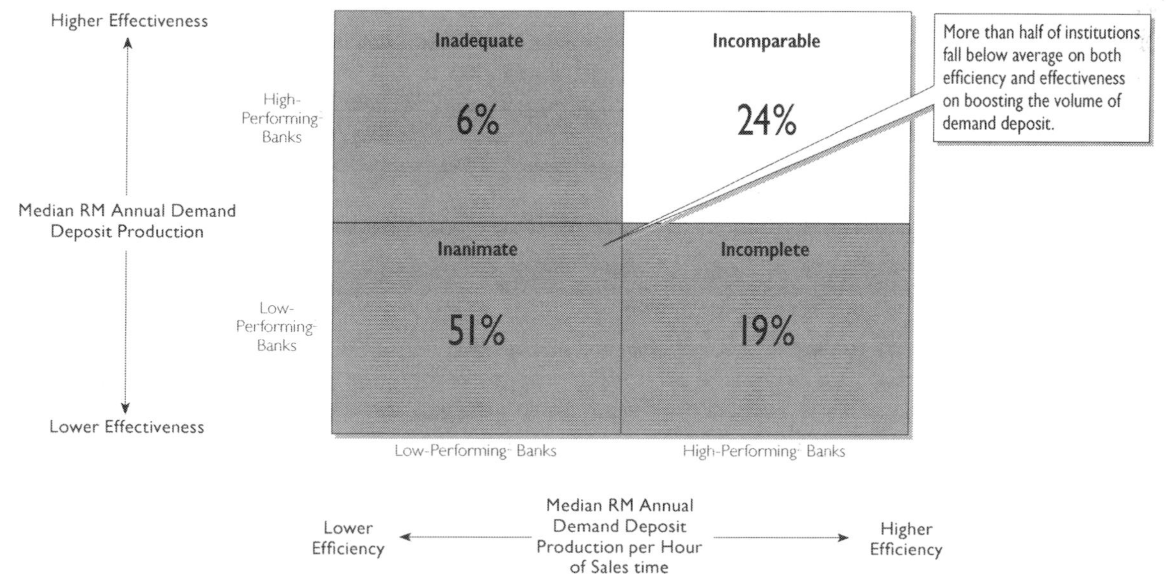

n = 44 institutions.

n = 4,211 RMs.

[1] Adjusted for variances in currencies, geographies, and customer revenue segments.

[2] Defined as above or below the average value of all median bank values.

Source: CEB Global Survey of Commercial Bankers; CEB Analysis; CEB research.

Slide: "Typical Scenario Planning Approach"

Rather than simply naming a number or percentage, this version of the 2D Segment layout embeds an abundance of qualitative data in each segment. On the right side of the chart, the 2x2 grid shows Research & Development Output divided into Centralized vs. Individual focus on the horizontal axis, and Incremental vs. Breakthrough Innovation on the vertical axis. The resulting four segments, beginning in the upper right and moving counter-clockwise, are Breakthrough Innovation and Individual ("Haves and Have Nots"), Breakthrough Innovation and Centralized ("Rationing Innovation"), Incremental Innovation and Centralized ("Payers Rule"), and Incremental Innovation and Individual ("Price Sensitive Patients"). In addition to a name in the heading, each of the four segments contains four to six detailed points describing the scenario.

To the left of the 2x2 grid, the presenter lays out the five steps in the scenario planning process that leads to the 2x2 segmentation. Each step is illustrated with a representative graphic.

Typical Scenario Planning Approach

Scenario planning often begins with several driving forces and ends with a 2x2 matrix

Process Steps

1. Define the Focal Issue
2. Identify Key Driving Forces
3. Craft Potential Scenarios
4. Determine Resulting Strategic Options
5. Set and Monitor Tripwires

Representative Output: Pharma Industry Scenarios, c. 2004

Lilly

R&D Output

Breakthrough Innovation

Centralized (Public or Private) ↔ **Individual (Patient/ Prescriber Focus)**

Rationing Innovation

- Tight formularies and utilization controls
- Innovation "rationed" to patients judged most likely to benefit
- Restrictions on off-label prescribing by MDs
- Right drug to right patient through accepted treatment algorithms developed by credible thought leaders
- Companies must demonstrate big improvements over current therapies to obtain price premium for new products
- Products in new therapy most likely to command price premiums

Haves and Have-Nots

- HSAs in widespread use; patients pay out-of-pocket for many Rx drugs
- Middle class and rich can supplement employer HSA contributions (pre-tax and after tax) to ensure access to new therapies; poorer consumers cannot
- Increased consumer price sensitivity and access inequities create pricing pressures on new therapies
- At same time, very expensive biotech products covered through high deductible catastrophic insurance plans, so pricing pressures on these products is less acute

Payers Rule

- Rx prices regulated by government (price ceilings)
- Very tight formularies and utilization controls
- Even with price regulation, companies must offer big discounts to "play" on formularies
- Restrictions on promotional spending and programs
- FDA focus on safety increases cost of clinical trials
- Massive pharma industry consolidation

Price Sensitive Patients

- Employers continue to pass ever larger share of health care costs onto employees, so patients are price sensitive
- Most seniors still have significant out-of-pocket drug costs
- Heavy use of generics, OTC products (FDA speeds Rx to OTC switching in many categories) and alternative medicines
- Small share of population willing to pay premium for branded products based on heavy DTC marketing efforts; most not
- Companies focus on NILEX and promotional efforts to drive sales

Incremental Innovation

Source: CEB research.

Slide: "The Best of All Worlds"

This version of the 2D Segment layout combines images and text in each segment, rather than only numbers or text as in the previous examples, and also shows movement to a desired end-state. The horizontal axis along the bottom is divided along Scope of Business Issues, from Single on the left to Multiple on the right. The vertical axis on the left presents a Scale of Solutions, from Narrow at the bottom to Broad at the top. Each individual element in the grid consists of an image and a title underneath it, like the Seminar in the upper left quadrant, or the Roundtable in the lower left quadrant.

This illustrative layout highlights three different tactics for growing a customer network by circling them, indicating how they can be best leveraged and combined for high impact. Separately the three tactics are less than optimal, but together they are worthy of the upper right segment: a broad scale solution that solves multiple issues. The company first determines their customers' sources of value creation, and the slide shows how the company then engineers customized and scalable value-creation tools—the details of which are listed in the upper right quadrant of the chart.

The Best of All Worlds

Skoll Bank* Network Value Signal

Illustrative

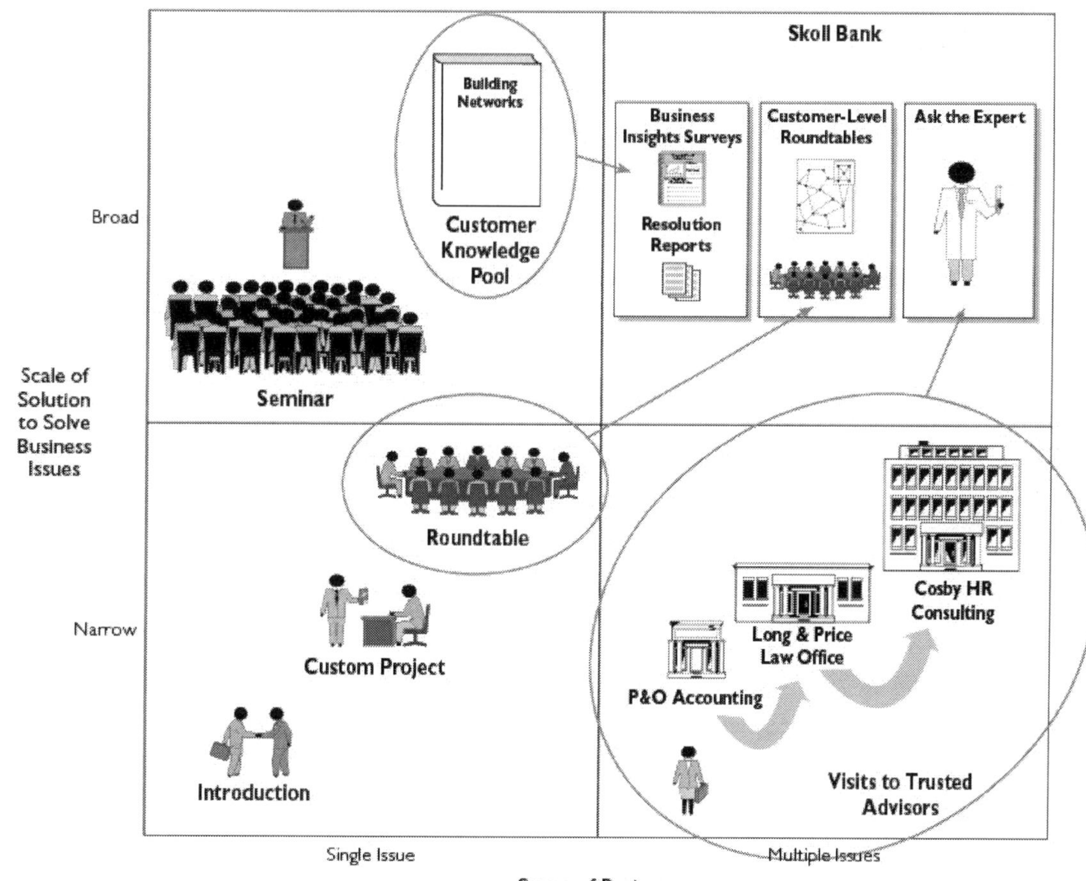

SOURCE: Skoll Bank; CEB research

Slide: "The Sum of the Parts . . ."

This version of the 2D Segment layout utilizes a 3x3 grid, with High and Low on each axis, and an implied Medium. On the left side the slide shows a suboptimal approach to segmentation—looking at the company's customers based on a broad industry view—and then reveals on the right side a more granular approach that yields actionable customer segments to target in different ways.

The vertical dimension of the grid on the right of the slide shows Strategic Fit—to what extent is serving this customer aligned with the company's strategy? The horizontal dimension of the grid is a scale of Opportunity—how large is the economic opportunity in serving this customer? The intersection of the High-(Medium)-Low values for the two dimensions yields nine customer segments which the company treats differently.

The audience's attention is drawn to the darkest shaded box in the upper right: the High Fit/High Opportunity segment that needs to be Developed or Defended, and is a portfolio-managed team account. The next tier has two lighter-shaded segments that are Priority Accounts: the High Fit/Medium Opportunity category in the top center needs to be defended, and the High Opportunity/Medium Fit category in the middle right needs to be developed.

The remaining six segments are not shaded and not emphasized: these third tier accounts are either defended selectively, maintained with limited resources, or withdrawn from—enabling the company to focus on accounts with greater fit and greater opportunity.

The Sum of the Parts...

When broad industry segmentation attempts fall short in clarifying where best to devote resources...

...Company A develops a granular customer selection tool to inform segment strategy

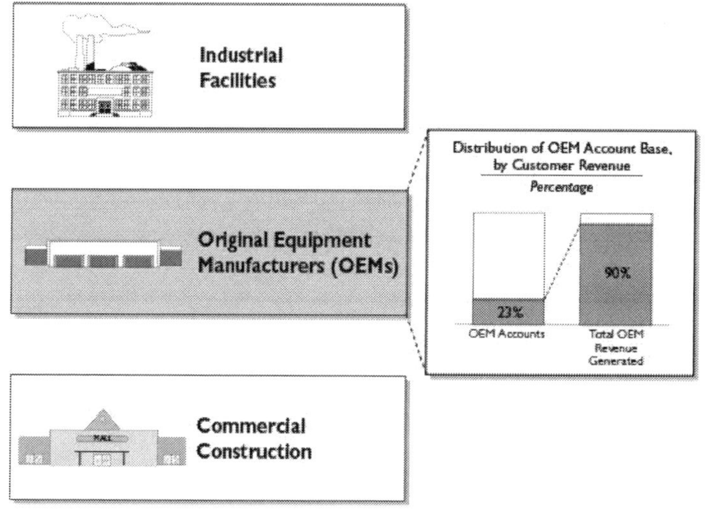

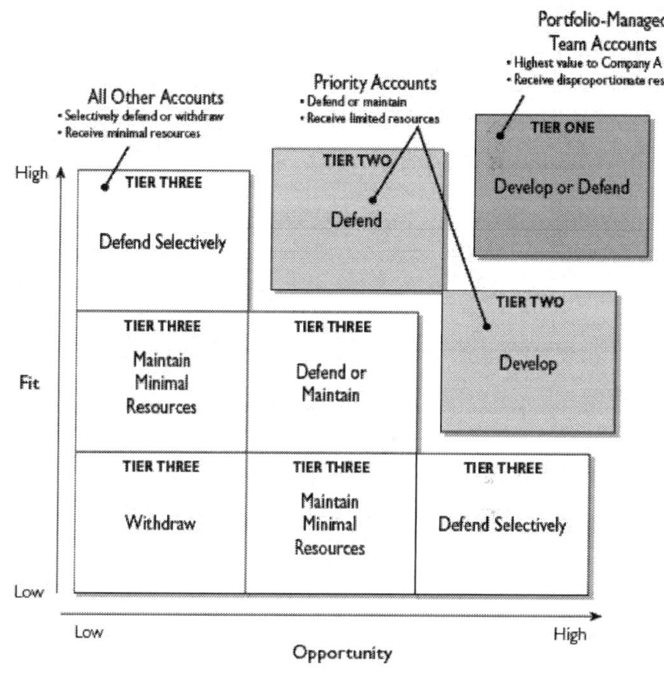

Source: CEB research.

Slide: "Textbook Segmentation"

In this 2D Segment layout, the standard high-low division of the axes is again augmented by a third, middle section, again breaking the resulting three-by-three matrix into nine segments. The vertical axis of customers' strategic "Fit" and the horizontal axis of market "Opportunity" define the nine sections, and enable the presenter to identify which targets are favorable or unfavorable. Some segments that are adjacent or touching share strategies, which allows for grouping of similar segments—and this leads to the pyramid on the right side of the page. The segmentation process displayed in the 3x3 grid on the left feeds into the company's service strategy for optimizing relationships and profits: the higher opportunity/fit segment in the matrix neatly maps to the upper tier of the pyramid, the middle segments to the middle tier, and the lower to the lower, as the arrows and the corresponding gray-shading show. The pyramid itself outlines the service strategy for the customer accounts, with details for each tier of the pyramid listed to the tier's right. (See also the Pyramid List chapter for relevant examples.)

Textbook Segmentation

By considering both market opportunity and customers' strategic fit with business model...

...the company ensures that resources go to accounts with the greatest relationship potential

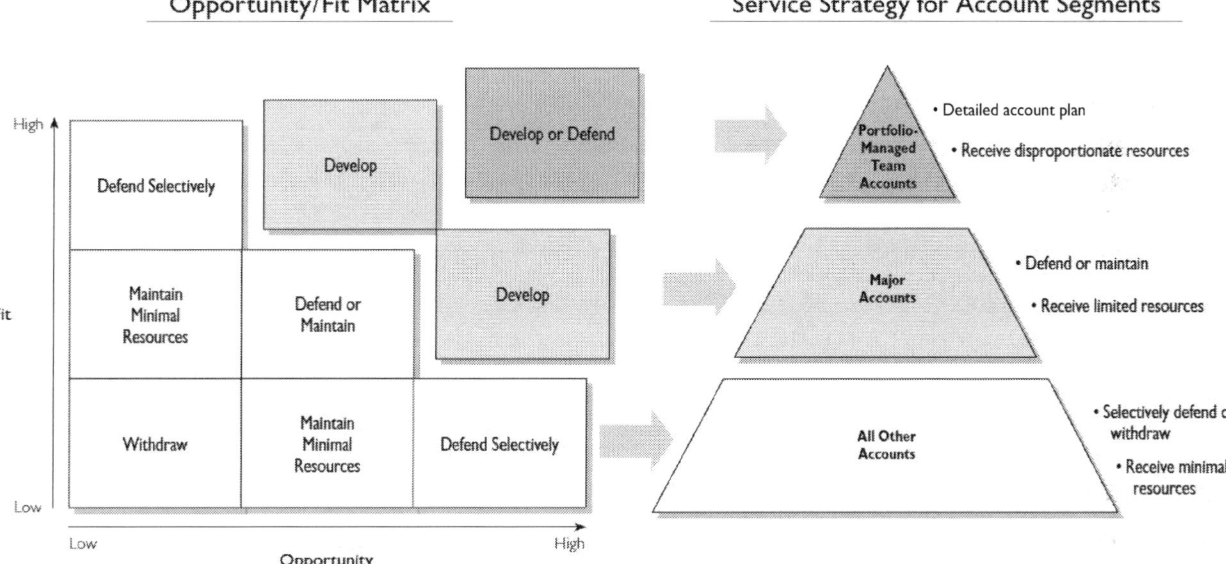

Slide: "Most Trusted Hands"

This 2D Segment layout utilizes a 4x4 grid to illustrate how some priority customers are extracted from telephone Interactive Voice Response (IVR) and placed in conversation with a live agent. The vertical axis ranks the customers from Top Priority down to Low Priority, and the horizontal axis divides according to the current wait time for a live agent, ranging from "0" (no wait time—a live person is ready to talk with the customer) to "120+ Seconds" (the customer has been waiting for two or more minutes). The resulting 16 boxes show how the company handles each incoming customer call based on customer importance and current wait time. For example, in the first column, when there is no wait time, all customers calling in are able to talk with a live agent; the higher priority customers are routed to Sales Specialists, and the lower priority customers to general Customer Service Representatives.

The top row of segments shows that if a Top Priority customer is calling in, even if the current wait time is up to 119 seconds, that Top Priority customer will be "extracted" from the queue and placed first in line to talk with the next available Sales Specialist.

The four call-out boxes around the segmentation grid annotate the figure and describe the process. Note how the labeling of A, B, C, and D provides a road-map for the audience's consideration of the process, moving from the upper left to the upper right, then to lower left and finally to lower right.

Prince Finance*

Most Trusted Hands

Behind the Extraction Protocols Sits a Well-Crafted Sales Strategy

Illustration of the Routing of Potential Extractees

Ⓐ Because the highest-performing agents have twice the conversion of general agents, Prince Finance directs the hottest prospects to these individuals.

	0 Seconds	1–59 Seconds	60–119 Seconds	120+ Seconds
Top Priority (1)	Sales Specialist	Sales Specialist	Sales Specialist	IVR
High Priority (2)	Sales Specialist	Sales Specialist	General CSR	IVR
Moderate Priority (3)	General CSR	General CSR	IVR	IVR
Low Priority (4)	General CSR	IVR	IVR	IVR

Ⓑ Sales specialists are chosen from the generalist pool and are the highest performers of that population.

Ⓒ Customers with less sales potential provide good learning opportunities for less experienced agents.

Ⓓ While moderate- and low-priority customers have lower conversion rates, they provide sales opportunities during slow periods in the contact center.

* Pseudonym.

Source: Prince Finance* Corporation; CEB research.

Slide: "Boosting the Return on Untapped Assets"

This conceptual variation on the 2D Segmentation layout uses a 5x5 grid, with the left vertical axis describing various bank assets, and the bottom horizontal axis listing a series of customer needs. To help focus the audience, rather than showing the resulting 25 possible segments, the layout shows only five—the ones where bank assets and customer needs intersect. The left axis is further separated into two subsections, with the traditional assets or products—"What Banks Sell"—listed at the bottom, and nontraditional assets—"Who Banks Know"—listed above. The effect is to reveal to the audience a vast area of core competencies that banks typically do not leverage, but which could serve a majority of customers' business needs. The gray boxes draw the audience's attention to those opportunity areas, and the contrast with the one, lonely white box in the lower right portion of the segmentation grid accentuates the narrow strategic focus of many banks.

Below the 2D Segmentation grid, the dictionary-style entry defining the word "network" emphasizes the importance of the bank using its privileged position to design a value-creating network that serves its customers and partners more fully.

Boosting the Return on Untapped Assets

Bank's Potential Solutions for Commercial Customer Needs

Conceptual

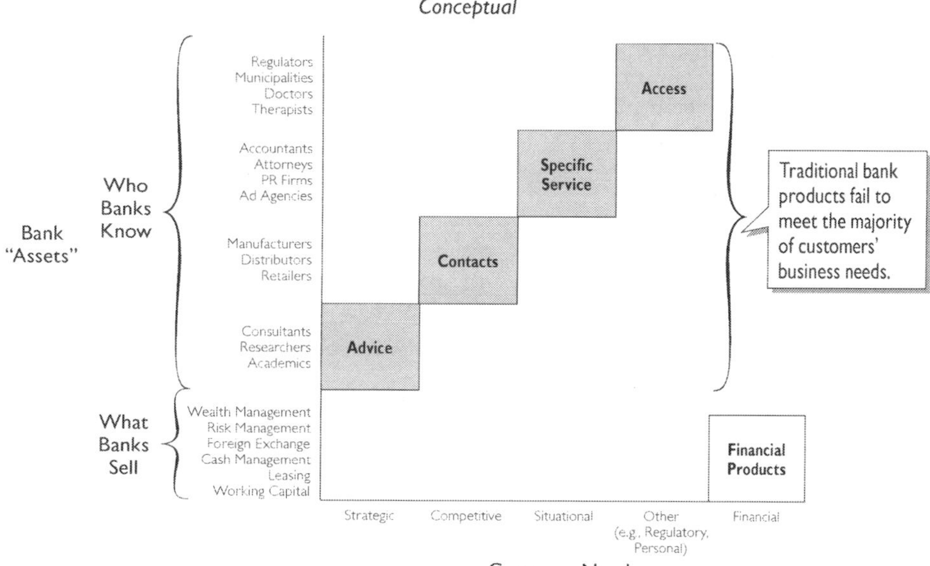

...that can be leveraged within the context of a network

> **network**
> *noun [c]*
>
> A large system consisting of many similar parts that are connected together to allow movement or communication between or along the parts or between the parts and a control centre.

Source: Cambridge University Press Dictionary; CEB research.

Slide: "Striking the Right Balance in Portfolio Stewardship"

This version of the 2D Segment layout emphasizes the importance of Chief Information Officers balancing executive judgment and process rigor when making systems project portfolio decisions. It does so by introducing a twist, or more accurately, a curve: a quarter circle that radiates up and to the right from the origin. The quarter circle is based on a fairly simple 2x2 conceptual motif, in which the left-hand vertical axis shows the Level of Executive Judgment, High at the top and Low at the bottom. Notice that there are no discrete lines dividing the levels—the implication is that the value of possible judgments is a continuum. The lower horizontal axis shows Process Rigor, also along a continuum of Low to High.

What makes this layout particularly interesting is that the segmentation is divided not into rectangular boxes but into radial cone segments. In the upper left, a high level of executive judgment combined with a low level of process rigor results in a situation characterized as "I know it when I see it." In the lower right, a high level of process rigor combined with a low level of executive judgment results in the contrary "Process Straightjacket" situation.

In a creative way, the presenter draws the audience's attention to the gray area, revealing that the right balance mentioned in the slide title is achieved not by merely resting in between the other two segments, but by combining them: the curved arrows at the top and the right of the layout indicate that ideally a CIO should balance executive judgment and process rigor, rather than favoring one or the other alone. The result is "Informed Intuition."

Striking the Right Balance in Portfolio Stewardship

The key portfolio governance challenge faced by CIOs is balancing business judgment and process rigor

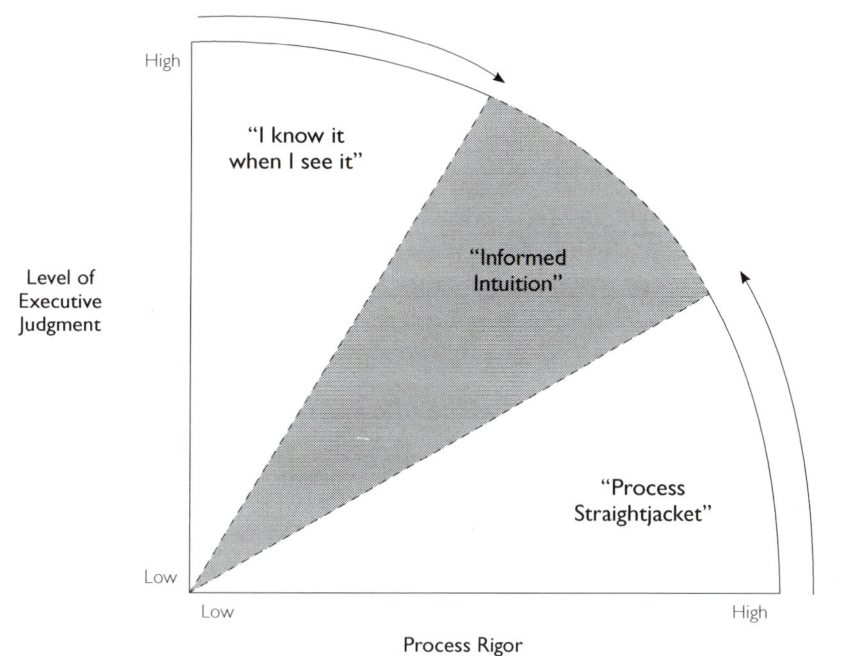

Portfolio Stewardship

Responsible management of the selection, execution, and adoption of an organization's collection of projects to provide value and further enterprise objectives.

Source: CEB research.

CI017R64BL

CHAPTER 2: "3D SEGMENT" LAYOUT

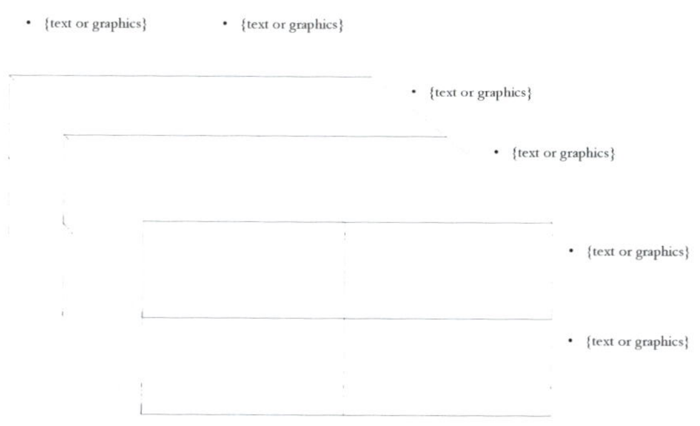

The 3D Segment layout enables the presenter to display data along three different dimensions at the same time; the intersection of specific values for all three of those dimensions results in an actual segment. This layout illustrates complexity of detail—sometimes over 100 data points—with a straightforward design.

How to draw the "3D Segment" Layout

Charteo

3D Cubes

Enter your subheadline here

Description 1
This is a placeholder text. This text can be replaced with your own text.

Description 2
This is a placeholder text. This text can be replaced with your own text.

Description 4
This is a placeholder text. This text can be replaced with your own text.

Description 3
This is a placeholder text. This text can be replaced with your own text.

www.Charteo.com
Concept charts, Cubes, 3D Cubes 10

Slide: "Customer Database Driven"

This 3D Segment layout shows a 3 x 3 x 3 customer segmentation cube, where the horizontal width axis shows recency of customer purchase, the horizontal depth axis shows the frequency of their visits, and the vertical height axis shows the monetary value of their purchases. The resulting 27 segments range from customers who have not purchased within the last 12 months, have only visited once, and whose purchases are between $0 and $99, to customers who have purchased within the last six months, have visited over 10 times, and whose purchases are over $1000. The specificity enables a company to target and serve different segments in very different ways.

Customer Database Driven: Segmentation created by analyzing your internal customer data as recorded on your databases. Primary types:

1   **RFM (Recency/Frequency/Monetary) Value** – Divides customers based on purchase variables – the recency of their last purchase, the frequency of purchases, and the monetary value of their purchases. Segments are groups of small businesses that display similar characteristics on these dimensions. For example, one segment might contain companies who have high lifetime spending but haven't purchased in 6 months. This is most useful for identifying groups of inactive or very active customers and designing tactics accordingly.

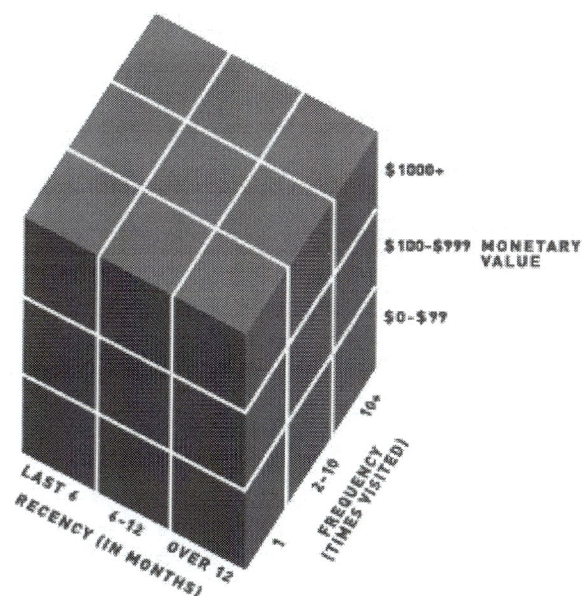

Slide: "Many Processes, Many Problems"

In this more complex example of the 3D Segment layout, it becomes clear that complexity can cause problems. The combination of three customer segments (height) by six products (length) by four variations (depth) yields 72 possible segments. The callout boxes further illustrate the issue: although in the 1980's the company had only one product for one customer type with one variation, it currently has 72.

Many Processes, Many Problems

Increased scope and complexity of products...

Picasso Life* Product Variations

Customer Segment: Large, Medium, Small

Products: Life, Vision, Disability, Dental, Section 125, Medical

Variations: HMO, PPO, POS, Indemnity

Product portfolio, 2003

Product portfolio, late 80s

...led to breakdowns in case setup process

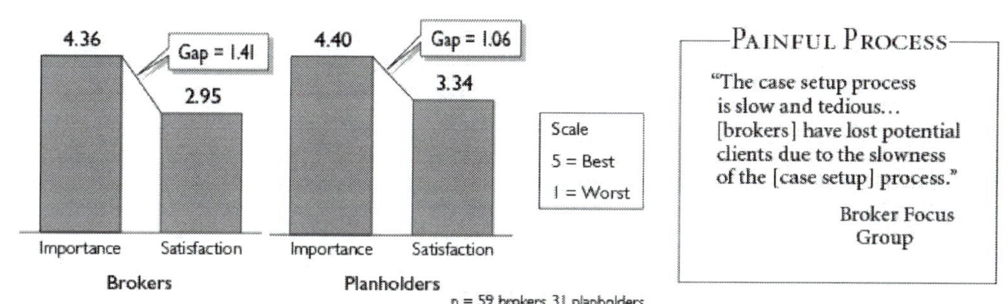

Painful Process

"The case setup process is slow and tedious... [brokers] have lost potential clients due to the slowness of the [case setup] process."

Broker Focus Group

*Pseudonym.

Source: Picasso Life.*

Slide: "Milking It"

This complex version of the 3D Segment layout portrays a three dimensional benchmarking tool that combines five key areas of focus, four levels, and seven performance dimensions, yielding 140 different segments. As strategy changes, the company can use a conceptual tool like this to migrate workforce skills to support the new strategic direction. Although the 140 possibilities demonstrate the very real complexity of benchmarking, the overall layout maintains a simplicity—that of a segmentation cube.

This overall layout also shows how the 3D Segment can map to a two dimensional chart: in the sample at the bottom of the slide, the Key Focus Area of "Account Planning" in the Performance Dimension of "Skills" is spelled out in detail on all four levels.

Milking It

Audit Phase Is Reliant on Comprehensive Benchmarking

Three-Dimensional Benchmarking Tool

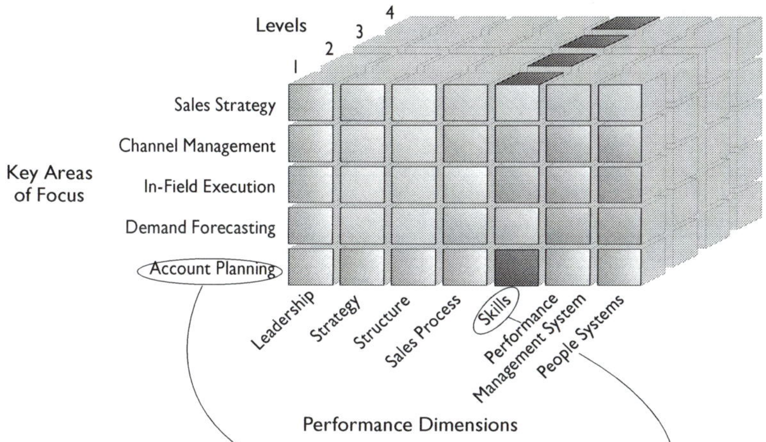

Sample Performance Definition

Area of Focus: Account Planning **Performance Dimension: Skills**				
	Level 1	**Level 2**	**Level 3**	**Level 4**
Skills	Highly developed planning skills are combined with an understanding of trends and drivers of channel structure. Ease with customer connectivity technologies and processes for global, national, and key regional sales management.	Generic business planning skills are provided by training programs as part of the management development process. Application to account development is provided through personal account management experience.	Exposure to the sales planning process and generic sales management training is the means to skill building. The complexity of planning and managing global/national accounts is not considered to require specific formally developed skills.	Skills focus is on sales execution. Planning skills are under developed with the context being resource scheduling. Skills development is individually motivated and managed.

Source: CEB research.

CHAPTER 3: "ALTERNATIVES – MULTIPLE" LAYOUT

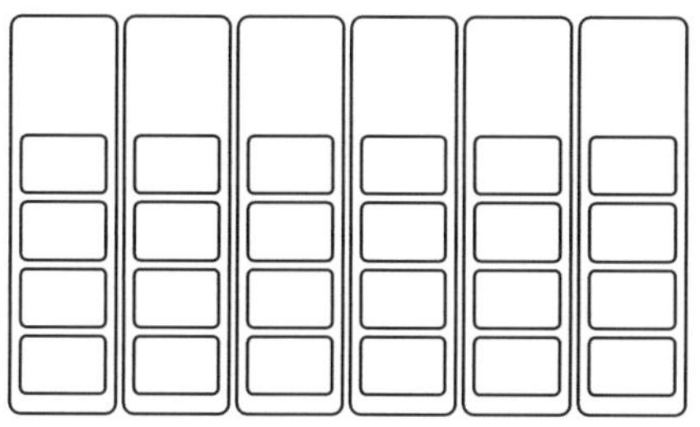

The Multiple Alternatives layout is used when several alternative options need to be compared, usually across multiple attributes. Usually the alternatives are presented with their different attributes listed vertically, allowing the audience to compare the alternatives side-by-side by means of the attributes. If the alternatives can be placed into any kind of order, they should be (as in "Slippery Slope," page 33), because this helps the audience to understand how the alternatives relate to one another.

The various dimensions of comparable attributes are listed vertically on the left side of the layout, typically in order of importance from top to bottom. With dimensions of attributes that are primarily text-based and lengthier, the comparison may work better if the alternatives are laid out horizontally (as in "Concession Stand," page 39).

The recommended or preferred option is usually highlighted somehow, either by drawing a box around it or by placing a gray shaded box behind it. Typically no other gridlines are used, to avoid visual clutter.

How to draw the "Alternatives – Multiple" Layout

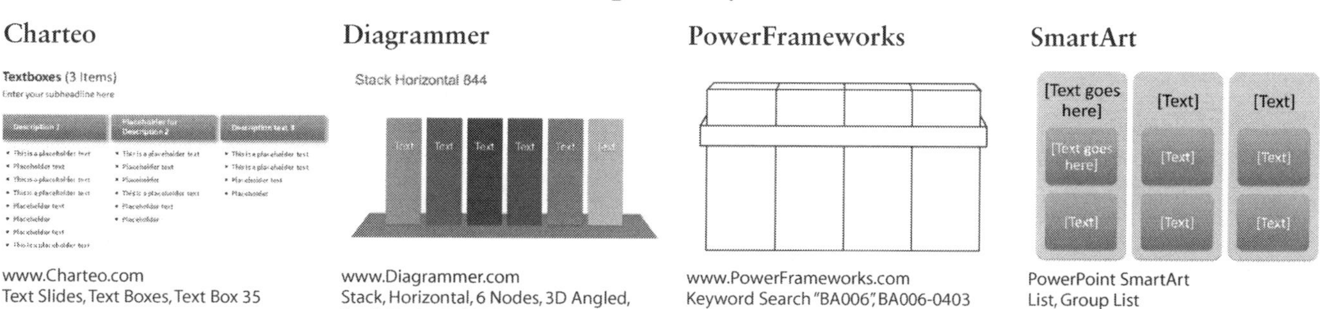

Charteo
www.Charteo.com
Text Slides, Text Boxes, Text Box 35

Diagrammer
www.Diagrammer.com
Stack, Horizontal, 6 Nodes, 3D Angled, Stack Horizontal 844

PowerFrameworks
www.PowerFrameworks.com
Keyword Search "BA006", BA006-0403

SmartArt
PowerPoint SmartArt
List, Group List

Slide: "HSAs Are More Attractive to Consumers ..."

The slide shows multiple alternatives for health spending accounts. The alternatives are presented in vertical columns, with each alternative listed in the header across the top and the various attributes to be compared running down the page. Along the left side the eight separate dimensions or questions about the alternatives are listed, allowing the audience to scan across the slide and compare all the alternatives, attribute by attribute. The first column is highlighted with a gray box, to draw audience attention to the main point of the slide, which is also reinforced in the slide's title, that the Health Savings Accounts option is superior to the three alternative options. Notice also that the other three options are not laid out chronologically, because the slide is designed not to show a timeline, but to contrast the attributes of each option.

HSAs ARE MORE ATTRACTIVE TO CONSUMERS AND EMPLOYERS THAN OTHER HEALTH SPENDING ACCOUNTS

	Health Savings Accounts (HSA)	Flexible Spending Accounts (FSA)	Health Reimbursement Arrangements (HRA)	Medical Savings Accounts (MSA)
Year created	2003	1978	2002	1996
Funds carry over year to year?	• Yes	• No	• Yes	• Yes
Contributions	• Employer and/or employee	• Employee only	• Employer only	• Employer or employee, not both
Portable?	• Yes	• No	• No	• No
Eligibility	• Those with high-deductible health plans under age 65 and dependents	• Employed individuals under 65 and dependents	• Employed individuals under 65 and dependents	• Employees of small employers (fewer than 50 employees) and the self-employed under 65 and dependents
Can you invest assets?	• Yes	• No	• No	• No
Replaced by HSAs?	• N/a	• No	• No	• Yes
Contributions taxed?	• No	• No	• No	• No

Sources: Medicare legislation; Hewitt Associates; UBS

Slide: "Companies must set their aspirations for how technology can add value ..."

The slide presents three strategic alternatives, laid out in a logical progression from left to right: "Stay in the race," "Win the race," and "Change the rules." Rather than working from a mere descriptive title (as on the previous page), each column has a conceptual heading which is reinforced by a photograph depicting the concept. Beneath each photograph are the three attributes—defined by the dimensions of focus, value, and risk—for each alternative. Given the amount of text in each attribute, faint gray lines are used to distinguish the attributes and facilitate comparison across the page. In this case, therefore, the gray lines are doing useful "work" for the slide, without adding clutter.

Companies must set their aspirations for how technology can add value, and then balance their portfolio of activities accordingly

	'Stay in the race'	'Win the race'	'Change the rules'

Focus	▪ IT is now the cost of doing business in this market, and a 'commodity' vs. a differentiator	▪ IT can help compete and win by differentiated products, services or prices, faster rollout or deployment, better margins	▪ IT can enable new markets or services, achieve significantly lower price points or change the industry value chain
Value	▪ Avoidance of revenue loss, operational failure or regulatory liabilities	▪ Med-high pay-off through improved performance of current business	▪ Highest pay-off through creating new market positioning
Risk	▪ Low-Med risks due to deployment challenges	▪ Med-High risks due to design & implementation	▪ Highest risks associated with innovation and disruption

Slide: "Slippery Slope"

This slide once again presents the alternatives in a logical order, in this case by contrasting extremes on a spectrum. The spectrum represents a range of sales representatives' behaviors. On the left of the spectrum, the sales rep is passive; on the right, aggressive; in the middle, assertive. Beneath each alternative the characteristic attributes are listed, emphasizing the problems with the passive and aggressive extremes and the benefits of the assertive mode in the middle. The summaries beneath the two extremes highlight the main point of the page, namely, (on the right) that sales leaders are afraid to encourage their reps to be assertive, for fear that they will become aggressive, while (on the left) passivity actually inhibits performance more than aggression does. The gradient shading of the arrow across the top reinforces this "too much / too little" message.

Because the (surprising) message of the slide is that passivity hinders sales success more than aggression does, the boxes across the bottom focus on the dangers of passivity. The summary along the left side of the slide recaps the slide's main points and provides an additional element of interest.

❯ Passivity inhibits performance more than aggression.

- There are three main reasons why reps are more passive than expected:
  - First, reps inappropriately assume that customers have more power in any given negotiation.
  - Second, economic conditions make reps believe they lack control of the outcome of a customer conversation—and loss of control is a common driver of increased passivity.
  - Last, organizations have encouraged reps to develop strong relationships with customers—instructions which can lead a rep to take the customer's side more than is desirable.

Who's Got the Power?
A survey of Fortune 500 Procurement and Sales Professionals (SP) showed that 75% of SPs think Procurement has more power in negotiations, while 75% of Procurement Professionals believe Sales has more power.

SLIPPERY SLOPE

Rep Behavior Spectrum, Passive to Aggressive

Passive	Assertive	Aggressive
▪ Subverts goals to the needs of others ▪ Allows personal boundaries to be breached ▪ Uses indirect, accommodating language	▪ Directly pursues goals in constructive way ▪ Defends own personal boundaries ▪ Uses direct language	▪ Pursues goals at the expense of professionalism ▪ Attacks others' personal boundaries ▪ Uses antagonistic language

Sales Performance Problem

Reps are often too passive with customers, seeking to resolve conflict whenever possible.

Common Sales Leadership Fear

Tell sales reps to be more assertive, and they may become aggressive.

Drivers of Passive Behavior

Perceived Customer Power

Reps think they want the sale more than the customer wants the sale, and therefore the customer dictates the terms and timing.

Erosion of Control

The current economic environment causes otherwise assertive people to become passive due to the perceived lack of control over the outcome of the sale.

Relationship-Focus

Instructions to sit on the customer side of the table and advocate for their needs are still hard to understand.

Source: BayGroup International

Slide: "Different Approaches Are Used to Drive Innovation ..."

Here, using several features from the preceding pages, we have an example of how much information can be usefully presented on a single slide that is laid out well. Five alternative approaches for driving innovation are offered. The alternatives are ordered logically from "close to the core business" on the left to "far from the core business" on the right. Defining details and the specific strategic intent are the aspects listed beneath each alternative.

The recommended alternative is boxed with a dotted line, and the right edge of the slide presents critical questions to aid the audience in leveraging the slide's information.

DIFFERENT APPROACHES ARE USED TO DRIVE INNOVATION, DEPENDING ON THE COMPANY'S STRATEGIC INTENT

Emerging model

Close to the core business ⟷ **Far from the core business**

	Traditional product development	Innovation unit (lab/center)	Incubator	Central R&D lab	Corporate venture capital
Definition	• Processes embedded in core businesses focused on innovations and development on existing products	• A distinct unit that is not part of core operations staffed by cross-functional teams to develop new products or services	• A facility (shared or part of a company) designed to help startup companies to grow through the use of shared resources, management expertise, and intellectual capital	• A central, corporate research facility focused on developing next-generation products and technology	• A dedicated fund that invests in early- and later-stage companies that might be acquired or spun off
Strategic intent	• To work on basic research and long-term product development	• To fill innovation gap created by shorter life cycles by bringing new products to market rapidly • To provide a structure for innovation in sectors that do not have R&D	• To closely develop and often co-develop multiple ideas that may be acquired to develop complementary or new products for existing or new customers	• To develop basic science that will lead to next-generation breakthrough products for existing and new customer segments	• To invest in strategic technologies and companies that will ultimately influence the business

Questions for a private bank

- How is the bank organized for innovation today?
- What is the most suitable innovation model for the bank?
- What role does/should IT have in the innovation organization?
- What organizational barriers (if any) prevent effective innovation in the bank?
- Are the right skill profiles involved in innovation today?

Slide: "Allocate vehicle mix using appropriate ..."

This version of the Multiple Alternatives layout carefully embeds complex detail conveyed through words, symbolic images, and graphics. The slide presents five alternative analytic approaches, arranged in a logical order, for allocating media vehicle mix in advertising. Beginning with the typical approach on the left, each subsequent alternative to the right requires a greater availability of data and analytic appetite—a fact that is reinforced by the rightward-pointing arrow above the five options. Within each column, each conceptual icon accentuates the title above it, and a verbal description of the column's approach is presented below.

At the bottom of the slide, detailed, data-driven graphics further elaborate the alternatives, indicating to the audience the type of analysis typically required for each approach. The level of detail in these graphics is worth noting. They include a waterfall chart at the bottom of the first column, stacked bars in the fifth column, and matrices and line charts in columns two through four. In particular, the second column's five-by-five matrix chart plots "quality of interaction" along the vertical axis vs. "cost per reach" along the horizontal. The fourth column's chart plots "short-term ROI" on the vertical axis vs. "long-term ROI" on the horizontal, and overlays a bubble chart to show the relative size of spend for each type of investment. Each chart presents an example, so the point here is not to convey the charts' actual details, but to use the images of the charts as a basis for discussion of what particular analyses entail.

The overall impact of using the appropriate approach is spelled out at the bottom center of the slide: significant revenue increase and cost reduction.

Allocate vehicle mix using appropriate approach(es) from a range of world-class techniques

Increasing availability of data and analytic appetite

A Typical approach last year +/- X%	B Reach-cost-quality	C Marketing mix modeling	D ST vs. LT ROI optimization	E "Full funnel" mix optimization
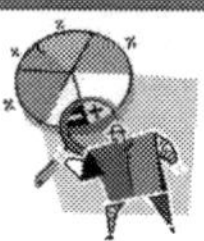				
▪ Apply management's best judgment to determine where to increase and decrease spend	▪ Optimize marketing investment on an apples-to-apples basis, comparing various, distinct marketing instruments	▪ Maximize short-term sales (or other objective) using econometric models to attribute historical sales results to various factors including marketing spend	▪ Monetize the return from investments in brand equity and evaluates trade-offs between these investments and those that drive short-term sales	▪ Maximize the health of the "full funnel", balancing short-term objectives vs. overall marketing funnel health, using predictive modeling based on tens of thousands of scenarios

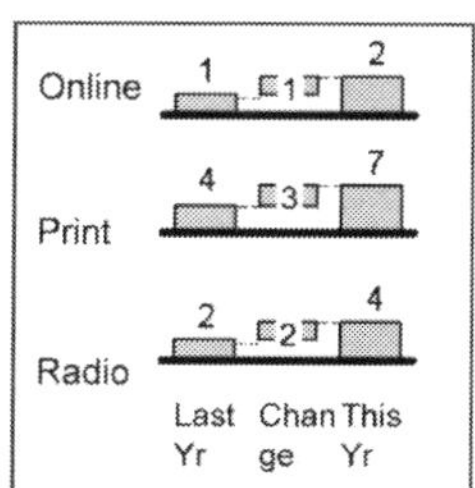

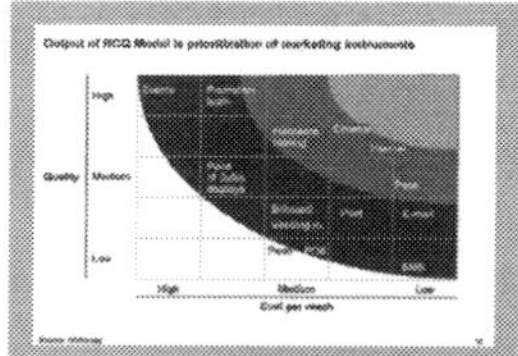

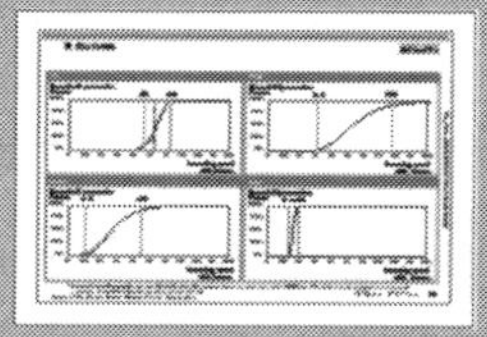

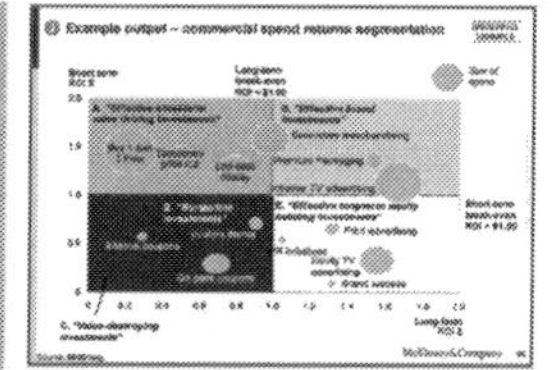

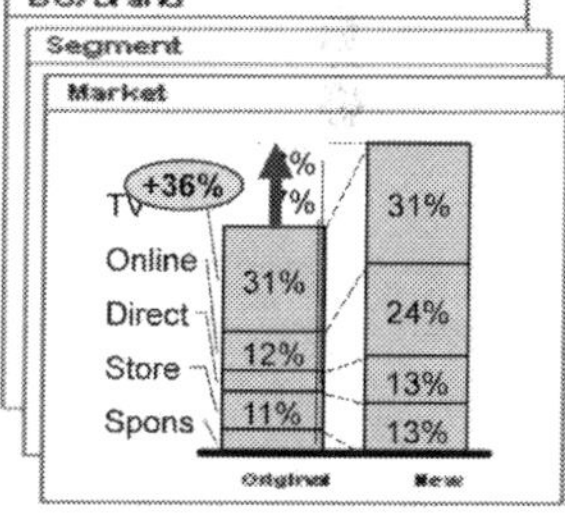

Impact: 7%-10% increase in revenue, 10%-15% cost reduction

Slide: "Concession Stand"

In this example, the alternatives are listed in rows rather than columns. Each alternative represents a pattern of making concessions during negotiation. The pattern name (Avalanche, Wrecking Ball, etc.) is on the left, along with its symbolic visual icon. In the middle the pattern is described, and on the right, the condition for its appropriate use. The curly brackets on the right side of the slide group the alternatives into two sets: three higher-risk alternatives at the top—for experienced negotiators only—and at the bottom two more long-term, relationship-oriented alternatives that anyone can use.

Text at the far left of the slide (separated by the thin vertical line) presents the slide's key takeaways. Along the bottom, a tracker indicates where this slide sits within the broader presentation.

This horizontal approach to the Multiple Alternatives layout should be used when attributes are all text-based and longer than two or three words each.

> **Understanding how different concession patterns impact customers helps reps maintain control without harming long-term relationships.**

- When exchanging value through concessions, knowing *what* trades to make and request is only half the battle. Knowing *when* and *how* to make them can have a significant impact on the outcome of the negotiation.
- The Avalanche, Wrecking Ball, and Sucker concession patterns signal to the customer that there is reasonable range of movement left in the negotiation, and increase their expectations of what the rep has to offer.
- Alternatively, the Martini and Ice Cream concession patterns signal to the customer that the rep is approaching their limit and closure is drawing near.

Experience and Reflect
During the skill building workshops, reps role play different concession patterns and then discuss how they feel when the negotiation ends, which illustrates the effect of different patterns on customers.

CONCESSION STAND

Concede According to Plan

Common Concession Patterns

Pattern	Description	Condition for Appropriate Use	
Avalanche	Size of concessions increase throughout the negotiation	Large number of potential negotiables	Higher-Risk Concession Patterns[1]
Wrecking Ball	All concessions made begrudgingly at the last minute	Few, but costly negotiables	Higher-Risk Concession Patterns[1]
Sucker	All concessions made up front	Competitive "take it or leave it" negotiations	Higher-Risk Concession Patterns[1]
Martini	Initial period of no concessions followed by a large concession and culminating in a tiny, reluctant concession	Expedited negotiations where momentum needs to be first generated and then shut down quickly	Long-Term Relationship-Oriented Concession Patterns
Ice Cream	Size of concessions diminish throughout the negotiation	Multiple rounds of negotiations	Long-Term Relationship-Oriented Concession Patterns

[1] Higher risk concession patterns require a more skilled negotiator to execute appropriately.

CHAPTER 4: "ALTERNATIVES – TWO" LAYOUT

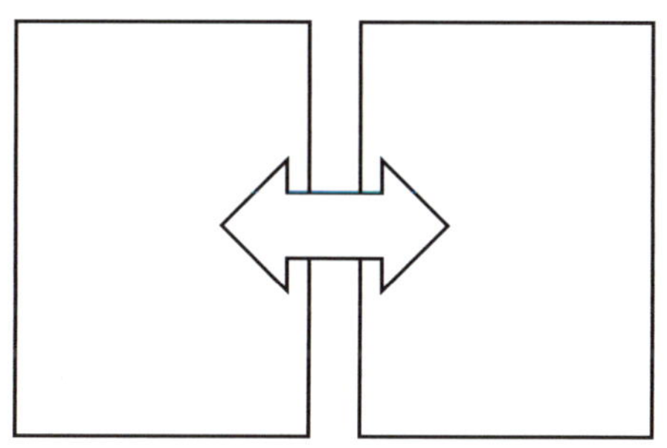

The Two Alternatives layout is a special case of the Multiple Alternatives layout, but worthy of its own chapter because the data so frequently require it. The two alternatives could be (among many other things) two sources of information, profiles of two competing options, or a contrast between two different outcomes. The layout helps the audience to visualize the differences at stake and to make an informed decision between the alternatives.

How to draw the "Alternatives – Two" Layout

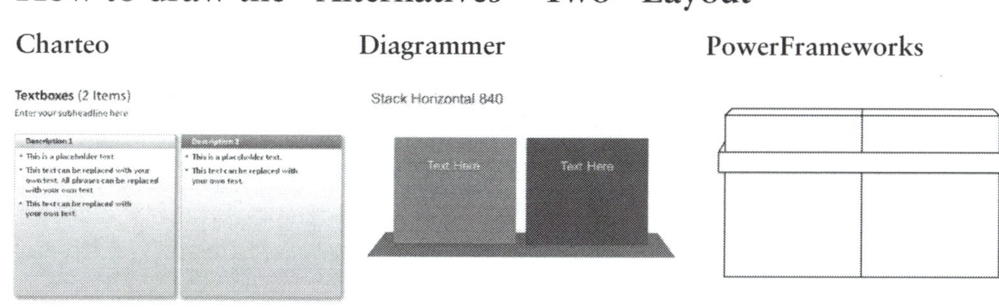

www.Charteo.com
Text Slides, Text Boxes, Text Box 1

www.Diagrammer.com
Stack, Horizontal, 2 Nodes, 3D Angled, Stack Horizontal 840

www.PowerFrameworks.com
Keyword Search "BA006", BA006-0203

Slide: "Relationships Don't Equal Sales"

This example of the Two Alternatives layout compares two types of sales representatives side-by-side: the "Relationship Builder" on the left and the "Challenger" on the right. At the top of each side, a verbal header profiles each type. The quantitative charts in the middle of each column present the potentially surprising conclusion that Challengers represent a much larger percentage of high performers than do Relationship Builders. At the bottom, specific attributes of each type are listed and grouped ("Gets along with others," etc.), highlighting the main differences between the two types. A summary of the slide is presented on the left.

Sales reps that focus on relationship building lose out.

- In the B2B environment, most companies are betting that sales reps who are adept at building relationships will win.
- They are wrong.
- A different profile—one that pushes customers—is more likely to outperform.

Sales Rep Profiles

Our research of thousands of reps surfaced five distintive types:

1. The Hard Worker
2. The Challenger
3. The Relationship Builder
4. The Lone Wolf
5. The Problem Solver

RELATIONSHIPS DON'T EQUAL SALES

Challenger Versus Relationship Builder Profiles

The Relationship Builder profile focuses on **resolving tension** in customer interactions to make situations more amicable and positive and encourage collaboration.

The Challenger profile focuses on **building constructive tension** in customer interactions to push the customer out of his comfort zone.

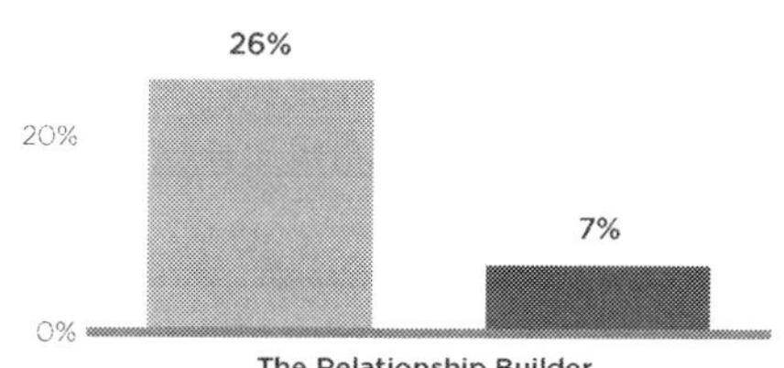

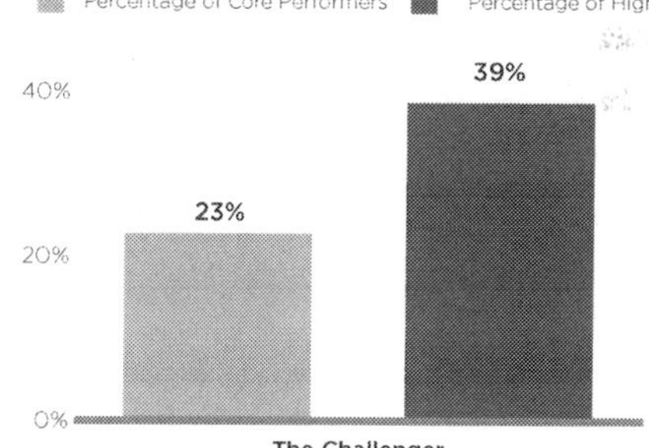

The Relationship Builder

Forms good relationships; Builds customer advocates; Builds cross-functional relationships	**Gets Along with Others**
Can work with anyone; Is genuine	**Likeable**
Accessible to the customer; Gives time to help others; Respects the customer's time	**Generous with Time**

The Challenger

Offers unique perspective; Two-way communication skills	**Teaches**
Knows customer value drivers; Can ID economic drivers	**Tailors**
Is comfortable discussing money; Can pressure the customer	**Asserts Control**

Source: CEB Rep Skills Diagnostic.

Slide: "Avoid Chartjunk"

This slide compares two versions of the same chart. The one on the left is clean: every word, line, and dot signifies something. The one on the right is burdened with "chartjunk"—Edward Tufte's word for visual embellishment that does not communicate anything; research has shown that chartjunk actually weakens communication. Here the Two Alternatives layout facilitates a clear comparison between these two fundamentally different approaches to chart design.

"Avoid Chartjunk"

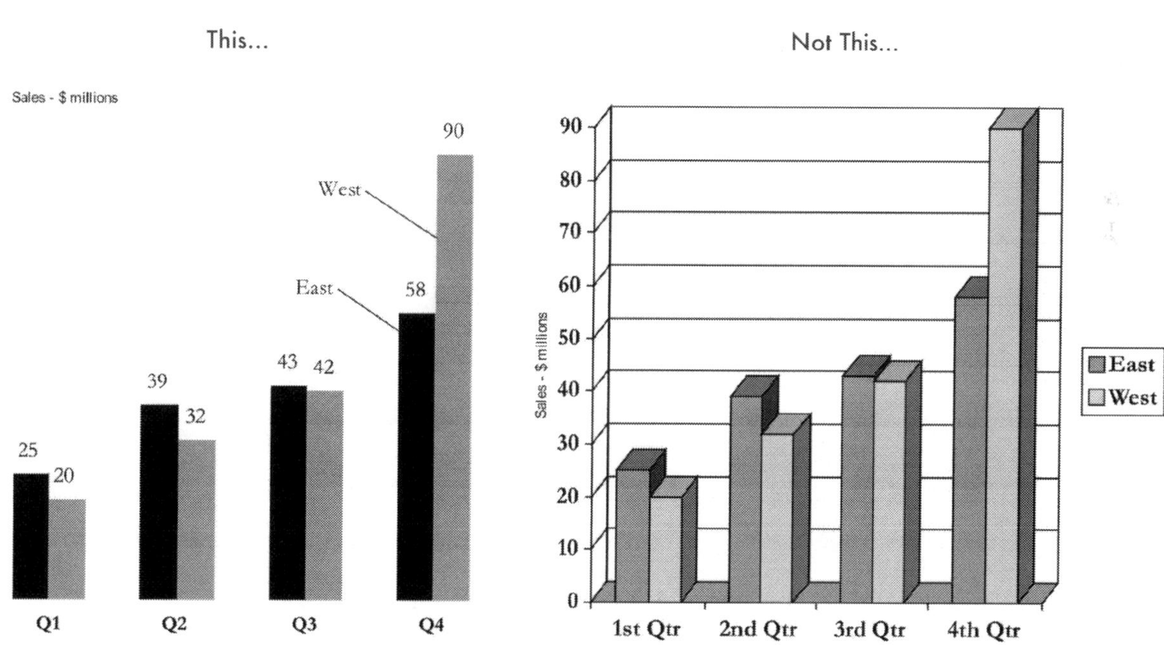

Source: The phrase "chartjunk" was coined by E. Tufte (in *The Visual Display of Quantitative Information*).

CHAPTER 5: "ANNOTATED OBJECT" LAYOUT

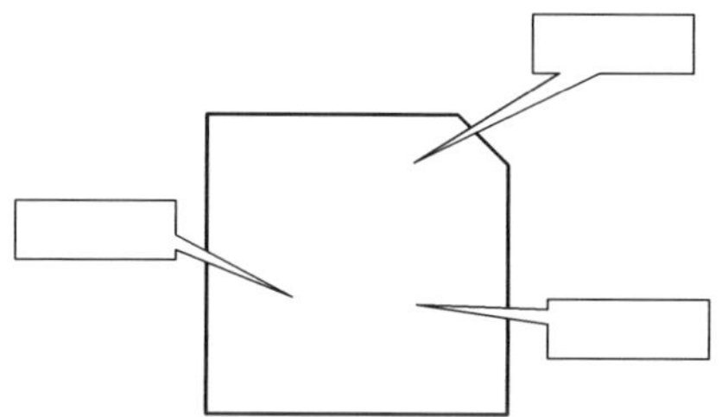

Annotated Object is a highly useful but surprisingly underused layout. It is ideal for explaining anything that can be presented as a single visual: a plan or map, a schematic diagram, a form, a webpage, etc. The object is placed in the middle of the slide and surrounded with callout boxes which highlight and explain various salient details.

How to draw the "Annotated Object" Layout

Charteo

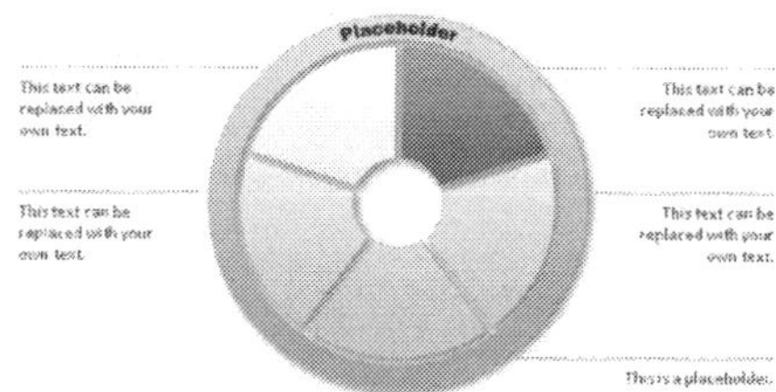

www.Charteo.com
Concept Charts, Circle Charts, Segmented Circle 15

Slide: "Helping Users to Help Themselves"

The annotated object can be almost anything—a sample contract, a customer's letter, a prototype for a product model, or a screen shot of a new system, as shown here. This sample is placed in the middle of the slide, and the callouts around the outside draw the audience's attention to the system's key elements: 1) monthly reminders, 2) sources used, 3) search functionality, and 4) security features. Notice how the numbering of the callouts begins on the upper left and proceeds counter-clockwise around the page. The presenter sets this sequence based on the desired flow of the presentation, and in other examples it can be clockwise, linearly down, or left to right. Besides guiding the flow of the discussion during a live presentation, the sequence also aids in directing the reader's attention if the slide is viewed without the benefit of a live presenter.

Helping Users to Help Themselves

Portal design focuses on ease-of-use

Home Page Screenshot

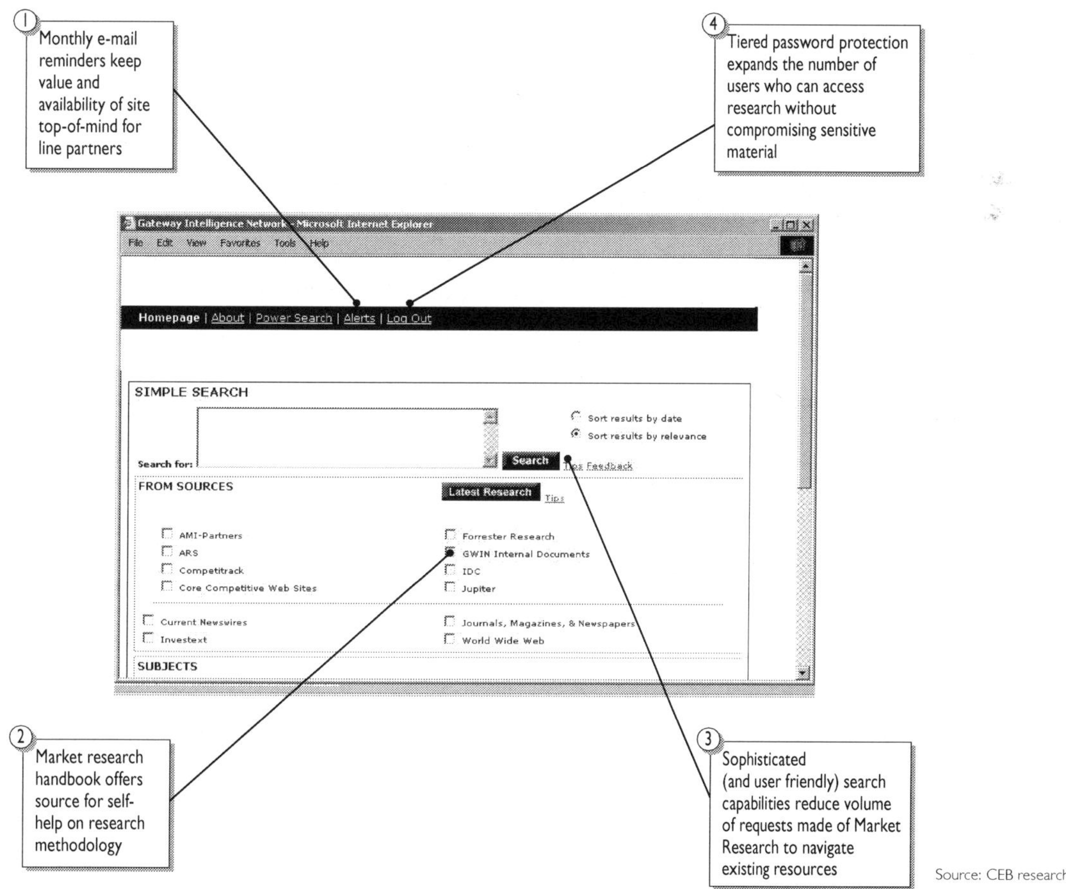

Source: CEB research.

Slide: "Setting Expectations"

Here the annotated object is a Research Request Form, with all the real-life details. The callouts specify how those details support the slide's overall message: that the requestor must justify the project request from the very beginning of the process. Here again the flow of the annotations proceeds from the upper left in a counter-clockwise direction. Note that the sequence of the flow does not map linearly down the page to correspond with the entries numbered 1 to 10; this is perfectly acceptable. The presenter first addresses callouts 1 to 4, and then, after the audience has a sense of the whole, circles back to deal with 5 and 6. The annotations enable the presenter to explain the important details and also the reasons why certain items are included on the form.

Setting Expectations

From the very moment they propose research, line partners must justify the project request

Research Request Form

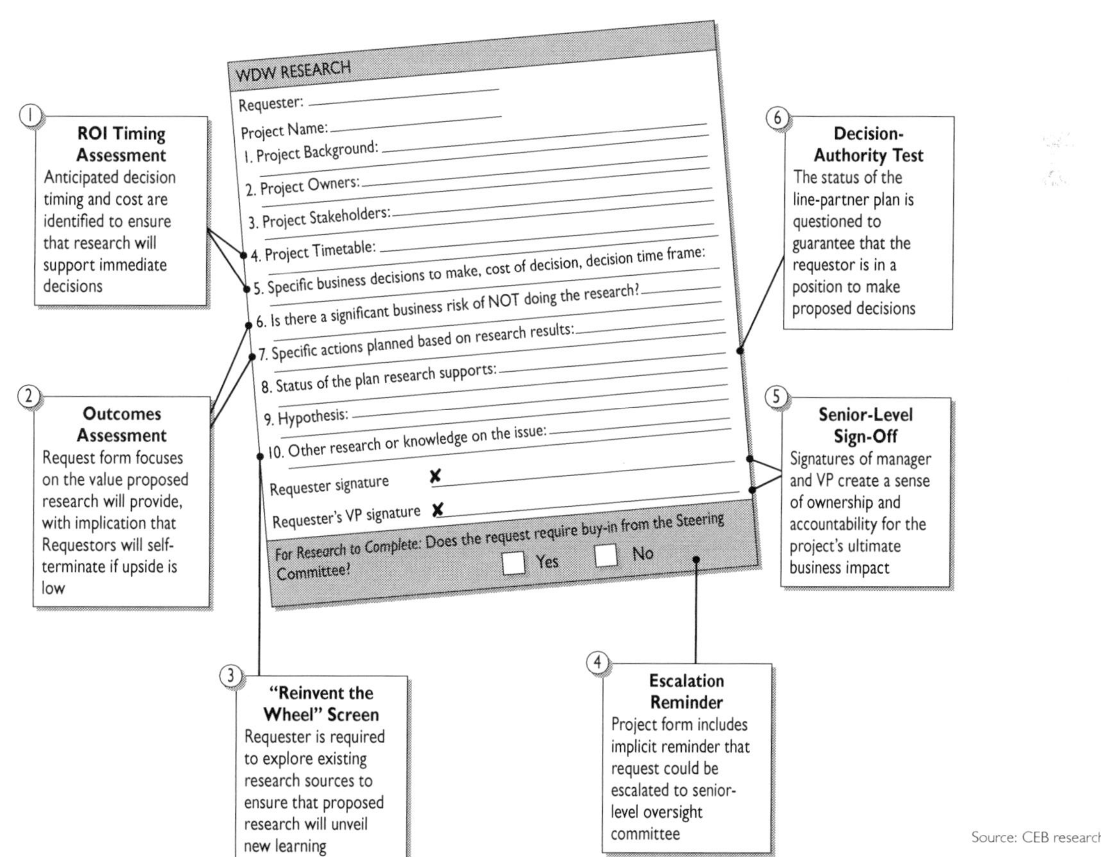

Source: CEB research.

Slide: "Framing the Professional Win"

The object at the center here is a stack of cards which prepares sales reps to understand the biases of certain types of customer, in this example, manufacturing. The card has four parts, highlighted by the four callouts. Although these annotations are not numbered, the sequence flows in a "Z": in the upper left of the card, Desired Outcomes points to number 1; in the upper right, Focus points to number 2; then down in the lower left, Concerns points to 3; and in the lower right, Potential Values points to 4.

To indicate that the manufacturing customer is only one of several types, we see four more cards behind the first card, the next of which is labeled "Functional Bias: Sales and Manufacturing." The audience understands that each card lists the main four areas of potential bias for a customer representing a different function of the organization. This underscores the usefulness for helping reps quickly understand the kinds of biases a given customer is likely to have, based on what function he or she represents.

The annotated object is flanked on the left by supporting information: the key takeaway in the upper left corner of the slide emphasizes the main conclusion, and the text beneath it offers further rationale for the cards used. Finally, in the bottom left of the slide, the presenter defines the term "Functional Bias."

> **Exposing the biases underlying decision making equips reps to articulate implications of action or inaction in customer terms.**

- Company A does not simply tell reps what to say, but helps reps understand why certain messages will resonate by teaching them how different functions are goaled and think about the world.
- Besides the rational outcomes which different functions are tasked with affecting, functional bias gets at the worries and worldviews of each customer, helping reps pull emotional levers and use relevant language.

"Functional Bias": The lens through which individuals in different functions interpret events as wins and losses and make decisions accordingly; a product of job goals and responsibilities, day-to-day worries, and the personalities/worldviews of people who tend to seek jobs in certain functions

FRAMING THE PROFESSIONAL WIN

Components of Functional Bias

Desired Outcomes
- High-level business outcomes for which they are responsible
- Shows the metrics reps must impact to get them to a decision

Concerns
- What they worry about day-to-day
- Allows rep to build empathy and credibility by appealing to fears and doubts

Functional Bias: Sales and Marketing

Functional Bias: Manufacturing

1. Decision Criteria
- Minimize costs
- Maximize yield
- Maintain plant
- Maximize throughput
- Improve operating latitude

2. Focus

On finished product leaving plant. Labor numbers and competence, current and mid-term. Being aware of equipment and process development to reduce cost/volume ratios, mid-term.

3. Concerns
- Do I have the right people for the job?
- Can I consistently produce to an end product specification?
- Is my plant well-maintained?
- Do my weekly production plans allow maximum length runs?

4. Potential Values
- Decreases rejects
- Minimizes rework
- Increases tolerance of process
- Expands equipment throughput
- Reduces need for capital investment
- Reduces total number of inputs

Focus
- Area of the business they care about and time frame for evaluation
- Steers reps to frame offering in terms of its impacts on these areas

Potential Values
- Specific levers to drive business outcomes
- Focuses reps on supplier capabilities most likely to create value

Slide: "Building Employment Brand Equity Through a Marketing Plan"

In addition to a standard object being annotated, this version adds a few more touches: the coffee mug, the pen, and the two partially hidden graphics labeled "Sensitive," all of which suggest that we are being offered a glimpse at the desk of an HR executive. The annotated object in the middle left, a marketing plan for an employment brand, has only titles showing—the callouts on the right side give all the details of the grayed-out text. Besides displaying details of the Situation Analysis, the Employment Objectives, etc., the callouts are further grouped into three components, indicating how they relate to each other and mapping them to the three parts of the product marketing plan (establishing clear objectives, planning marketing communication strategy and action steps, and measuring and assessing progress). The text at the top of both sides describes the slide's overall narrative and context. Although the material here was originally designed for a two-page layout, it can work well on one slide.

Building Employment Brand Equity Through a Marketing Plan

The key to effective marketing and brand building in the product market is a solid marketing plan. A marketing plan for the company's employment value proposition(s) and resulting employment brand(s) serves as an important guide for the corporation and its brand management team, as compelling offers are structured within the company and communicated to employees or the labor market—thus building employment brand equity.

An employment brand marketing plan will have three components that are common in product marketing plans. First, the plan should clearly establish what corporate objectives are to be pursued through the plan—such as decreasing turnover or increasing recruitment. Second, the plan should lay out the marketing and communication strategy to be used, as well as specific actions various groups within the company need to take. Finally, an effective plan needs to establish a control process that identifies how progress is to be measured and assessed, as well as how changes will be made in the plan or the employment offer.

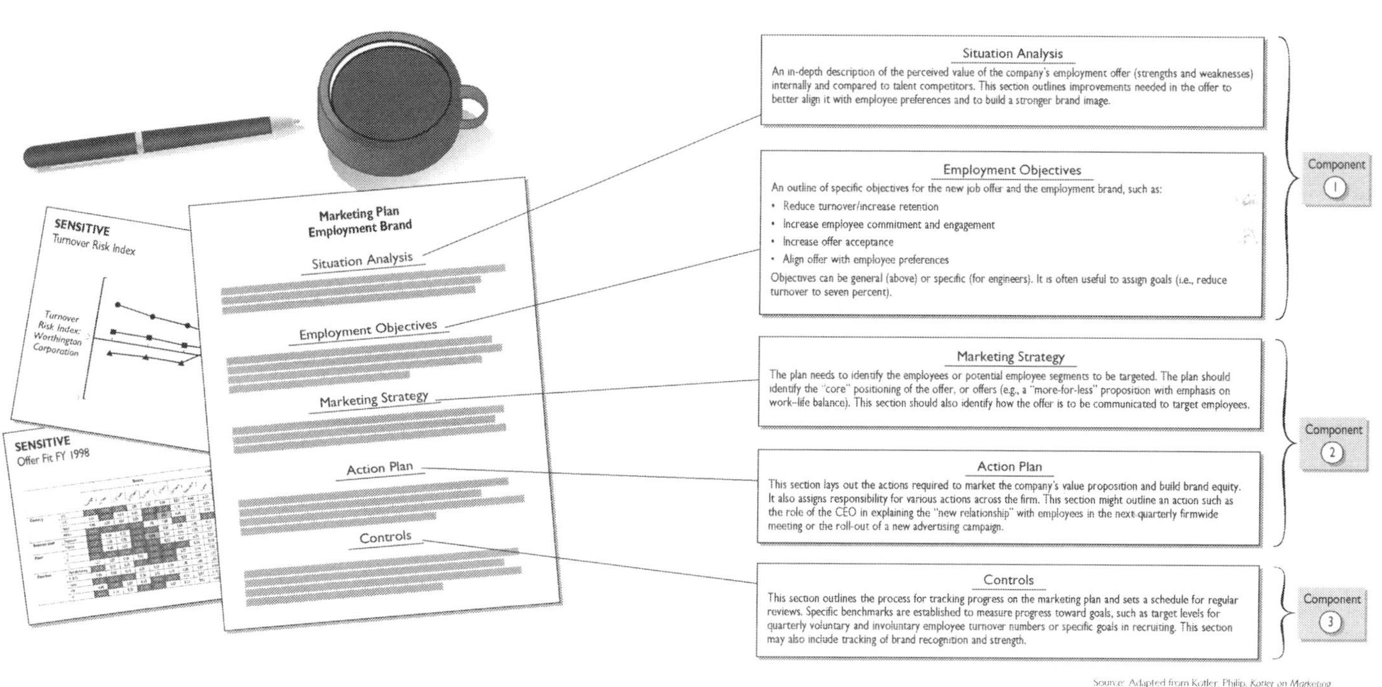

Source: Adapted from Kotler, Philip. *Kotler on Marketing.* New York: The Free Press, 1999, pp. 167–175.

Slide: "A Place of Our Own"

The annotated object depicted here appears at first to be a room, but closer inspection reveals it to be a virtual workspace. The concrete image of a room enables the presenter to be very specific and visual in labeling different "parts"—document management systems, a message board, etc. Once the five callouts have clearly explained these various parts in the upper portion of the page, the entire virtual room itself flows into the screen in the middle, showing that these are elements of a collaborative research portal. At the bottom of the page, a visual metaphor of a work group table shows the varied composition of the team that developed the portal (for more examples, see the Metaphor layout chapter).

Notice also the nice touch of the binary code "wallpaper," which further indicates that the room is virtual.

A Place of Our Own

Multiple Features Ensure a Highly Effective Collaboration Tool

Depiction of Virtual Collaborative Workspace

Illustrative

① **Document Management Systems**
Version-control ensures that users edit correct versions of documents.

② **Secure Permission-Based Access**
Owners control access to the workspace, allowing teams to work with the most sensitive information.

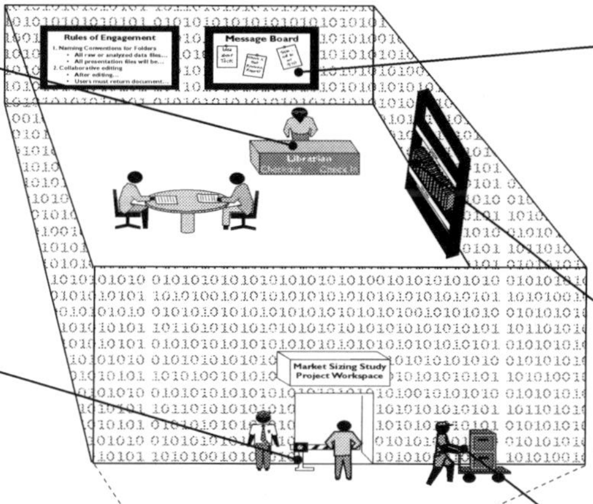

③ **Single Storage Space** limits other information storage options, compelling researchers to use the collaborative workspace to ensure use.

④ **Standardized Folders**
Consistent content architecture facilitates collaboration and seamless assimilation of new talent as needed.

⑤ **Message Board**
Message Board allows users to share and save ideas in parallel, removing friction of communication.

Rules of Engagement

Message Board

Librarian

Market Sizing Study Project Workspace

Collaborative Research Portal

Composition of Portal Development Team

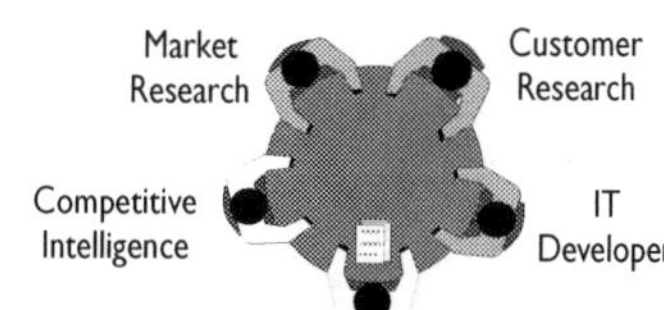

Source: CEB research.

Slide: "Anatomy of a 'Conference Room' Style Presentation"

The idea here is to describe conference room style presentations on one page. A typical one-slide presentation is featured in the middle, and the ten most significant features of conference room style are highlighted, by pointing (where possible) to the specific feature on the slide.

Anatomy of a "Conference Room" Style Presentation

Use a Conference Room style presentation when you are trying to persuade or educate a small group—e.g., seeking approval for an initiative, selling a product, service, or idea, or pitching a new venture or investment.

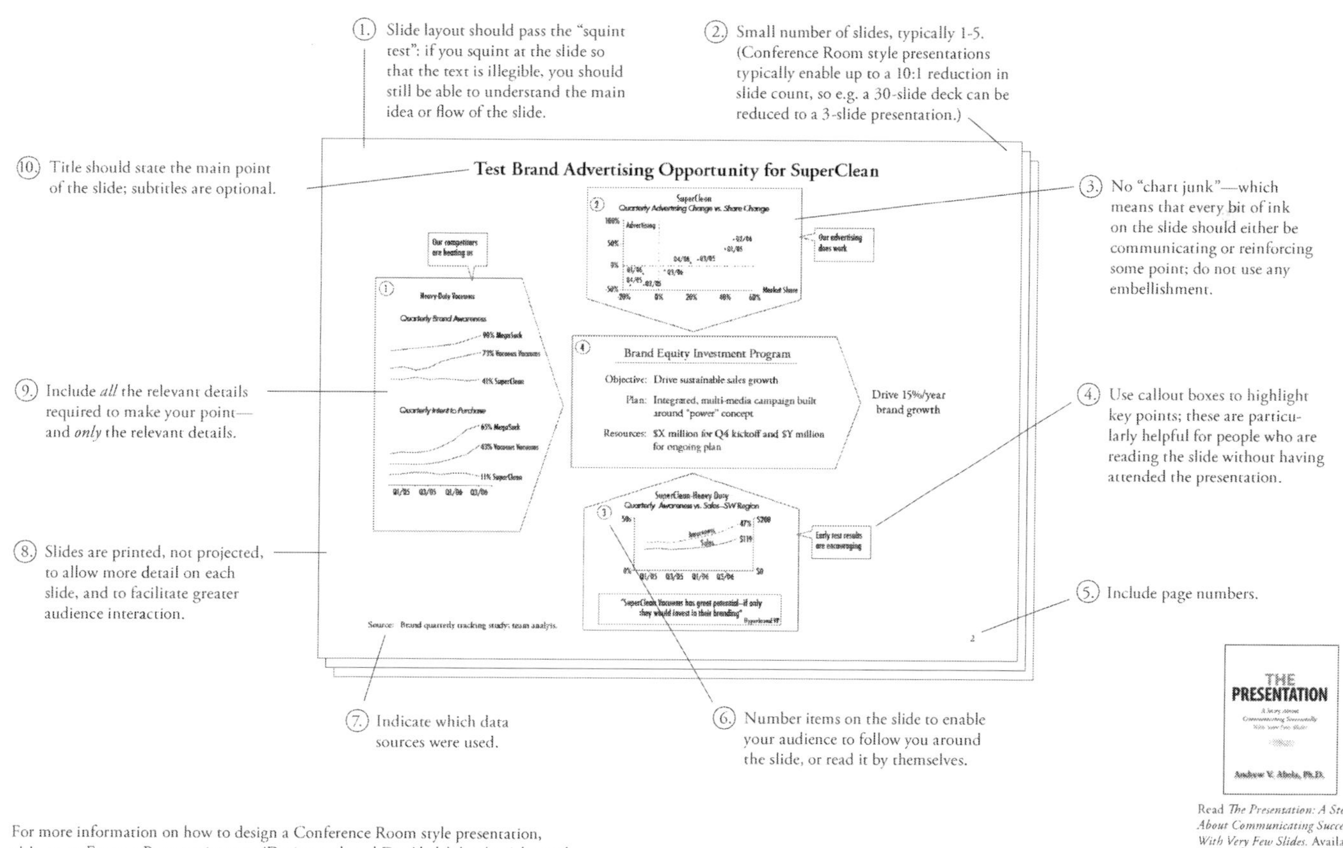

For more information on how to design a Conference Room style presentation, visit www.ExtremePresentation.com/Design and read Dr. Abela's books *Advanced Presentations by Design* and *The Presentation*.

Read *The Presentation: A Story About Communicating Successfully With Very Few Slides*. Available on Amazon.com for US $7.50.

CHAPTER 6: "ASPECTS – MULTIPLE" LAYOUT

The Multiple Aspects layout uses a matrix to describe in some detail the various aspects of a particular idea or situation. The aspects can be laid out vertically or horizontally, and described directly or in terms of various related factors. Matrices are very space-efficient, permitting the inclusion of extensive detail, as the examples demonstrate. The Multiple Aspects layout differs from Multiple Alternatives in that instead of suggesting a choice among several alternatives, it describes several facets of one topic or issue. This distinction is further clarified by the addition of visual cues, such as an object radiating outwards towards all the aspects for Multiple Aspects (see page 63), versus highlighting one alternative in the Multiple Alternatives layout.

How to draw the "Aspects – Multiple" Layout

Diagrammer

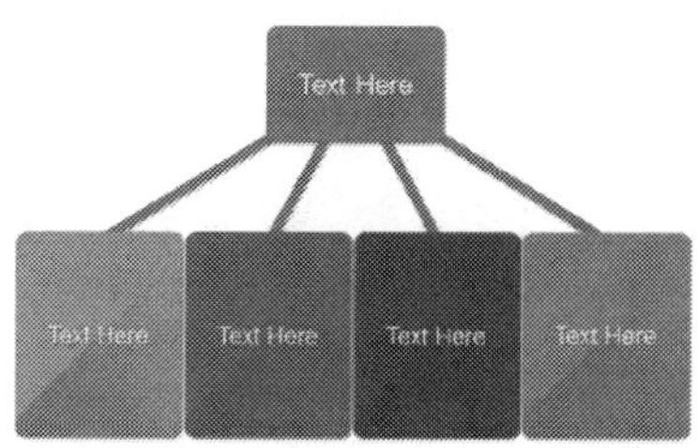

www.Diagrammer.com
Network, Flare, 4 Nodes, 2D Angled, Network Flare 3

Slide: "If left unaddressed, organizational issues can generate significant performance challenges"

This slide illustrates a characteristic Multiple Aspects layout. The main idea, "Key performance challenges," is highlighted in an oval at the top of the slide. The four aspects of the idea, or the four main categories of challenges—talent management, process management, value capture and behavioral—radiate outwards below it. The details of each aspect are captured in columns, without any categorization. The text along the bottom, embedded in a dark background that spans all four aspects, highlights the finding that these challenges occur across cultural differences.

If left unaddressed, organizational issues can generate significant performance challenges

Key performance challenges

Talent management	Process management	Value capture	Behavioral
▪ Executive turnover ▪ Attrition of high-performing employees	▪ Breakdown of decision making ▪ Excessive internal focus and time lost ensuring coordination	▪ Slowed value capture (loss of ability to convert revenue, cost, and capability synergies) ▪ Reduced innovativeness and opportunity capture ▪ Disruption of core business performance	▪ Passive-aggressive behavior, insufficient cooperation and sabotage ▪ Erosion of common values and vision ▪ Inconsistent interaction with customers

Common across cultural differences

Slide: "Businesses are employing technology trends to create competitive advantage across each of their primary activities"

This example demonstrates how much detail a single slide can comfortably convey in the Multiple Aspects layout. Three aspects of technology use—in this case, three primary business activities—are laid out horizontally with their headings listed down the left side of the slide: Managing talent, Managing capital/assets, and Managing information. The details for each aspect or activity are categorized into three groups, presented in columns. The first column describes the driving force behind the use of technology in that activity. The second and third columns provide case examples of companies that have used technology to either "Win the race" in that activity (thus succeeding in their existing business) or to "Change the rules" for that activity (by using technology to create a whole new market approach). Once again, this example is differentiated from Multiple Alternatives by the absence of any attempt to highlight one of the aspects.

Businesses are employing technology trends to create competitive advantage across each of their primary activities

	Driving force	'Win the race'	'Change the rules'
Managing talent	▪ Labor force is expanding beyond employees to include customers, collaborators and volunteers	▪ **JetBlue** has been able to use "work at home moms" for all of its reservation agents, leveraging VoIP	▪ **InnoCentive** is a marketplace for companies to post chemistry or biology problems to be solved by anyone for a price. Originally setup by Eli Lilly, it is now used by a number of companies ▪ **iStock Photo** is an online stock photography portal, where prosumers are very active. Along with similar sites, it has reduced the cost of stock photos by ~100x
Managing capital/ assets	▪ Companies are increasingly opening their value chains to leverage scale ▪ Advances in automation are enabling new types of activity and information collection	▪ **Wal-Mart** is aggressively implementing RFID for product tracking throughout its supply chain and will shortly expand it to in-store products	▪ **Mobile phone companies** have opened up their networks and billing systems to allow others to resell branded services (aka Mobile Virtual Network Operators) ▪ **Amazon's** "Simple Storage Service" and "Elastic Compute Cloud" enable companies to use Amazon's global infrastructure for storage and processing
Managing information	▪ Increases in data collection and mining techniques are allowing businesses to improve internal operations; enhance customer acquisition and retention; and create new revenue streams	▪ **Progressive** and **Capital One** use massive amounts of data to micro-segment offerings and price-points for customers ▪ **Amazon.com** has created a historical pricing offering which allows access to 3 years of sales data for books, music, videos, and DVDs for a fee	▪ **Norwich Union** has begun offering "Pay as you drive" auto insurance, using GPS monitoring to set rates based on where, when, and how far policyholders drive ▪ **Barclays Capital** built a new electronic exchange for interest rate swaps, creating a transparent and efficient market, and capturing share from other platforms

Slide: "Exploring Disrupters"

In this example, four types of industry pressure (suppliers, competitors, disruptors, and buyers) are listed in vertical columns, with details about the pressure categorized in rows. The details show the implications for the airlines industry stemming from each source of pressure. The left margin, set off by a thin vertical line, provides a brief synopsis of the slide.

EXPLORING DISRUPTERS

Simplify "future exploration" by focusing on potential disrupters to its value chain.

- Instead of focusing on macroeconomic and social or political trends, use business drivers to explore possible future changes.
- That exploration focuses on plausible industry disruptions that would impact near-term decisions.
- For each scenario, develop implications—including threats and opportunities.

Competitive Dynamics Modeling Exercise

2001

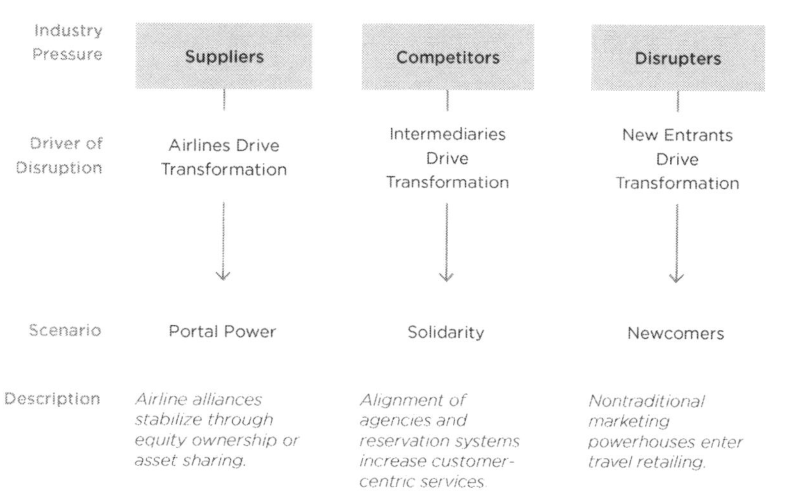

Industry Pressure	**Suppliers**	**Competitors**	**Disrupters**	**Buyers**
Driver of Disruption	Airlines Drive Transformation	Intermediaries Drive Transformation	New Entrants Drive Transformation	Socioeconomic Retrenchment Drives Transformation
Scenario	Portal Power	Solidarity	Newcomers	Global Cocooning
Description	*Airline alliances stabilize through equity ownership or asset sharing.*	*Alignment of agencies and reservation systems increase customer-centric services.*	*Nontraditional marketing powerhouses enter travel retailing.*	*Economic, political, and social turmoil reduce appetite and ability to travel.*
Implications	• Defend against airline strategies that adversely impact nondirect channels. • Invest aggressively in operational and marketing CRM.	• Operational efficiencies enable intermediaries to lower distribution and marketing fees. • Regulatory environment constrains airline consolidation.	• Create new business models and align with innovative intermediaries to meet customer service and distribution needs.	• Reservation systems and travel agencies consolidate and survive on significantly reduced revenue streams. • Improve ease and comfort of travel experience.

SOURCE: CEB research.

Slide: "Stall Factors Rest on Common Flawed Assumptions"

This example presents six factors or causes of corporate growth stalls and the false assumptions underlying each cause. The causes are listed horizontally; the assumptions upon which they rest, vertically. Each list begins with a title and an illustrating icon. Beneath the icon, the various false assumptions are listed. At the very bottom, horizontal brackets are used to group the causes by the type of false assumptions upon which they are based. Note that this slide was originally designed to be printed on two 8-1/2 x 11" portrait pages side-by-side, and has been shrunk to fit our page here; the text is not intended to be read in this size.

Stall Factors Rest on Common Flawed Assumptions

Premium Position Captivity

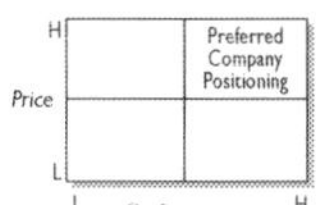

Specific False Assumptions

Customer Priorities

- Core customers will never be willing to trade better product performance for lower prices
- Core markets will continue to value the company's proven ability to innovate

Competitor Capabilities

- Low-end players will never meet performance demands of mainstream customers

Competitive Benchmark

- Traditional primary rival should remain the company's competitive benchmark

Non-Product Entry Barriers

- Advantages such as brand equity, experienced sales force will thwart inroads by low-end rivals

Advent of Disruptive Technology

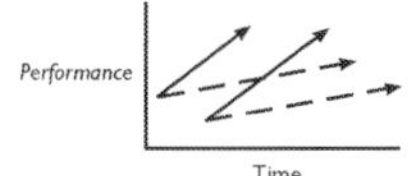

Specific False Assumptions

Competitor Capabilities and Industry Structure

- Low-end players will never meet performance demands of mainstream customers; low end of market is severable

Customer Priorities

- Core customers will never be willing to trade better product performance for lower prices

Product Innovation

- Continued product innovation runs only small risk of "overshooting" market needs
- Self-cannibalization of products rarely desirable

Errors driven by premium positioning or disruptive technologies principally due to faulty assessments of customer priorities and capabilities of low-end rivals

Senior Team Composition

Senior Management

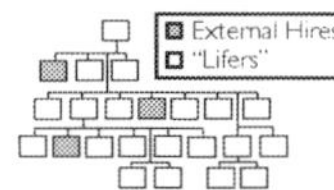

Specific False Assumptions

Talent Sourcing Policy

- Managers who know the company's business model and customers will always outperform newcomers
- Strict adherence to promote-from-within policy needed to maintain *esprit de corps*

Management Competencies

- Managerial skills adaptable across business situations and entire industries

Team Dynamics

- Benefits of highly cohesive management teams generally outweigh risk that groupthink will inhibit objectivity

Groupthink often driven by incorrect assumptions about appropriate senior team profile

Premature Core Abandonment

Focus of Investment

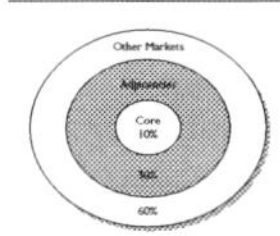

Specific False Assumptions

Market Potential

- Prevailing industry growth delimits possible company growth rates
- Operational shortcomings in the core indicate that growth should be pursued elsewhere

Growth Goals

- Prudent to treat once high-growth business units as "cash cows"

Reinvestment Requirements

- In mature markets, high-dividend payout ratios do not risk underinvestment
- Acceptable to reduce reinvestment in advertising, R&D and capital to boost profits, fund noncore initiatives

Strategic Diffusion

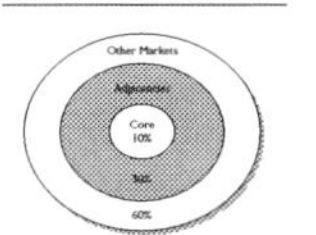

Specific False Assumptions

Core Competencies

- Core competencies have broad applicability, are easily leveraged into adjacent market opportunities

Portfolio Management

- Major mergers or acquisitions often best enablers of future core business growth
- Even moderately cyclical businesses must be hedged through diversification

Managerial Capabilities

- Senior managers can effectively manage many strategic initiatives simultaneously
- Highly dissimilar businesses can be managed by a single team with a single set of systems, controls

Errors of core abandonment and strategic diffusion principally rooted in poor understanding of market opportunity and the limits of portfolio management

Innovation Management Breakdown

Product Pipeline NPV

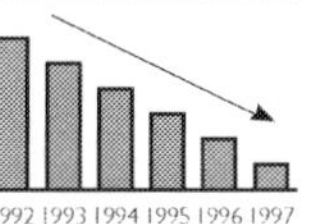

Specific False Assumptions

Business Definition

- Innovation should occur within narrow business definition

Product Proliferation

- Product differentiation will not confuse customers and drive up costs

Investment Requirements

- Short-term cut in R&D spending to improve earnings will not hurt long-term growth

Organizational Structure

- Decentralized R&D can produce long-term, high-risk successful investments
- New products should be placed in the same unit as the products they will replace

Innovation management breakdown driven by mistaken assumptions across all stages of the innovation process

Source: CEB, *Stall Points: Barriers to Growth for the Large Corporate Enterprise*. CEB research.

CHAPTER 7: "BALANCE/OUT OF BALANCE" LAYOUT

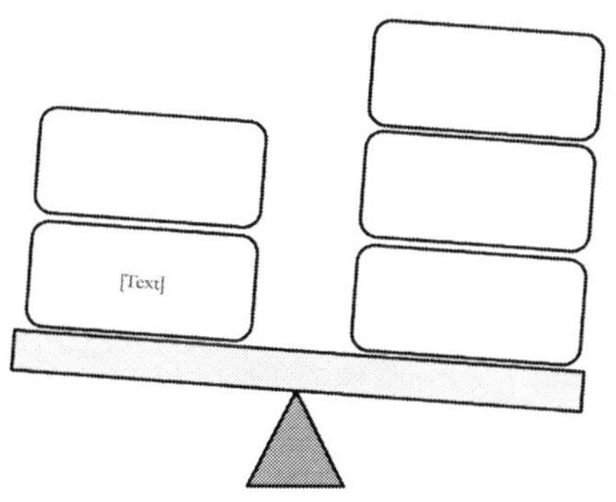

The Balance/Out of Balance layout effectively shows the audience that there is too much of something on one side of the balance, or too little on another. The image of a balance scale loaded with unequal (or equal) weights provides the conceptual structure for this layout.

How to draw the "Balance/Out of Balance" Layout

Charteo

Weight scale

www.Charteo.com
Graphics and Metaphors, Scales, Weight Scale 7

SmartArt

PowerPoint SmartArt
Relationship, Balance

Slide: "Everybody Wins"

The Balance/Out of Balance layout is used here to show not that something is wrong, but rather that something is right: by working together, the Wealth Manager and the Brokerage Advisor can better serve the client and can build overall revenue. The thought bubbles of the Wealth Management Advisor on the left of the slide show him trying to determine how best to serve a specific client, whose critical information is detailed on the tear-out paper beneath the Advisor's table. Because he is offered an equal incentive for choosing either option, the Advisor is able to combine perspectives on both platforms in order to partner most effectively with the client.

The balance on the right side of the slide depicts the fact that combining both approaches results in a greater benefit to the client and to the company. The benefits are listed beneath the two partnering figures whose combined weight registers in the nearer scale, and the deficiencies of the weaker (and lighter) Solo approach are delineated in the scale on the upper right.

Everybody Wins

Gramercy Financial's* compensation structure makes wealth management advisors platform neutral...

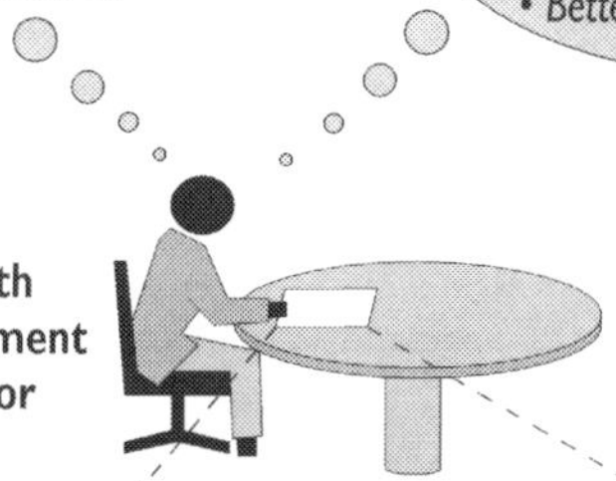

...and encourages ongoing teamwork between brokerage and wealth management

Factors to Determine Optimal Platform for Clients

Gramercy Financial

Benefits of Partnership

Gramercy Financial

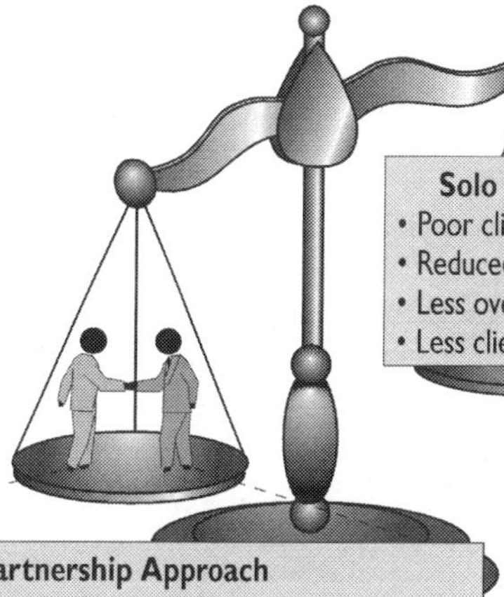

* Pseudonym.

SOURCE: Gramercy Financial; CEB research.

Slide: "Tipping the Scales?"

This version of the Balance/Out of Balance layout introduces uncertainty: the balance scales here hold factors of unknown weight, leaving the audience unsure as to which side of the scale will prevail. The question in the title of the slide further reinforces the uncertainty of the outcome. This layout helps the presenter to discuss both the advantages and the disadvantages of an action, method, or idea, and can invite the audience into the discussion to help answer the questions. In this slide, the reasons behind the disadvantages are laid out on the right, above the perplexed person sitting at the table. The quotation at the bottom of the slide offers one manager's perspective as to why the advantages can outweigh the disadvantages.

Tipping the Scales?

The advantages of proactive hiring manager outreach are often counterbalanced by the disadvantages...

Advantages and Disadvantages of Hiring Manager Outreach

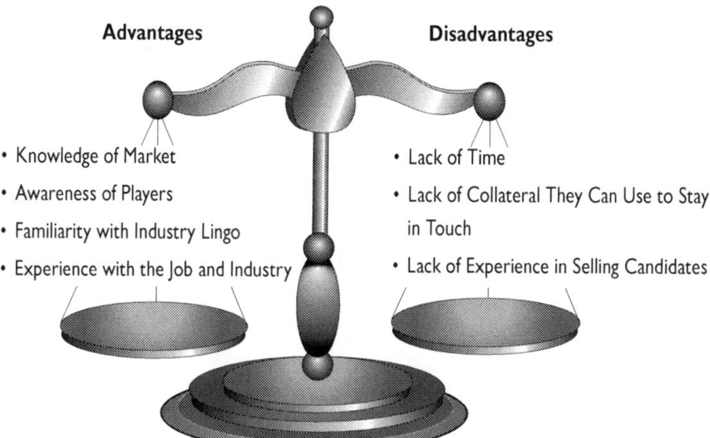

...which often stem from a lack of resources and training

Voice of the "Typical" Hiring Manager

"If only I had **talking points,** I might be able to have this type of conversation..."

"Maybe if there were **specific objectives** for the conversation..."

"Well I wouldn't even know **how to position** such a **conversation**..."

"Even if I got them engaged, I wouldn't have **anything interesting to send** them to keep them interested over time..."

Walk the Walk

"Our hiring leaders know the role better than anyone and can quickly build rapport with candidates by talking in specifics. They can anticipate questions that prospective candidates might have and this helps us quickly identify leads for these positions."

Phil Haynes
Sourcing Strategy Manager

SOURCE: CEB research.

CHAPTER 8: "BARRIER" LAYOUT

The Barrier layout helps the presenter describe how some project or process is being blocked or stifled. This layout typically shows an arrow or a process driving up to and stopping at a vertical line, which acts as a visual barrier. If the presenter wants to portray something "hitting a wall," this is the right layout. The simple overall design quickly communicates the main point of the page, and also allows for many details explaining the process, the thing opposing it, and the reasons for the opposition.

Slide: "Feeling Left Out"

The lower half of this page uses the Barrier layout to demonstrate three common obstacles to internal stakeholder adoption of recommendations based on market segmentation research findings. The interesting change here is that the barriers are not plain vertical lines or boxes, but the proverbial brick wall. The research study findings themselves reside in the lower left of the slide, and the arrow points from the findings towards the target consumer—but through the barrier of the brick wall. The complexity and difficulty of adopting the findings is demonstrated by the fact that there are three consecutive barriers: (1) The findings are too complicated to understand; (2) even if the end-user can understand the findings, they are not credible; and (3) even if the first two barriers are overcome, the findings may not be actionable.

This Barrier layout is embedded within the overall slide—the upper portion of the slide shows typical attempts to involve stakeholders in the segmentation process, and the quotation at the bottom offers a big-picture perspective on some of the reasons behind the failure to adopt study findings.

Feeling Left Out

Despite Research's efforts to involve stakeholders in segmentation analysis...

Standard Stakeholder Engagement Efforts

Illustrative

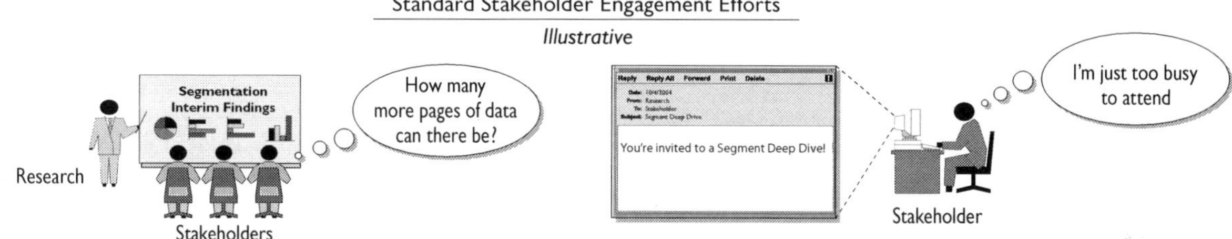

...stakeholders feel a limited sense of study ownership that drives resistance to adopting study recommendations

Obstacles to Adoption of Segmentation Recommendations

Illustrative

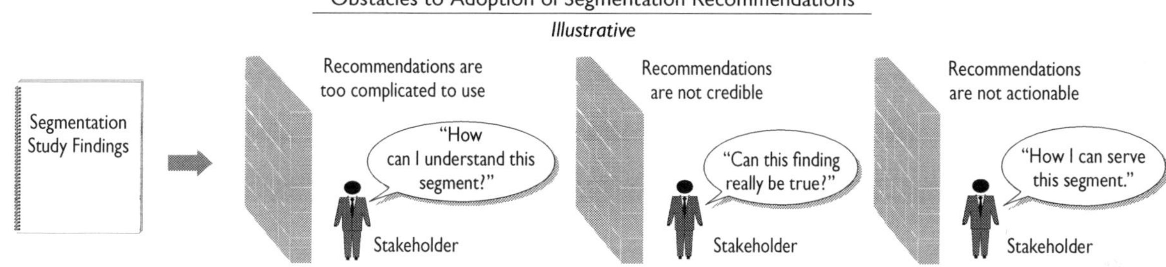

Pattern Recognition

"From reviewing previous segmentation studies, it became clear that our traditional embedding plan left end users feeling detached from the process and thus inclined to question the usability of the findings."

Senior Director, Research

SOURCE: CEB research.

Slide: "Lost in Translation"

Here's an alternative version of the Barrier layout: the barrier here is not a physical presence, but the absence of a bridge between the two sides. On the left side, the research team has generated some major insights as symbolized by the large light bulb. In trying to translate these insights for their internal stakeholders—a move symbolized by crossing the chasm between the two sides—much is lost. The impact of the insight decreases (represented by the decreasing size of the light bulb) as contextual details like Consumer Voice are lost or "fall down into the gap" in the insight delivery process. By the time the light bulb reaches the internal stakeholder, it has not only shrunk in size but has also cracked.

The overall point of the slide is clear: the lost contextual details are essential if the line manager on the right is to adopt the research insight in business decisions.

Lost in Translation

Research Efforts to Translate Insights for the Line Invariably Omit Important Contextual Details Necessary for Applying the Insights

Impact of Split Ownership for Insight Generation and Adoption of Insights

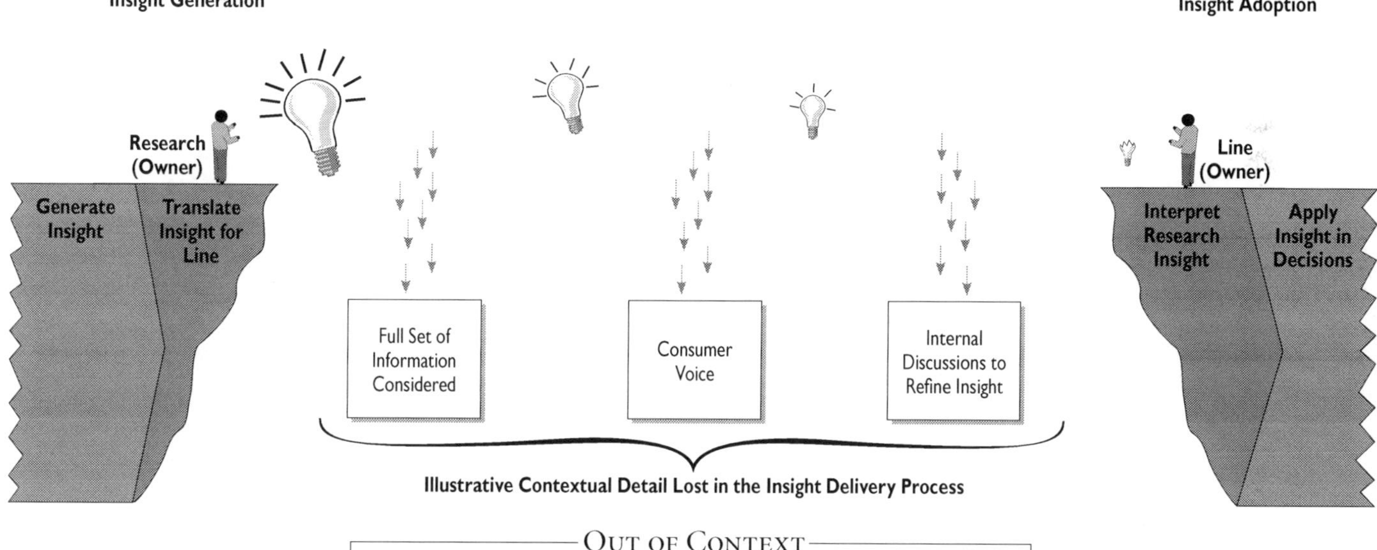

Out of Context

"It had reached the point where people were getting totally confused about what to do with insights."

Head of Research
Consumer Packaged Goods

SOURCE: CEB research.

CHAPTER 9: "CONVERGING ISSUES" LAYOUT

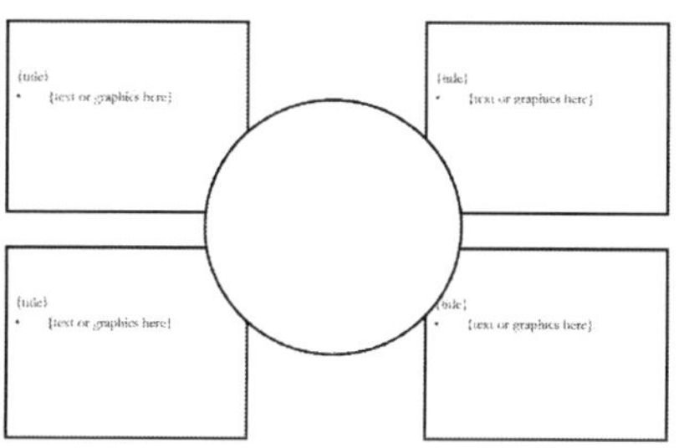

The Converging Issues layout takes some focal point and surrounds that focus with a handful of separate issues which impact it. This layout is very useful when (for example) the presenter needs to show many factors influencing a decision. It is one of the most commonly used layouts, as seen in the multiple examples in this chapter.

How to draw the "Converging Issues" Layout

Charteo

www.Charteo.com
Concept Charts, Circle Charts, Segmented Charts, Segmented Circle 60

Diagrammer

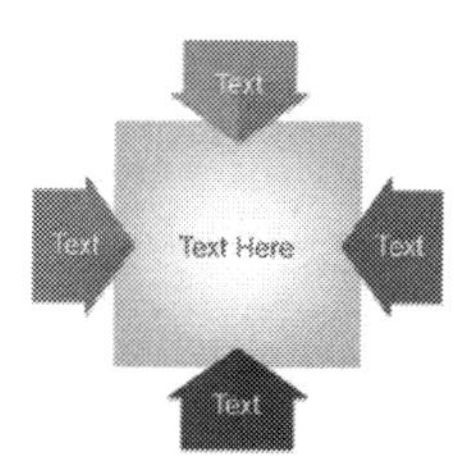

www.Diagrammer.com
Flow, Merge-Divide, 4 Nodes, 2D Angled, Flow Merge and Divide 552

PowerFrameworks

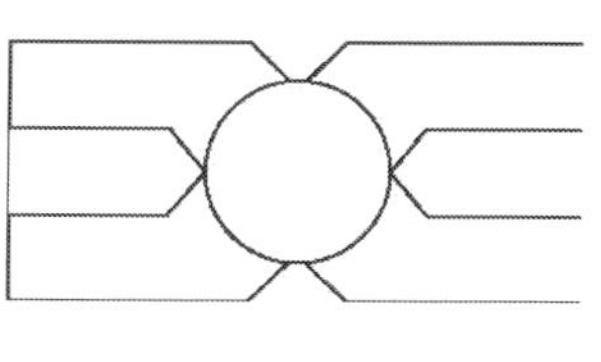

www.PowerFrameworks.com
Keyword Search "AV009", AV009-0203

SmartArt

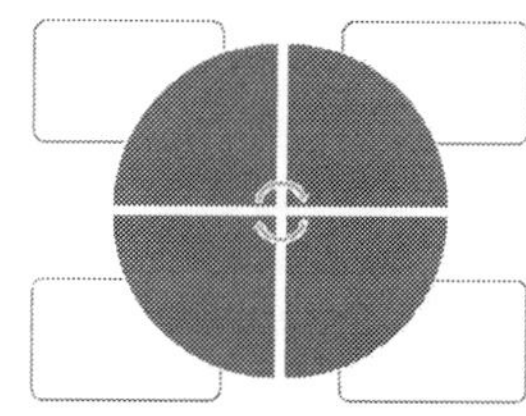

PowerPoint SmartArt
Matrix, Cycle Matrix

"Converging Issues" Layout

Slide: "Developing a technology-enabled business vision requires a holistic assessment of the environment"

This Converging Issues layout focuses on the vision of how the company will create competitive advantage; this focal point is surrounded by the four issues of Business strategy, Current capability assessment, Technology trends and impact, and Competitive assessment and market needs. Each of the four areas is embedded within a chevron pointing toward the focal point in the middle of the page, and within each chevron are two or three questions relevant to developing the company vision.

This layout shows how the four outlying issues impact the company vision at the center, with a clarity that could not be achieved by placing each of these issues on separate slides, or even by embedding them as four quadrants on one slide.

Developing a technology-enabled business vision requires a holistic assessment of the environment

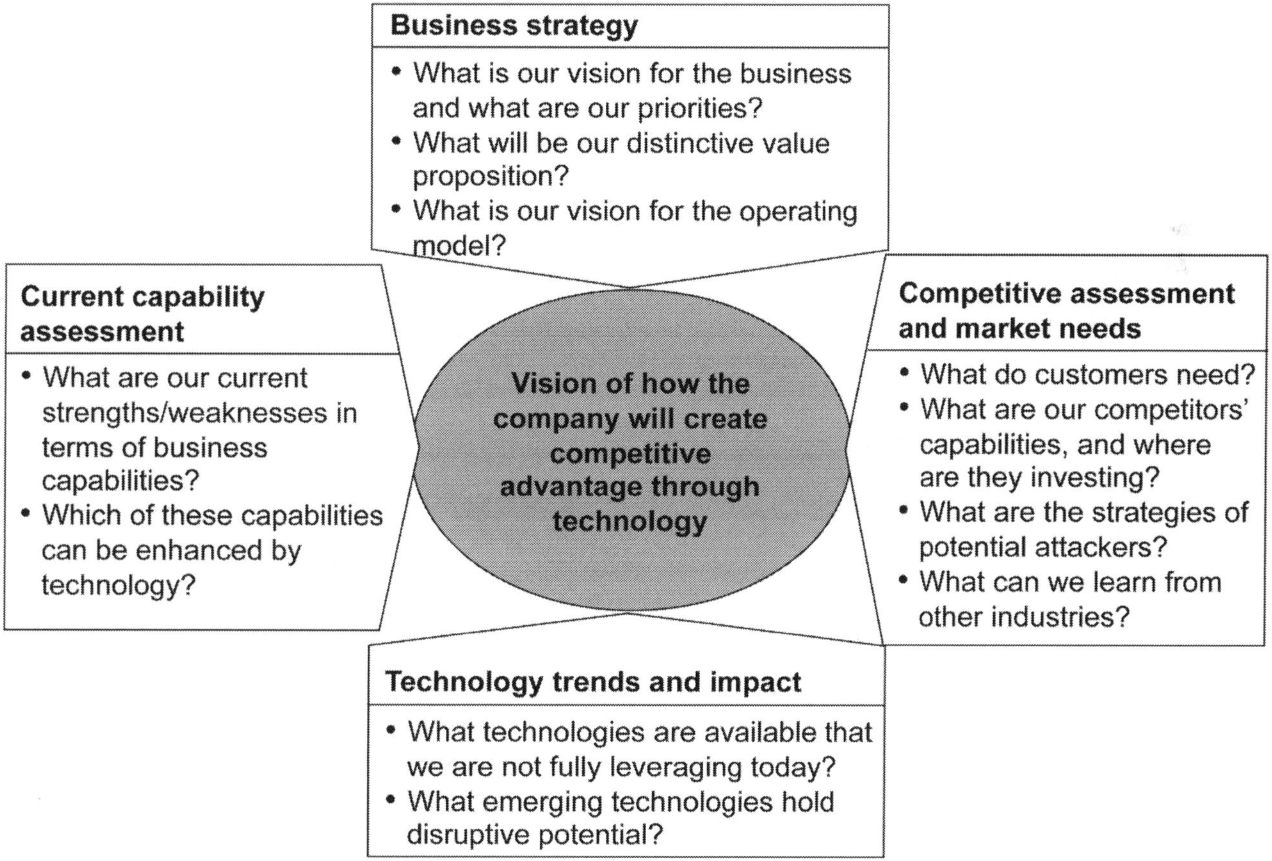

Vision of how the company will create competitive advantage through technology

Business strategy

- What is our vision for the business and what are our priorities?
- What will be our distinctive value proposition?
- What is our vision for the operating model?

Current capability assessment

- What are our current strengths/weaknesses in terms of business capabilities?
- Which of these capabilities can be enhanced by technology?

Competitive assessment and market needs

- What do customers need?
- What are our competitors' capabilities, and where are they investing?
- What are the strategies of potential attackers?
- What can we learn from other industries?

Technology trends and impact

- What technologies are available that we are not fully leveraging today?
- What emerging technologies hold disruptive potential?

Slide: "Short Memories"

The central focus of this Converging Issues layout is the learned behavior of managers during financial crises, and the issues around the outside are four factors that decay or weaken that learned behavior. Each factor's title is bolded and accompanied by a quotation representing the attitude of a manager experiencing this factor. To further depict the destructive factors' corrosiveness, the morbid skull-and-crossbones symbols "eat away" at the central focus—the positive learned behavior. The main conclusion of the page, given at the top of the left column, is followed by background and summary narrative explaining the slide.

Although this slide resembles an Annotated Object layout (see that chapter for examples), it is a genuine and appropriate example of Converging Issues, because the four outlying factors are not merely labeling the central object, but impacting it both visually and conceptually.

> **Without a crisis or deliberate effort, individuals are likely to revert to old behaviors.**

- Human psychology makes it hard for us to adopt and maintain new behaviors.
- Managers are no exception. With the economic crisis behind them, the motivation to continue with newly learned practices may fade.
- The result: smart behaviors wrongly discarded.

SHORT MEMORIES

Factors Leading to "Managerial Recidivism"

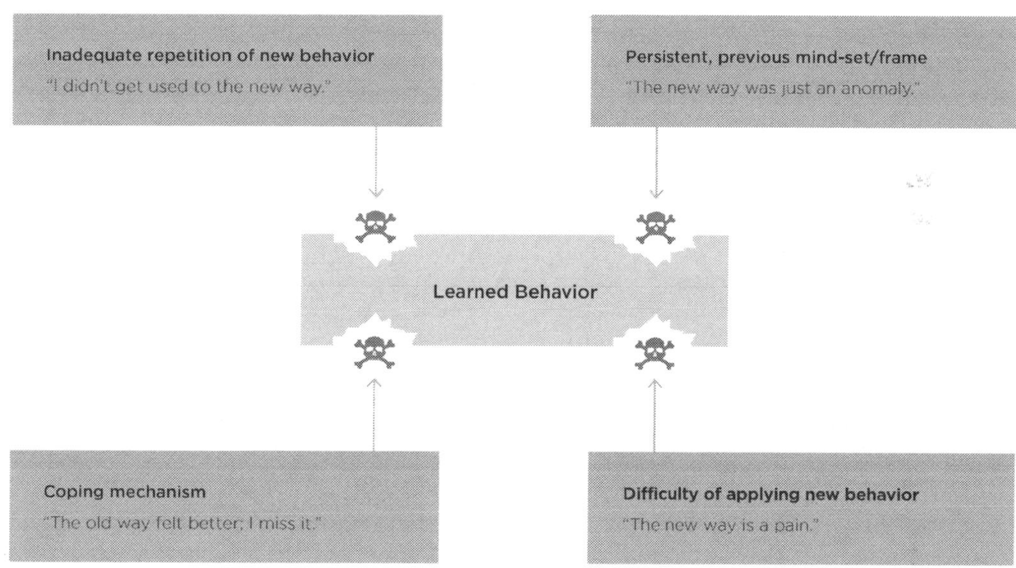

Source: Deutshman, Alan, *Change or Die*, Fast Company, 19 Dec 2007; Bregman, Peter, *The Easiest Way to Change People's Behavior*, Harvardbusines.org, 11 March 2009

Slide: "In the Line of Fire"

Although it adds more graphical detail, this example preserves simplicity of design: three key pressures surround a frazzled marketing executive at the center of the slide. Each of the converging pressures is summed up by a title, a conceptual graph or icon, and a text description. The graphs show visually what the titles identify: for example, for "Pressure # 3: Speed of Market Change," the graph shows how much more quickly new products decline in price, compared to older product introductions. A straightforward example of Converging Issues, this layout delivers its main message quickly by reinforcing the slide title, "In the Line of Fire," through the overall layout—the arrows are aimed at the marketing executive.

In the Line of Fire

Three Pressures Increase the Complexity of the Marketing Executive's Job

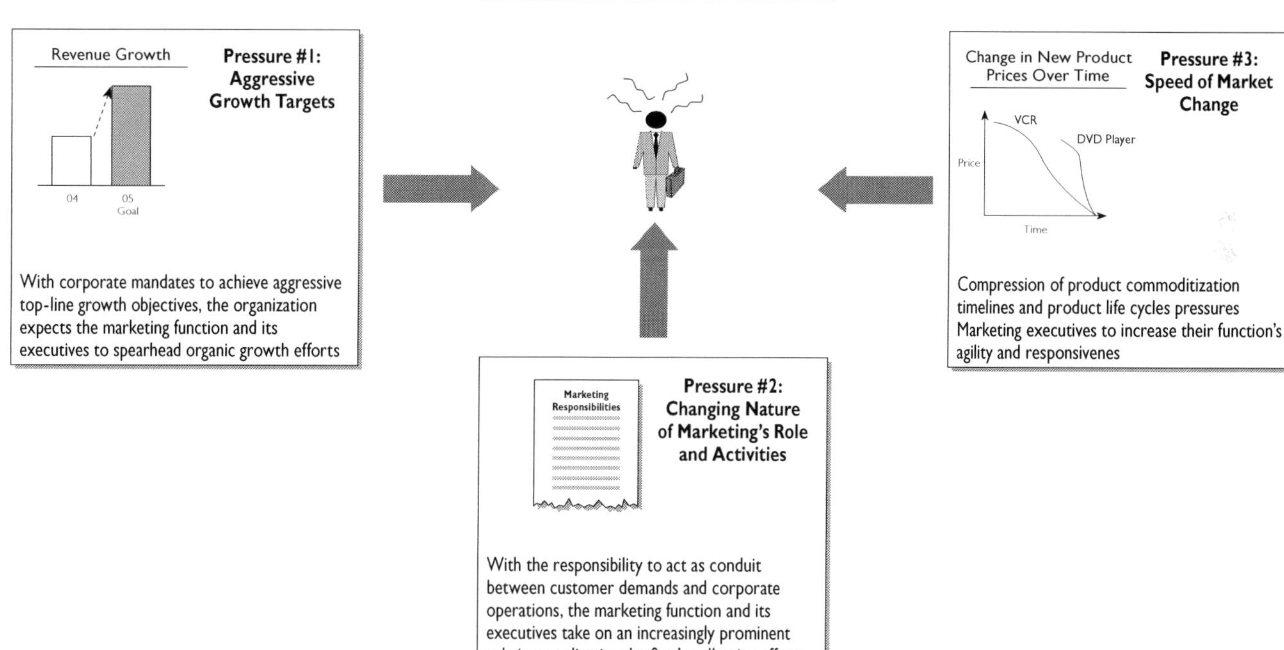

SOURCE: CEB research.

Slide: "Which Trees? What Forest?"

A further example of the Converging Issues layout, this version surrounds an executive with seven factors: various questions and demands, in areas that range from pricing to customers to peer executives to the CEO. The stacks of paper on the desk and floor depict the stress of the beleaguered executive, implying that this person already has too many projects and responsibilities. The title of the page should normally capture the slide's main message, but in this case the catchy title (playing on the aphorism that one "Can't see the forest for the trees") is followed by a descriptive subtitle which does indeed deliver the main message of the slide.

Which Trees? What Forest?

New Executives Face the Dual Challenge of Defining and Prioritizing Both Strategic and Operational Improvement Opportunities

Representative Demands on New Marketing Executive

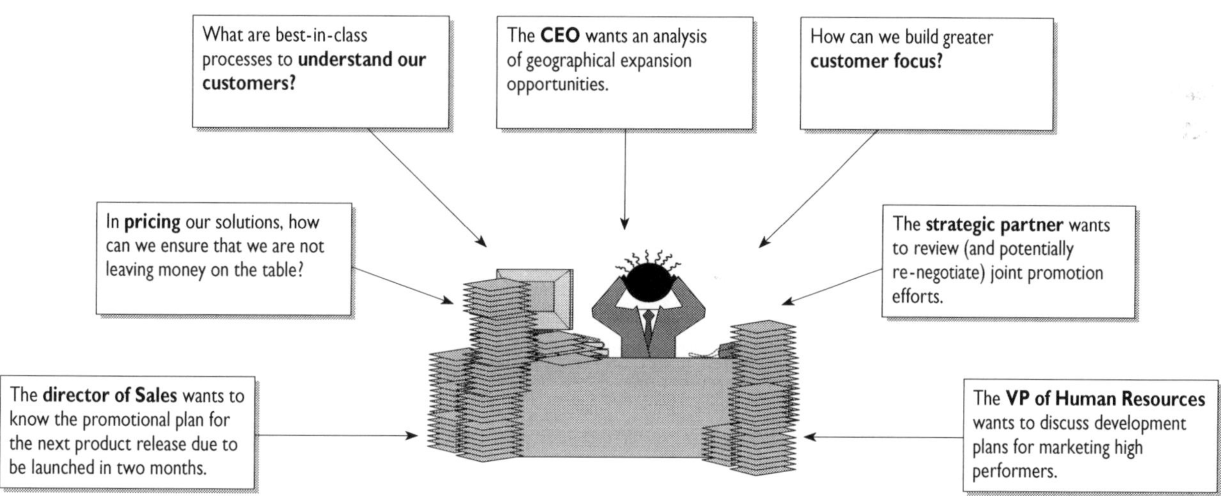

SOURCE: CEB research.

Slide: "Covering All Bases"

This slide, a clear example of the Converging Issues layout, embeds an extra layer of detail. To show how much input goes into evaluating the sales organization, the layout surrounds the sales rep with seven different constituencies grouped into four categories: Customers, Supply/Partner, Line Management, and Executives. A box for each of the seven constituencies not only details the kind of feedback the constituency gives, but also provides a concrete quotation, verbatim from a survey or interview—which is a great way to show pertinent detail. The slide's conceptual title is followed by a descriptive subtitle, and the subtitle's reference to a "360 degree perspective" is reinforced by the inner circle surrounding the sales rep.

Covering All Bases

Critical input from multiple constituencies provides 360 degrees of perspective on sales organization performance

Constituencies Targeted for Interviews

Customers
Feedback on overall supplier performance and field staff skills:
"Your sales reps need to be business consultants who help me grow my top and bottom line and improve my company's customer satisfaction levels."

Suppliers
Feedback on sales processes:
"Lack of transparency in your sales processes makes it difficult for us to work with your organization and to deliver on our promises."

Vendors
Feedback on working with the sales organization:
"It is impossible to propose solutions to a sales organization mired in paralysis. There is no vision or road map for us to deliver against."

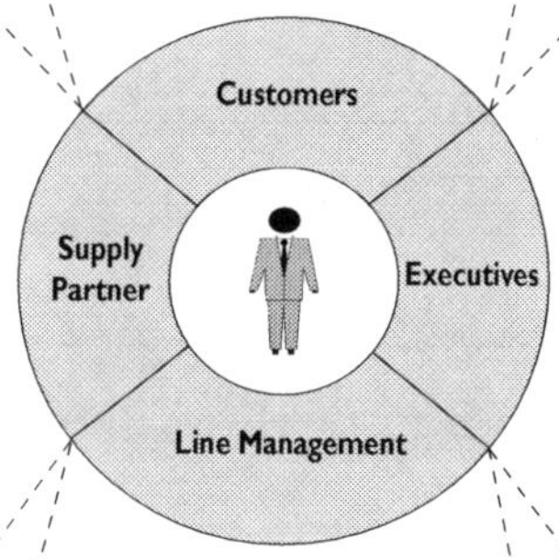

Customers
Supply Partner
Executives
Line Management

Executive Leadership (CEO, COO, CFO)
Feedback on executive mandate and firm's market position:
"Bring the sales organization back into the firm."

Division VPs/P&L Executives
Feedback on cross-functional interactions and service:
"The sales organization is out of synch with the rest of the company, so there is no value for the cost allocated to my P&L."

Regional Managers
Feedback on sales management and process problems:
"We have no way of measuring our progress against a plan. There are no targets and no feedback on performance."

Field Reps
Feedback on customer-centric problems:
"Priorities change every month. I don't know what the company wants us to do and sell."

Slide: "Studying an Arts Degree at Monash University"

This version of the Converging Issues layout might be more relevant for a poster or large handout, but it does show the kind of detail that can be successfully communicated in a well laid-out slide. The six main issues here are questions that proceed in a clockwise manner, surrounding the central focus, i.e. studying a Global Arts degree at a certain university. Each of the six questions is answered through graphics, charts, maps, tables, quotations, and/or text—evidence of a thorough and research-based response. For example, the second question, "Why International Studies?", is answered via a metaphorical picture of a bridge connecting two continents, two data charts, and a global map, all accompanied by explanations in text. The answers to the six questions converge towards the middle, inducing the audience to recognize the value of this degree. A layout like this is more visually engaging than a simple list of frequently asked questions.

01 What is the Bachelor of Arts (Global)?

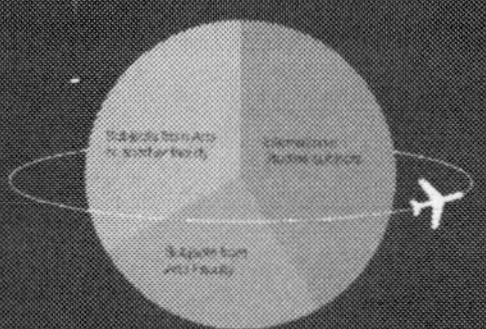

A 3 year degree with a focus on International Studies and broadening the educational and cultural experience of our students by giving them the opportunity to study overseas.

02 Why International Studies?

Globalisation means our competitiveness in the international marketplace of products, ideas and knowledge relies on understanding cultural differences and minimising the divide.

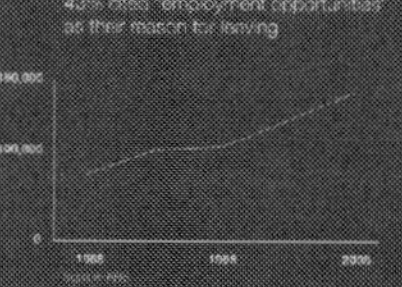

Globalisation means greater integration of business & trade and an increase in migration and mobility.

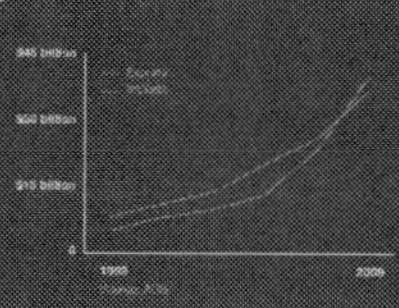

"Increasingly, organisations ...are becoming aware of the gap between what they need in an employee and what they are getting."*

Monash is an international university with campuses in Sth Africa and Malaysia and connections with 120 universities around the world. We have a wide variety of overseas study opportunities.

06 What kinds of careers can I go into?

Graduates enter a wide range of careers in government, NGOs and private practice. (See over)

Skills employers are increasingly looking for:

- Written and verbal communication
- Teamwork- Interpersonal skills
- Leadership skills
- Intercultural understanding
- Critical thinking

Studying an Arts Degree at Monash University

Discover the advantages of choice

MONASH University

Arts

03 What does a Bachelor of Arts (Global) look like?

Major: This is the area that you specialise in. It's compulsory and takes up one third of your degree.

Minor: This is made up of four units, from a different area of study to your major.

Sequence: In first year you have to complete one arts sequence. It's like doing half a minor. If you like it you can keep doing it in 2nd and even 3rd year.

Electives: You can choose whatever you like to do for your electives.

Core Units: Global Studies are core units in the BA Global.

Mapping an Arts degree

	Major	Minor	Electives	Electives
Semester 1	International Studies	Philosophy	Japanese	Marketing
Semester 2	International Studies	Philosophy	Japanese	Marketing
Semester 1	International Studies	Philosophy	Global Studies	Marketing
Semester 2	International Studies	Philosophy	Anthropology	Marketing
Semester 1	International Studies	International Studies	Global Studies	Criminology
Semester 2	International Studies	International Studies	Writing	Writing

04 Double degrees double your options

	Major	Minor	Electives	Electives
Semester 1	International Studies	Philosophy	[illegible]	[illegible]
Semester 2	International Studies	Philosophy	[illegible]	[illegible]
Semester 1	International Studies	Philosophy	[illegible]	[illegible]
Semester 2	International Studies	Philosophy	Global Studies	[illegible]
Semester 1	International Studies	[illegible]	[illegible]	[illegible]
Semester 2	International Studies	[illegible]	[illegible]	[illegible]
Semester 1	International Studies	[illegible]	Global Studies	[illegible]
Semester 2	International Studies	[illegible]	[illegible]	[illegible]

← **Double degrees**

In a Double Degree 16 units must be from Arts, and 16 are from your other degree.

05 What can I study?

International Studies

↓ Global disasters, impact, inquiry and change

↓ Ethics of Global Conflict

↓ Travel and global cultures in history

Monash Arts has 58 areas of study. International Studies segues across many of these.

CHAPTER 10: "CONVERGING RADIAL" LAYOUT

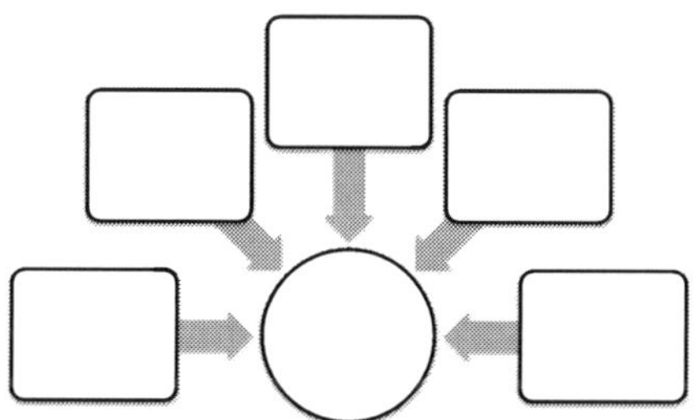

The Converging Radial layout enables the presenter to place multiple items around the central focus, with an arrow pointing radially inward from each item to show how it impacts the main concern. Because the arrows are separate from the outlying items and do not need to be large enough to contain them, this layout can be used even when the surrounding items include large amounts of text.

How to draw the "Converging Radial" Layout

Diagrammer

www.Diagrammer.com
Flows, Merge-Divide, 5 Nodes, 2D Angled, Flow Merge and Divide 459

PowerFrameworks

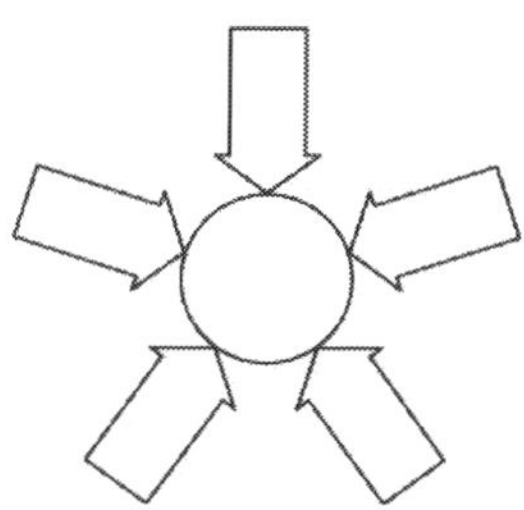

www.PowerFrameworks.com
Keyword Search "FR004", FR004-0500

SmartArt

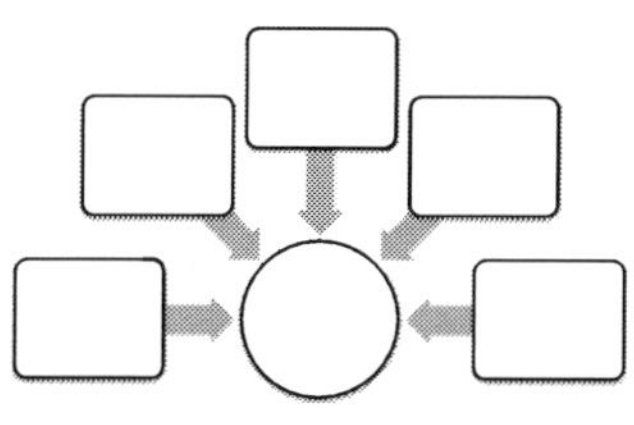

PowerPoint SmartArt
Relationships, Converging Radial

Slide: "Employer Interest in HSAs Will Be Driven by at Least Five Factors"

In this example, a bold text description anchors each radial, summarizing the issue and drawing the audience's attention inward. Further out, behind and beyond each anchoring description, a larger cluster of questions provides additional detail on the each of the five issues. Some issues have only one question, others have up to three; it is one of the advantages of this layout that it allows for variation in the size of each cluster.

EMPLOYER INTEREST IN HSAs WILL BE DRIVEN BY AT LEAST FIVE FACTORS

How many employees does a company have?

How many different plans does the employer offer? How generous are they? How are they priced?

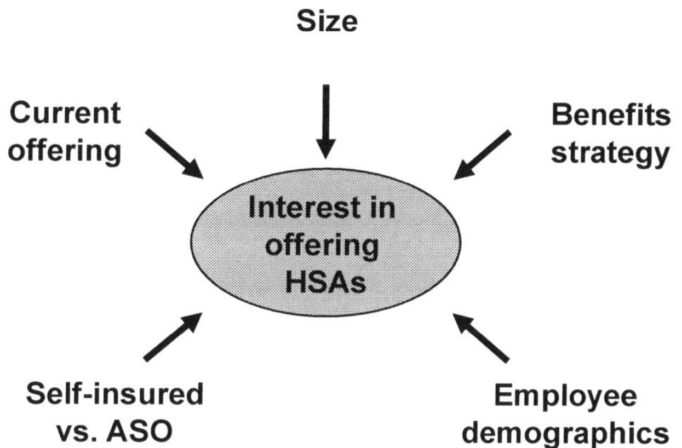

Does an employer's benefits strategy prioritize minimizing costs, maximizing options, attraction and retention, etc.?

Does an employer prefer to self-insure?

Is the employee base young and healthy, or older and more likely to get sick? Is there significant variability, or are people somewhat homogenous?

CHAPTER 11: "COUNTERBALANCE ARROWS" LAYOUT

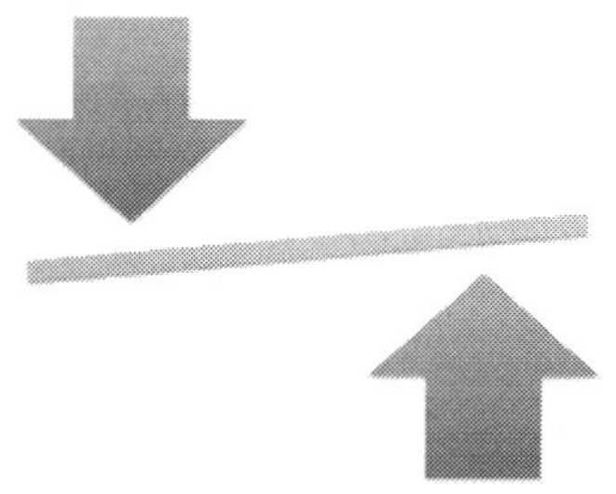

The Counterbalance Arrows layout shows at a glance that two elements are at odds: one is going up, the other going down. These elements could be differing trends, for example, or opposing financial results. The two arrows can be pointing left and right instead of up and down—counterbalancing each other horizontally instead of vertically; in either case the layout shows that two forces are going in different directions. The arrows provide order to the details of the trends or results presented on the slide, enabling communication of a richness of detail within an overall simplicity of design.

How to draw the "Counterbalance Arrows" Layout

Charteo

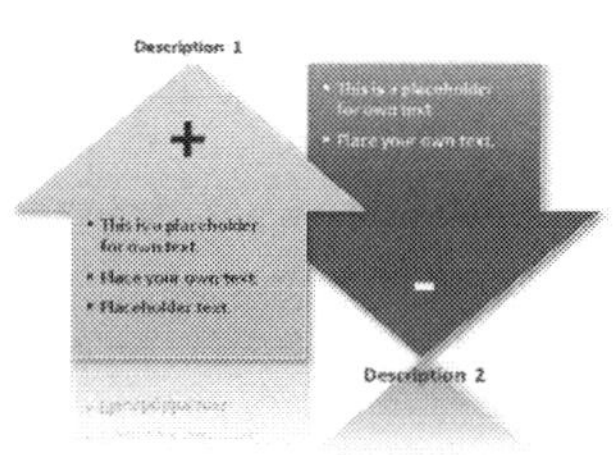

www.Charteo.com
Concept Charts, Arrows, 2D Arrows 1

PowerFrameworks

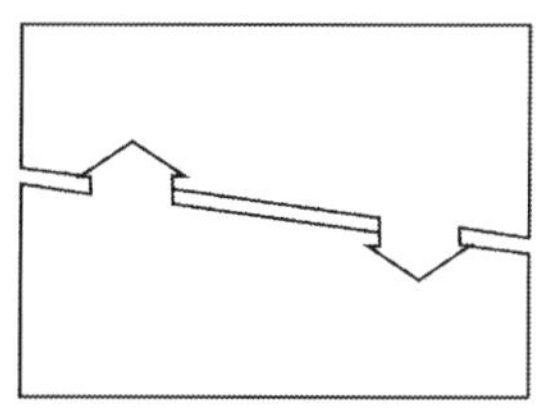

www.PowerFrameworks.com
Keyword Search "FR003","FR003-fr003_0002"

SmartArt

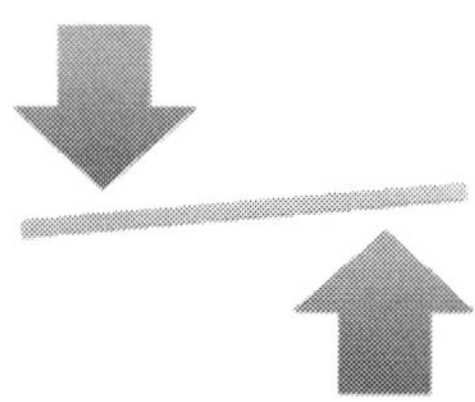

PowerPoint SmartArt
Relationship, Counterbalance Arrows

"Counterbalance Arrows" Layout

Slide: "Changing of the Media Guard"

This version of the Counterbalance Arrows layout shows a trend on the left—the effectiveness of traditional media channels—going down, while a trend on the right—the rise of alternative communication tactics—goes up. Overlaid in front of the arrows are the details: boxes with a representative icon on the left, and two or three bullets of facts and data on the right. The backdrop of the two arrows tells the overall story, and the boxes in front provide specific examples and statistics which support the overall trends and make them concrete.

Changing of the Media Guard

As the effectiveness of traditional channels continues to decline...

Effectiveness of Traditional Channels

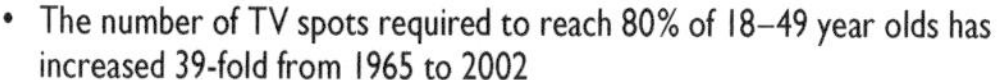

TV

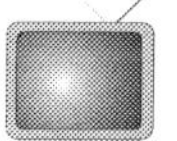

- The number of TV spots required to reach 80% of 18–49 year olds has increased 39-fold from 1965 to 2002
- Digital Video Recorder penetration expected to reach 34% of the U.S. population by 2007
- When Digital Video Recorders are in "playback" mode, consumers skip 75% of non-programming content

Radio

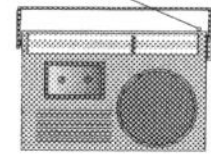

- 13% decline in weekly hours dedicated to radio listening since 1993
- 22% fewer 18–49 year olds listening to radio since 1999

Print

- 5% decline in U.S. newsprint circulation over the first four months of 2005
- 4% decline in daily newspaper consumption over the first four months of 2005

...companies turn to alternative forms of communication to engage consumers

Select Alternative Communications Tactics

Podcasting

- Volvo sponsors www.autoblog.com and underwrites the launch of the blog's podcast
- Nestlé Purina podcasts animal sound ring tones
- Music label, BMI, launches podcasts to promote its new artists directly from its corporate Web site

Blogging

- Unilever develops video Weblogs in the spirit of reality TV shows to promote its male body spray—Axe
- Levi's allows visitors to its pan-European Web site to create video messages and compose mobile ringtones

Branded Experience

- P&G's Charmin division builds a mobile "experience" center featuring its Charmin Ultra product
- Coca-Cola develops branded Internet cafés and Coke lounges in Singapore
- ConocoPhillips launches Breakplace—a branded convenience store experience for consumers

Source: Audit Bureau of Circulation; Arbitron; Aldrich, Lester "Global Newsprint: Lower Circulation Behind Demand Drop" *Dow Jones Newswire* (29 June 2005); Van Duyn, Aline "Why the Mays Have Faith in Radio Go-Go" *Financial Times* (9 May 2005); Peers, Martin "Buddy, Can You Spare Some Time?" *The Wall Street Journal* (26 January 2004); Television Bureau of Advertising; The Media Center at the American Press Institute; Mann, Charles "The Resurrection of Indie Radio" *Wired Magazine* (13 March 2005); Feakins, Kathryn and Michael Zea "Designing the Branded Experience: How Conoco Broke the Convenience Store Mold" Lippincott Mercer (2004); Kiley, David "Mad Ave's Rush to Podcasts" *Business Week* (25 May 2005); CEB research.

Slide: "Going with the Flow"

This version of the Counterbalance Arrows layout shows the downward and upward flow of processes in an organization. On the left side, the downward arrow shows the flow of control and command from the top down, starting at the level of the CEO and descending through Strategy/Planning, Goal Setting, and Monthly Goals, down to Daily Rates and Errors. On the right of the slide, the arrow shows the upward flow of information and reporting, from Daily Reports, through Weekly and Monthly Reports, to Aggregated Reports.

Two particularly interesting features help to communicate visually. First, the breaks in the arrow on the right show that the reporting process is not seamless. Second, the organizational chart in the middle of the slide helps the audience to see which level in the company is responsible both for the control and command on the left and for the reporting on the right. The quotation at the bottom of the slide further highlights the problems caused by the suboptimal reporting process depicted on the right.

For further examples, see Org Chart chapter.

Going with the Flow

Control and Information Flows

Brokerage Operations

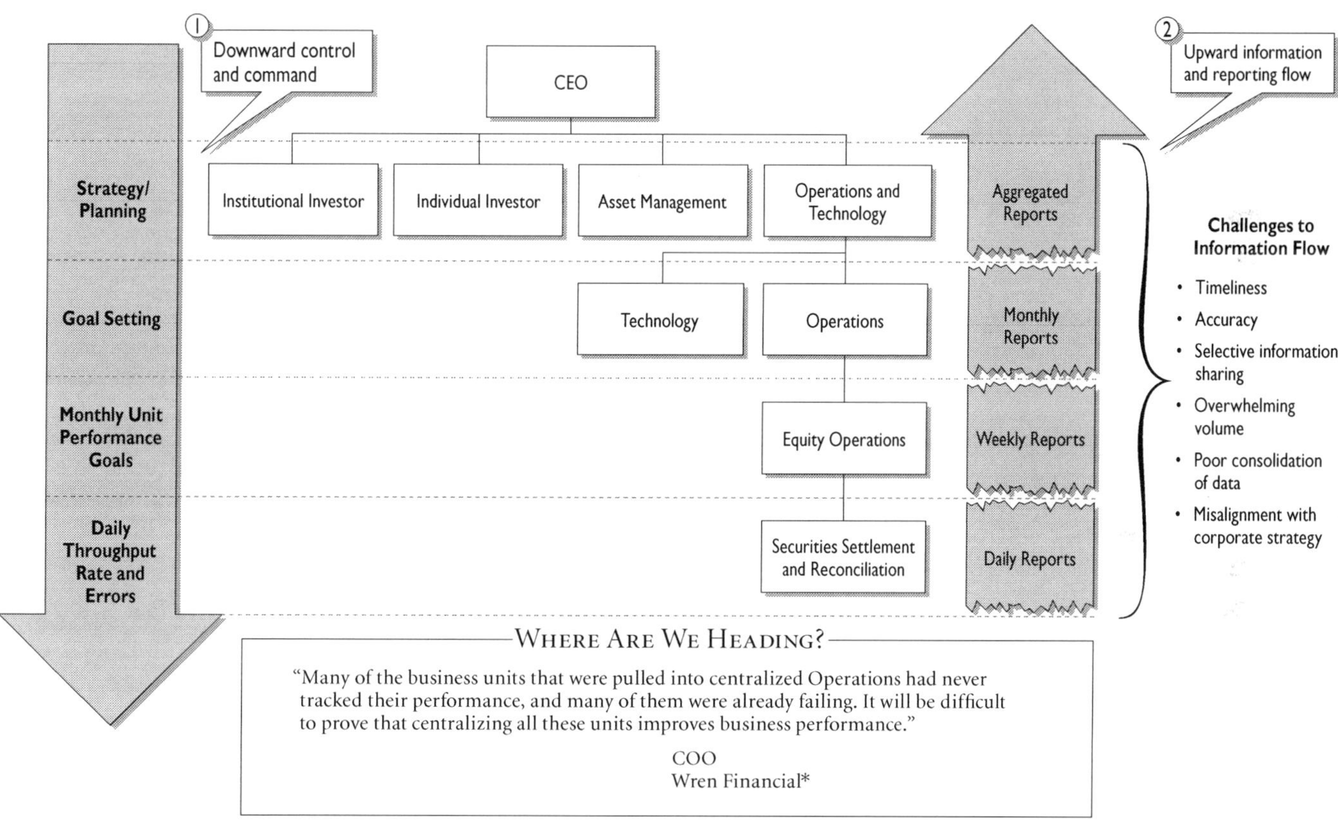

Where Are We Heading?

"Many of the business units that were pulled into centralized Operations had never tracked their performance, and many of them were already failing. It will be difficult to prove that centralizing all these units improves business performance."

COO
Wren Financial*

* Pseudonym.

Source: Wren Financial; Lowell, Bryan L., and Claudia Joyce McKinsey, "The 21st-Century Organization," *Quarterly* 2005, Number 3, pp. 21–29; CEB research.

Slide: "Now, the Hard Part"

This version of the Counterbalance Arrows layout utilizes horizontal arrows instead of the more typical vertical ones, in this case to contrast two opposing approaches to market research insight generation. The upper arrow depicts the old process—beginning with insights generated by research—and flows from left to right, where it bears an uncertain relationship to the end goal, the "Decision to Be Made by Line." The broken head of the arrow, the dotted outlines at the arrow's end, and the cloud of "Decision Ambiguity" all illustrate this uncertainty. In contrast, the new way (depicted by the arrow at the bottom of the page) begins with the decision to be made by the line and flows to the left, resulting in insights produced not by Research alone, but by the firm as a whole. Both arrows have three parts, each part labeled with a header, depicted by an image, and explained by text. The numbering of the headers over each part helps to reinforce the left-to-right flow of the upper arrow and the right-to-left flow of the lower arrow.

The two boxes on the right of the slide show that this new, counterintuitive process has challenges of its own; each challenge is named and described, and is accompanied by the icon of a company that has overcome the challenge.

Now, the Hard Part

To establish a decision focus, Research must fundamentally reverse its existing issues orientation…

Schematic of an Issue-Focused Research Model

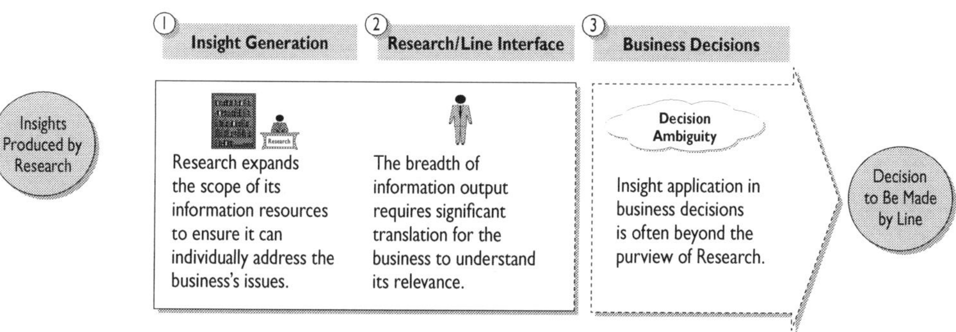

Schematic of a Decision-Focused Research Model

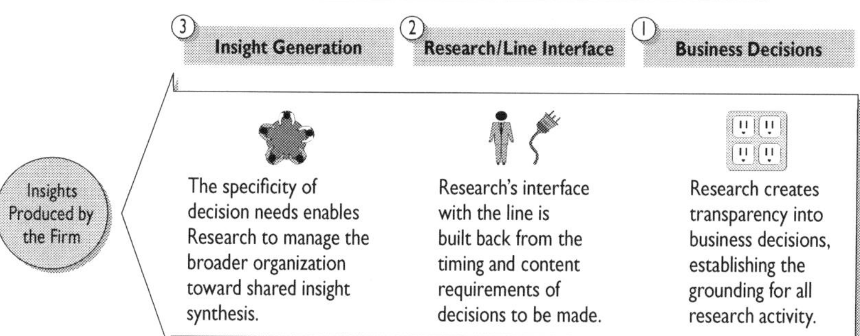

…yet, doing so presents a new set of challenges

Challenges with a Decision Focus

Challenge #1

Constituents Cannot Articulate Their Decisions

Research's attempts to surface constituents' decisions yield responses that either are not actual decisions or are decisions, but too broad to be useful or too narrow to be relevant.

Challenge #2

Research's Decision Support Is Inconsistent

Research lacks the transparency into decision making to determine the appropriate level of support it should provide across decision-making stages.

Source: Market Research Executive Board research.

CHAPTER 12: "COURSE CHANGE" LAYOUT

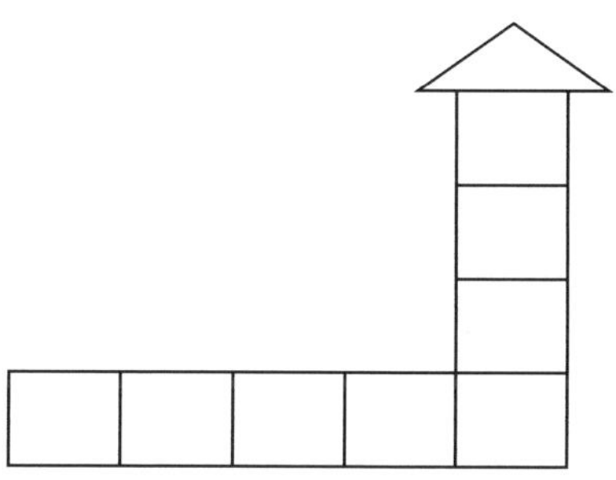

The Course Change layout can be used effectively when the main message of the slide is that there either has been or needs to be a major shift in the direction of a project or strategy. The layout shows a process or line which proceeds straight initially—but then turns, either to avoid a bad result or to achieve a new goal which could not have been attained without the dramatic change. A single slide can sometimes portray more than one change.

How to draw the "Course Change" Layout

Charteo

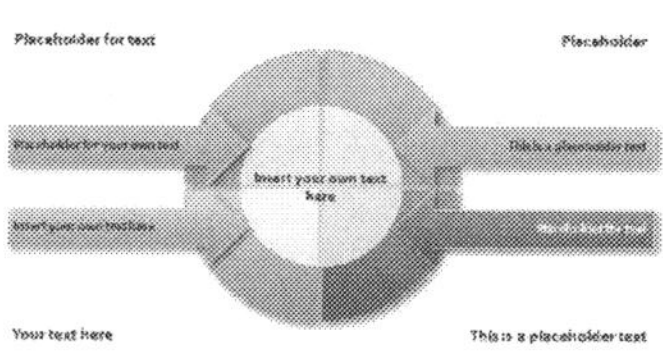

www.Charteo.com
Concept Charts, Arrows, 2D Arrow 63

Slide: "Sharp Curves Ahead"

This Course Change layout begins with the depiction of a phone call in the lower left corner of the slide and proceeds to the right and up, along a road which curves 90 degrees four different times, and ends in re-routing the customer call based on the situation. The presenter has made use of the metaphor of driving along a road, by placing guardrails at each turn, thereby indicating that the actions depicted by the turns help the company to manage risk.

Sharp Curves Ahead

Company A Sets Careful Guardrails to Manage the Risk of Internal and External Resistance

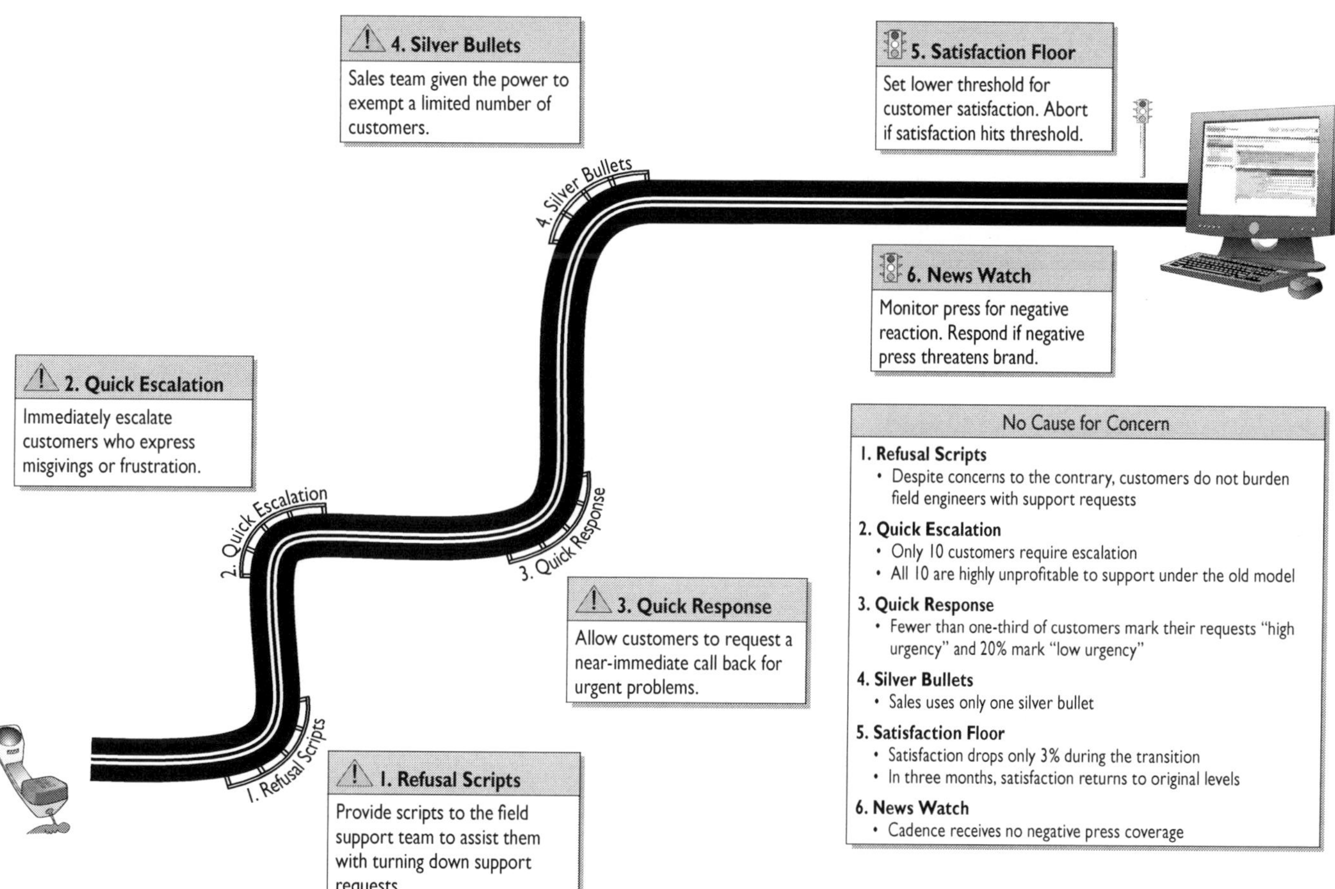

No Cause for Concern
1. Refusal Scripts • Despite concerns to the contrary, customers do not burden field engineers with support requests
2. Quick Escalation • Only 10 customers require escalation • All 10 are highly unprofitable to support under the old model
3. Quick Response • Fewer than one-third of customers mark their requests "high urgency" and 20% mark "low urgency"
4. Silver Bullets • Sales uses only one silver bullet
5. Satisfaction Floor • Satisfaction drops only 3% during the transition • In three months, satisfaction returns to original levels
6. News Watch • Cadence receives no negative press coverage

Source: CEB research.

Slide: "Where the Road Divides"

This version of the Course Change layout shows three alternative directions for retailer strategy. The movement begins at the bottom of the slide and flows upwards. In the Zone of Customer Focus, the retailer can execute many attributes perfectly, but without satisfying the needs of certain segments which the retailer serves. As the audience follows the road up the slide, it diverges into three paths, dividing along customer segment lines. The layout invites the audience to consider what path the retailer ought to choose—i.e., which customer segment the retailer should aim to satisfy. A slide like this can lead to a productive conversation, as it explores possibilities for the future while visually implying that the audience must choose a path.

Where the Road Divides

Segment Focus Goes Substantially Beyond the Elimination of "Dissatisfiers"

Elements of Customer and Segment Focus in Experience Strategy

Illustrative Consumer Electronics Retailer Example

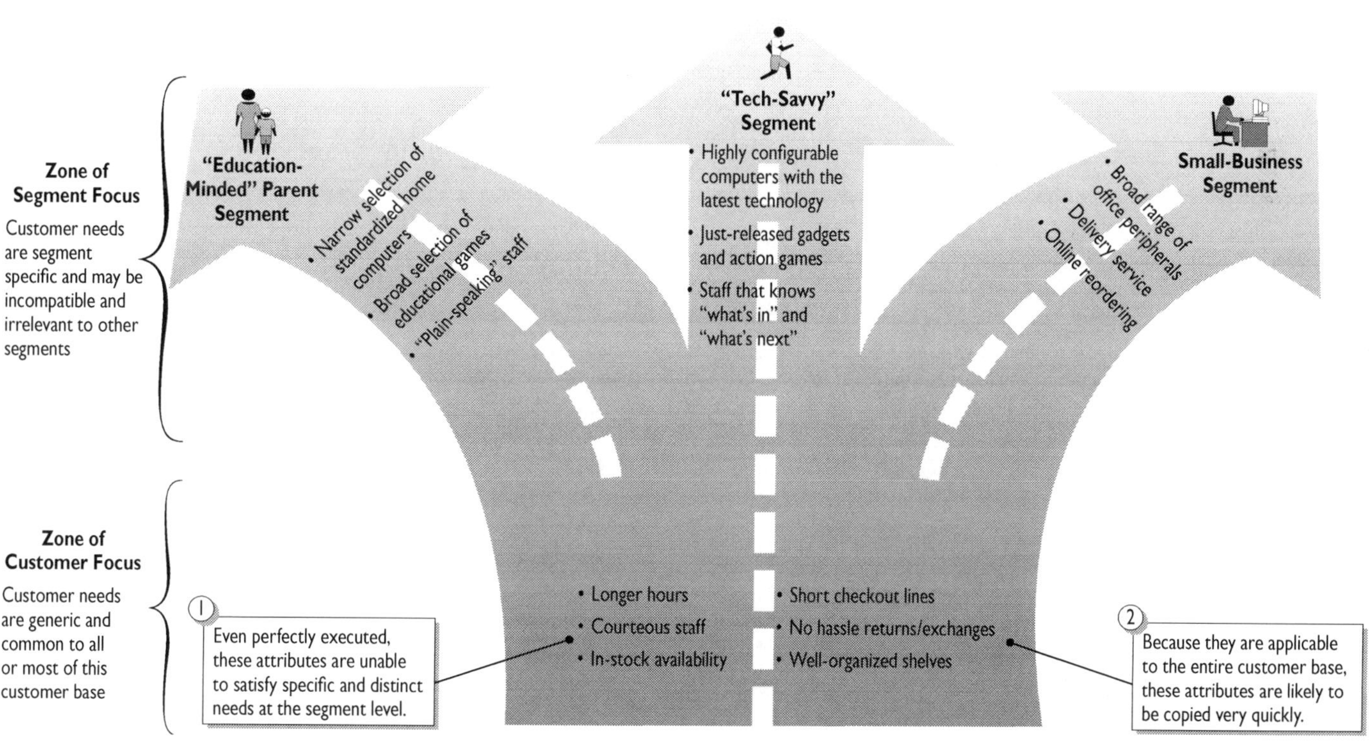

Source: CEB research.

Slide: "A Call to Change"

This Course Change layout combines the turns of the arrows with stop signs inserted at key points, showing how a project in process must halt and undergo rework in order to achieve its goal. Two key features visually accentuate the frustration the company must feel. First, the course changes in the project are not merely 90 degrees, but closer to 135 degrees—showing how arresting each change is, and how it pushes the process back to the beginning. Second, each of the thick gray arrows starts from the same horizontal point, a placement which reinforces the fact that the project repeatedly has to "start over"—a problem which is reemphasized by the thin black arrows pointing back from each stop sign, labeled "Rework."

Along the left of the slide, three separate calls to three separate groups are shown leading to the interruptions in the process. The calls are mirrored on the right of the slide by three key negative outcomes: loss of money, diminished business value, and inability to fill customer commitment. Finally, warning signs in the lower left corner of the slide highlight the three key causes for this kind of project mishap.

A Call to Change

Inadequate Decision-Making Framework for Managing Proliferating Customer Requests Leads to Poor Business Outcomes

Ad Hoc Project Execution

Illustrative

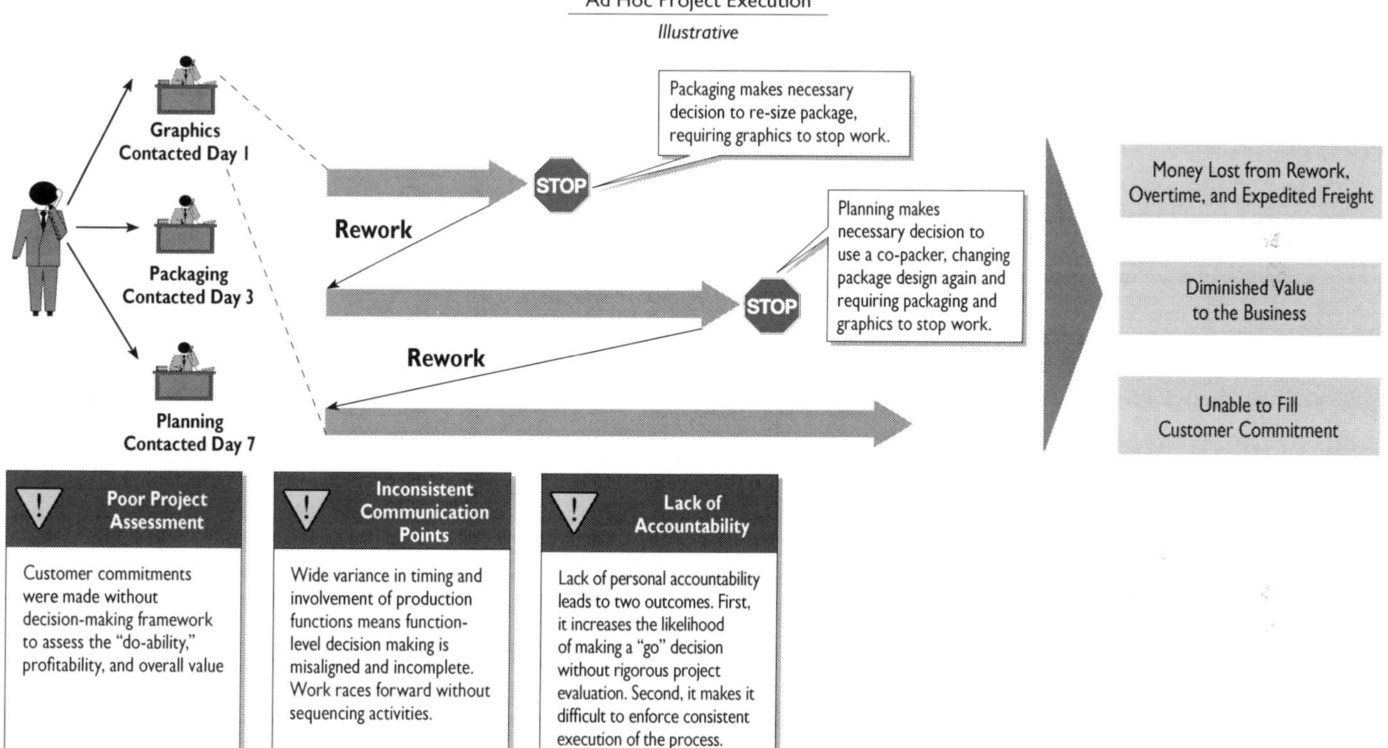

MLB1AKKEJD

Source: CEB research.

CHAPTER 13: "CYCLICAL PROCESS" LAYOUT

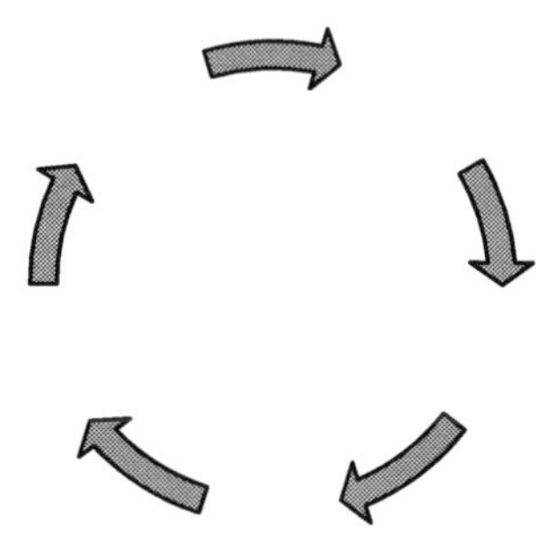

The Cyclical Process layout is used when the presenter needs to show a series of steps in a recurring process. The steps can be numbered or lettered, to indicate a beginning and an end, but the visual layout implies that the process continues after the final step, starting over again – either in a new time period or at a greater depth.

How to draw the "Cyclical Process" Layout

Charteo

www.Charteo.com
Processes and Flows, Process-Circular, 2D Arrow 63

Diagrammer

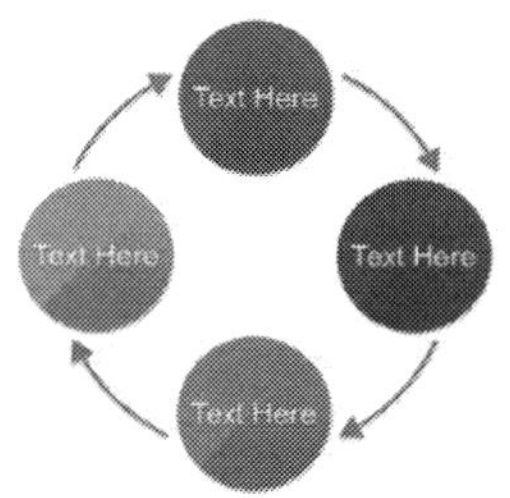

www.Diagrammer.com
Flow, Loop, 4 Nodes, 2D Curved, Flow Loop 73

PowerFrameworks

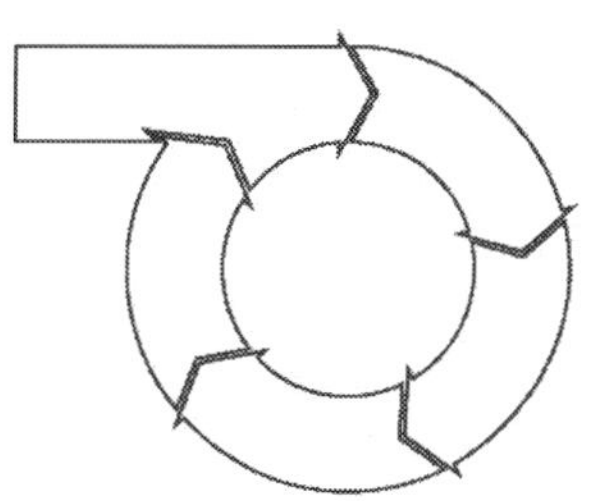

www.PowerFrameworks.com
Keyword Search "CF012", CF012-0401

SmartArt

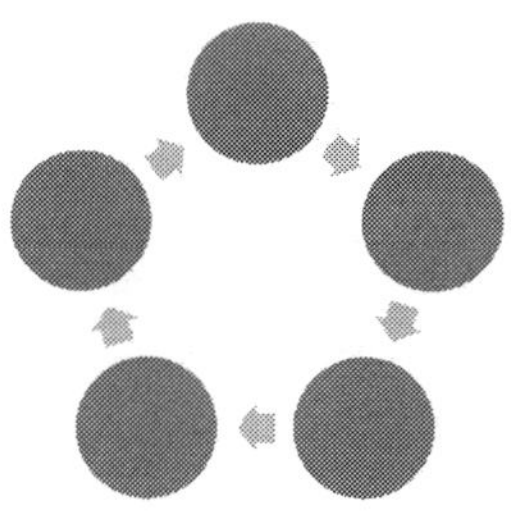

PowerPoint SmartArt
Cycle, Basic Cycle

Slide: "Business technology strategy should be integrated with overall strategy design"

This Cyclical Process layout presents a three-step cycle, drawn as three curved chevrons. The process has no beginning or end—it continually refreshes itself, passing through step A on the right: "Assess business and technology context," then step C: "Create strategy," then step E: "Execute strategy," and back to step A. The cyclical layout emphasizes the point that strategy development and execution is an ongoing process.

Business technology strategy should be integrated with overall strategy design

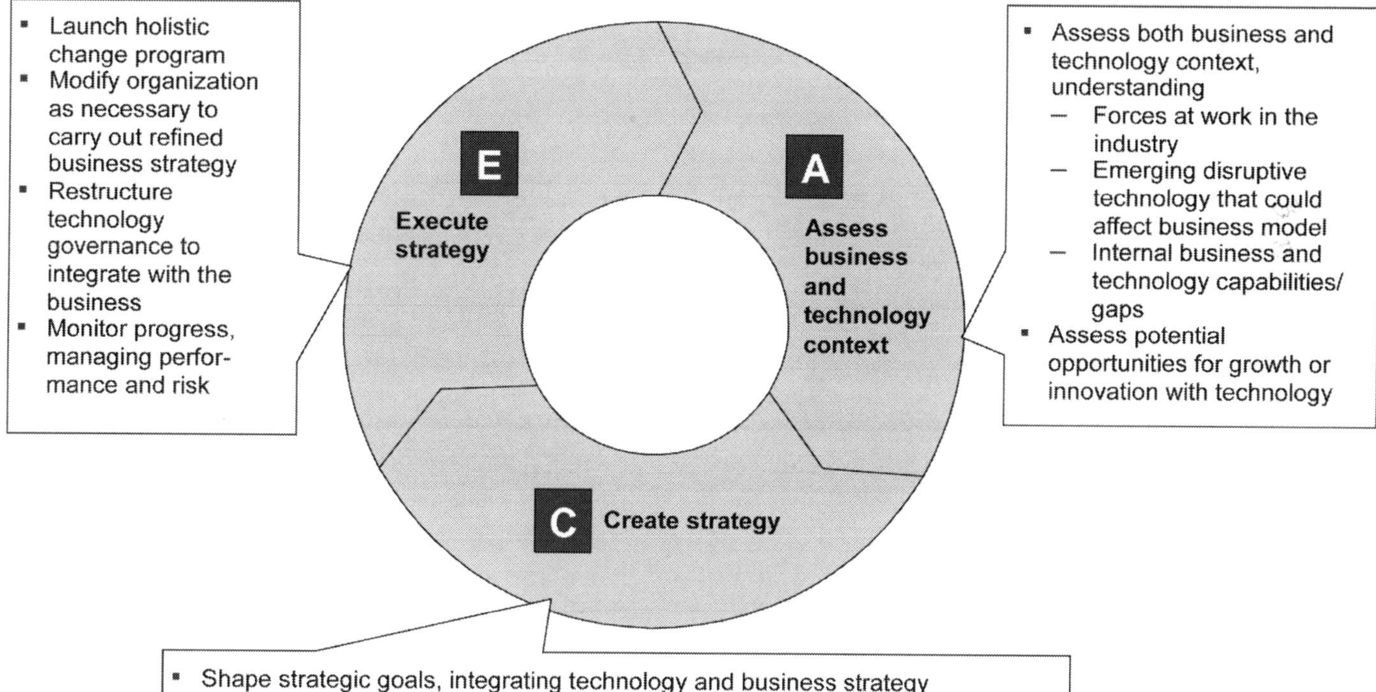

Slide: "Ring Around the Customer"

This version of the Cyclical Process layout shows six steps in an annual customer planning process. Here the step details are placed in boxes in between the arrows, rather than embedded in the arrows themselves, enabling the presenter to include more detail in each step: a title, icons visualizing what occurs in the step, and text offering a brief narrative. Step 2, for example, has five different icons showing the various sources used to gather customer insights. After step 6, the process continues to step 1, where the company reassesses the performance gap and prepares for the coming year. The quotation at the center describes how the customer is "at the beginning, in the middle, and at the end" of the process. The catchy title has a more descriptive subtitle that makes reference to a 360-degree customer view, further emphasizing the circular nature of the process.

Ring Around the Customer

Tesco's 360-Degree Customer View Generates Holistic Customer Insights That Are the Basis for Focusing Customer Priorities Each Year

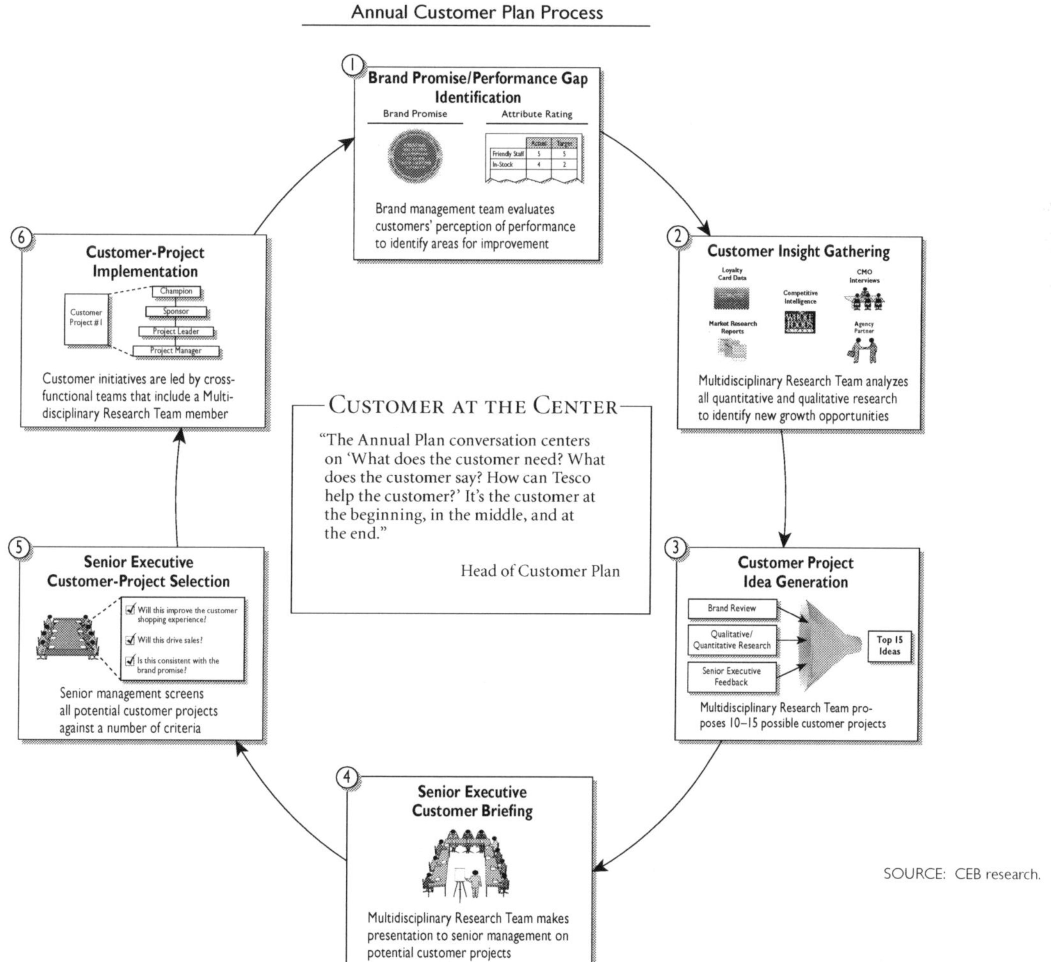

SOURCE: CEB research.

CHAPTER 14: "DECISION TREE" LAYOUT

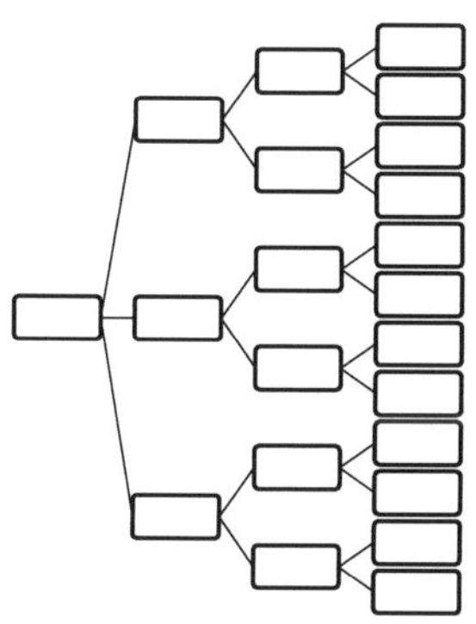

The Decision Tree layout is used to portray a decision and its various alternatives. Typically the tree begins with one node and proceeds into multiple options, which may then in turn flow into further options. It is a particularly useful layout for structuring a conversation about an impending decision, or for highlighting a specific recommendation.

How to draw the "Decision Tree" Layout

Charteo

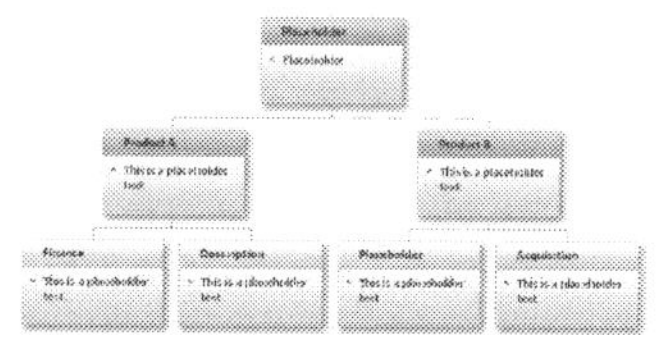

www.Charteo.com
Concept Charts, Org Charts, Org Horizontal 24

PowerFrameworks

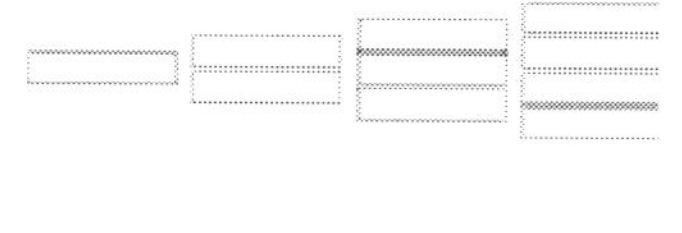

www.PowerFrameworks.com
Keyword Search "PF001", PF001-0404

SmartArt

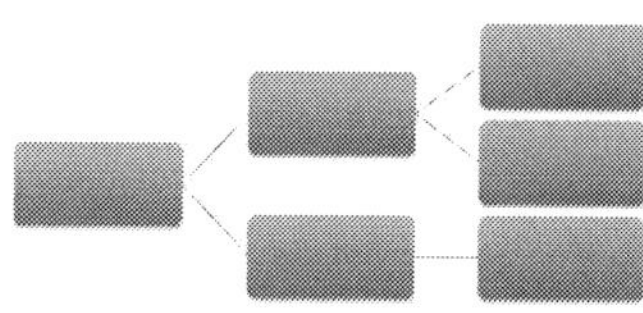

PowerPoint SmartArt
Hierarchy, Horizontal Hierarchy

Slide: "Hard to Handle"

This example of the Decision Tree layout flows from left to right, beginning with the bolded questions in the middle-left of the page. Each question branches out into two options to the right: the answers Yes and No. These answers or options are each clarified by additional text. The rectangles around the two Yes-answers in the middle of the slide draw the audience's attention there, and their proximity enables the audience to recognize that both Yes-answers present negative conditions. The arrow flowing from this pair of Yes-answers to the far right points the audience to the difficulties that these two responses can cause: trouble with focus, problem solving, and decision making.

On the far left of the slide, the main point of the slide is summarized, followed by a narrative explanation of the decision tree's findings.

Current conditions can take a toll on managers' performance.

- When managers struggle to make sense of change, or to act in an uncertain environment, their performance often suffers.
- There are two ways this commonly occurs. In one, a manager feels overwhelmed by demands placed on him or her (relative to resources), creating a perceived threat.
- In the second, managers can't reconcile events or inputs with their world views or standard decision rules, creating confusion and doubt.
- Either can take a toll on focus, problem solving, and decision making.

HARD TO HANDLE

Causes and Effects of Selected Performance Variables on Managers

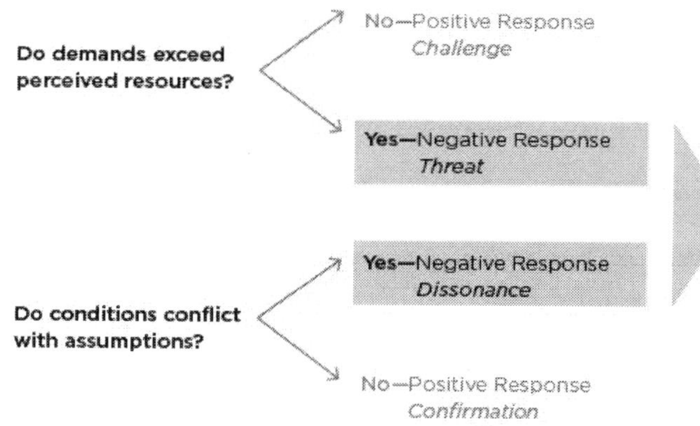

SOURCE: Driskell, James and Eduardo Salas (eds.), Stress and Human Performance, 1996.

CHAPTER 15: "DISAGGREGATION" LAYOUT

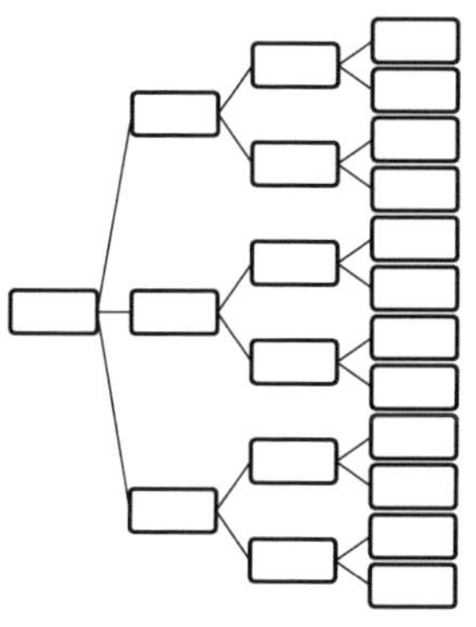

The Disaggregation layout, or tree, shows how a large and/or complex issue can be broken down—"disaggregated"—into smaller component parts. Classically, each fork in the tree presents two or more sub-issues that are mutually exclusive and collectively exhaustive ("M.E.C.E."): there are no overlaps and no gaps.

How to draw the "Disaggregation" Layout

Charteo

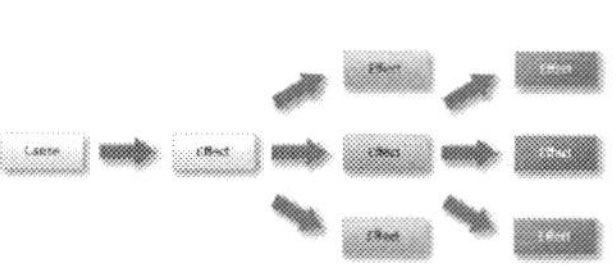

www.Charteo.com
Processes and Flows, Cause and Effect Diagrams, Cause and Effect Chart 1

Diagrammer

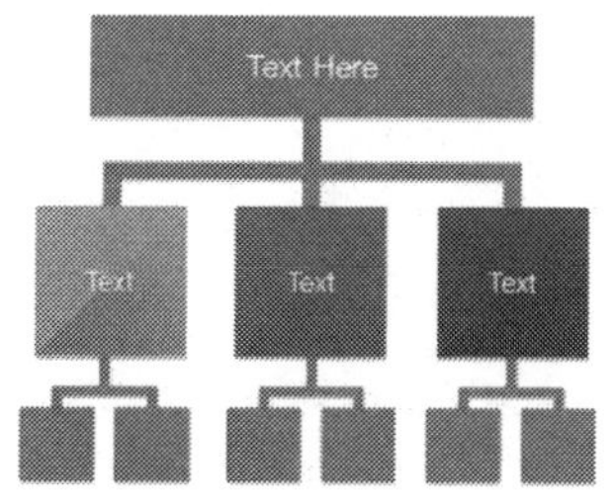

www.Diagrammer.com
Network, Flare, 3 Nodes, 2D Angled, Network Flare 36

PowerFrameworks

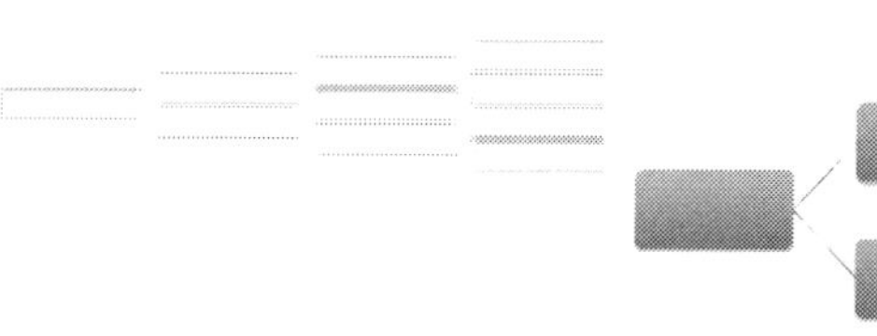

www.PowerFrameworks.com
Keyword Search "PF001, PF001-0404

SmartArt

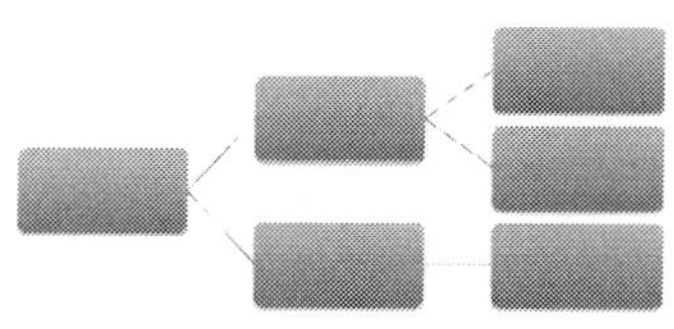

PowerPoint SmartArt
Hierarchy, Horizontal Hierarchy

Slide: "Business Problem-Solving"

This example disaggregates the root causes of inadequate return on investment (ROI). It begins at the top of the page, where the two possible sources of inadequate ROI are presented: if ROI is inadequate, this is either because investment is inadequate, to the left, or because profit is inadequate, to the right. Each of these is then further disaggregated: inadequate profit is caused by costs that are too high, or revenues that are too low, and so on. At each node, the root causes presented always cover all the possibilities, without any overlaps, so that they are M.E.C.E.

[3] Business Problem-Solving

Does Your Presentation Make a Clear Contribution to Solving an Important Business Problem?

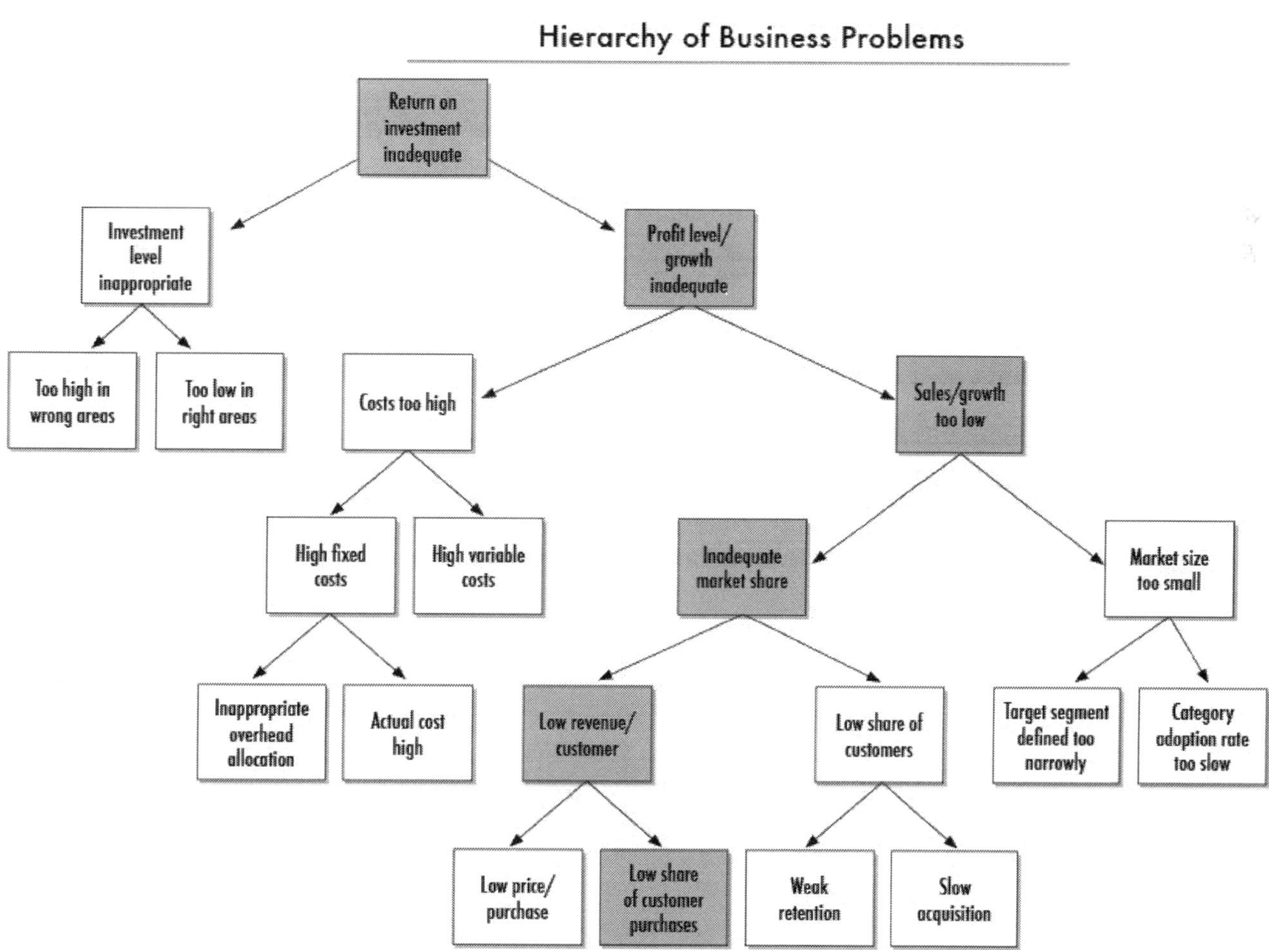

Slide: "Developing Metrics for the 'Approach Speed' of the Future"

In this slide, the corporate strategy for a regional bank, first described in the box on the left of the slide, is disaggregated into three key assumptions immediately to the right. These assumptions are then further disaggregated into indicators or "signposts" that act as evidence that can validate or invalidate each assumption. To the right of these signposts are "tripwires," or specific metrics representing threshold levels for each signpost.

At the bottom left, the terms "signpost" and "tripwire" are defined comprehensively.

Note that this slide was designed to be presented on two side-by-side portrait pages within a book, which is why there is a white gutter down the middle, and why the type size appears small when reproduced here on a single page.

DEVELOPING METRICS FOR THE "APPROACH SPEED" OF THE FUTURE

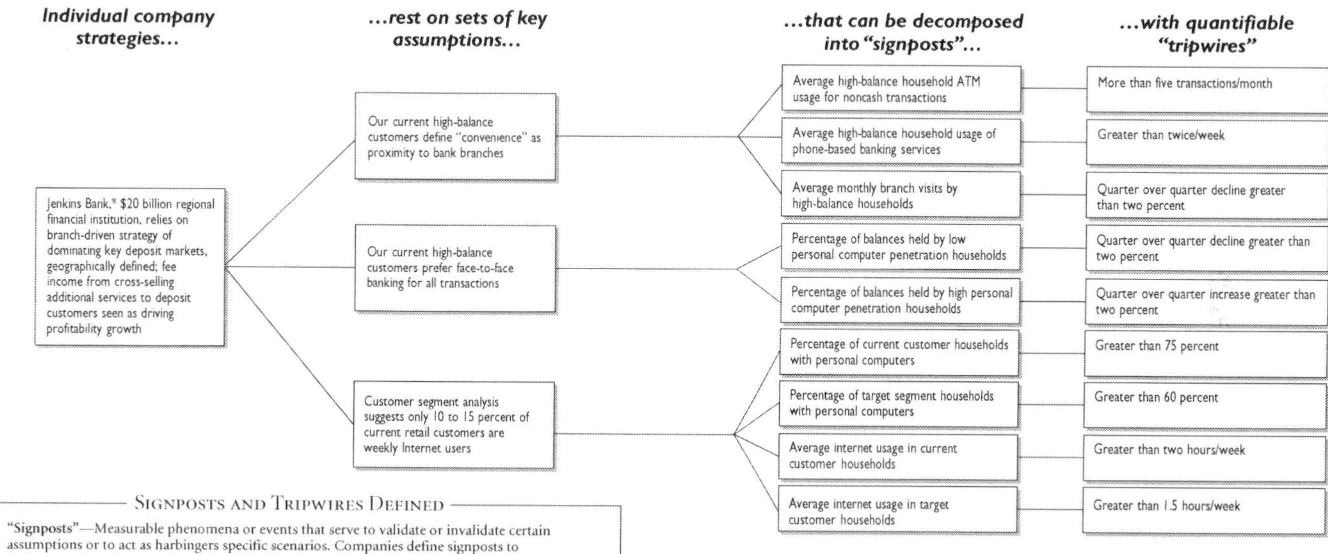

SIGNPOSTS AND TRIPWIRES DEFINED

"**Signposts**"—Measurable phenomena or events that serve to validate or invalidate certain assumptions or to act as harbingers specific scenarios. Companies define signposts to facilitate the monitoring of critical external factors; changes in the signposts indicate important changes in global assumptions or scenarios.

"**Tripwires**"—Threshold levels determined for each signpost indicate certain assumptions are being invalidated or certain scenarios are unfolding. Companies use tripwires as objective warning signs to indicate that certain phenomena or events have progressed sufficiently (beyond the threshold level) to warrant immediate review or action.

* Hypothetical case.

Slide: "Understanding Premium Position Captivity"

This slide uses a version of the Disaggregation layout to explain the concept of "Premium Position Captivity"—the inability of a company with premium-priced positioning to react quickly enough to changes from new competitive activity and/or their customer base that threaten that positioning.

The box at the top left of the slide names and briefly describes the concept, which is then disaggregated into the variety of causes. Placing the problem description in the upper part of the slide, above the list of its causes rather than directly to the list's left, frees up space on the right of the slide for detailed case examples of each cause, including company name and logo, date, and a description of the threatening changes and the consequences to the case company.

Understanding Premium Position Captivity

"Premium Position Captivity" Has Multiple Root Causes That Have Tripped up Even the Most Well-Respected Companies

Premium Position Captivity
Failure or inability to shift tactics in response to the advent of a low-cost competitor or changing customer preferences

Root Cause	Company	Manifestation	Consequence
Disruptive Competitor* Price/Value *Competitor's market entry that significantly displaces the existing market leader's proposition on price/value*	Toys "R" Us 1992	Wal-Mart moves aggressively into retail toy sales, expanding toy shelf space and using toys as loss leaders to build foot traffic in stores.	Wal-Mart surpasses Toys "R" Us in 1998 to become the largest toy retailer; Toys "R" Us is acquired in 2005.
Overestimation of Brand Protection *False security derived from perception of power of brand image to retain a loyal customer base*	Kellogg's 1992	Overconfidence in customer loyalty to withstand competitive pricing pressures from store brands and General Mills.	Before restructuring to become cost competitive, company is forced to slash prices to keep market share, ending 51 straight years of revenue increases.
Gross Margin Captivity *Self-restriction of top-line growth opportunities to only those that shore up or enhance current gross margins*	1988	Pursues a high-price strategy to earn higher margins across all product lines.	High prices reduce Apple's market share and isolate software developers on whose packages Macintosh sales depend.
Premium Escalation *Premium-captive firm shifts toward even higher-premium market niche to protect margins*	SEARS 1969	Responds to discount retailers' inroads with a premium response—raising prices and stocking more upscale goods.	Premium response confuses Sears's customers and sales continue to decline.
Premium Replication *Pursuit of only premium niches in multiple markets leads to inability to address full range of growth opportunities*	3M 1980	Company is ill-equipped to compete on cost and accept market maturity; had not placed enough bets in less adjacent categories that valued innovation.	CEO Lehr leads major reorganization leading to business model improvements including better cross-unit coordination and reduction of divisional fragmentation.
Missed Strategic Inflection in Demand *Failure to recognize and respond appropriately to material changes in the value proposition preferences of customers*	Reebok 1991	Misses shift in customer demand from fashion and comfort to high-performance athletic shoes.	Nike consistently widens a market share lead across the 1990s.

* Similar to Clayton Christensen's topic described in *The Innovator's Dilemma* (1997).

Source: CEB research.

CHAPTER 16: "DIVERGING APPROACHES" LAYOUT

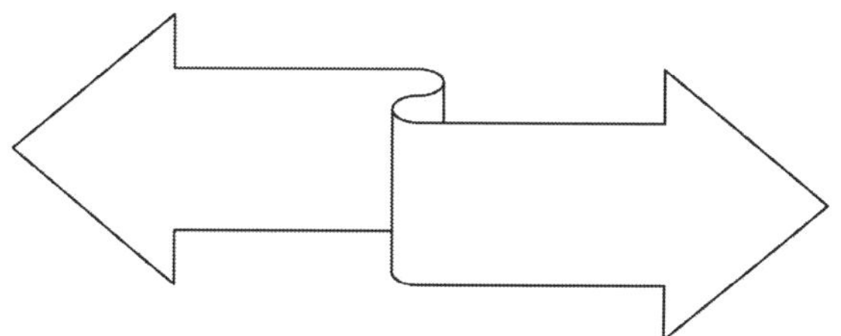

The Diverging Approaches layout enables the presenter to contrast two main options; these could be two possible decisions, or two conflicting strategies, or two mutually exclusive paths. The visual effect of the diverging arrows or chevrons emphasizes the "either/or" character of the two approaches being distinguished.

How to draw the "Diverging Approaches" Layout

Charteo

SmartArt

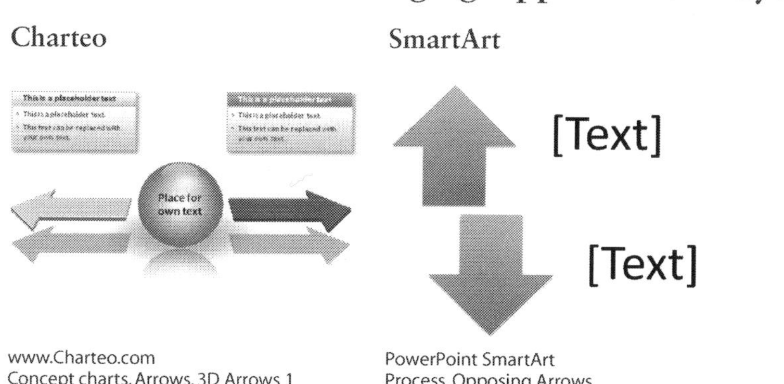

www.Charteo.com
Concept charts, Arrows, 3D Arrows 1

PowerPoint SmartArt
Process, Opposing Arrows

Slide: "We see culture as a product of specific practices ..."

This example of the Diverging Approaches layout embeds the contrasted items within the two chevrons, which in this case represent two views as to what constitutes organizational culture. Each chevron's heading describes its content. The concluding text beneath the diverging chevrons— "Culture is a science, not an art"—is visually reinforced by the loose, unstructured, "artsy" layout of the general words on the left, versus the linear, structured "scientific" layout of the specific questions on the right.

Notice also the seismic rift in the middle of the slide, which further implies that the two views are breaking away from each other, and are worlds (or continents) apart.

We see culture as a product of specific practices that determine organizational health

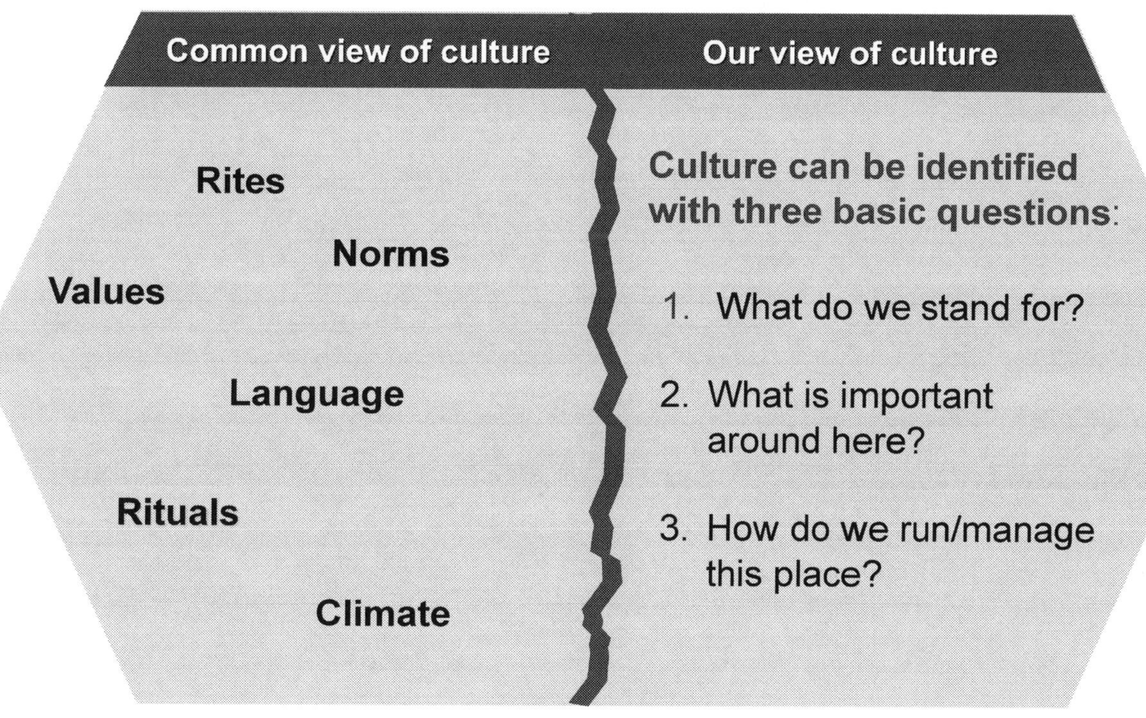

Culture is a science, not an art

CHAPTER 17: "DIVERGING RADIAL" LAYOUT

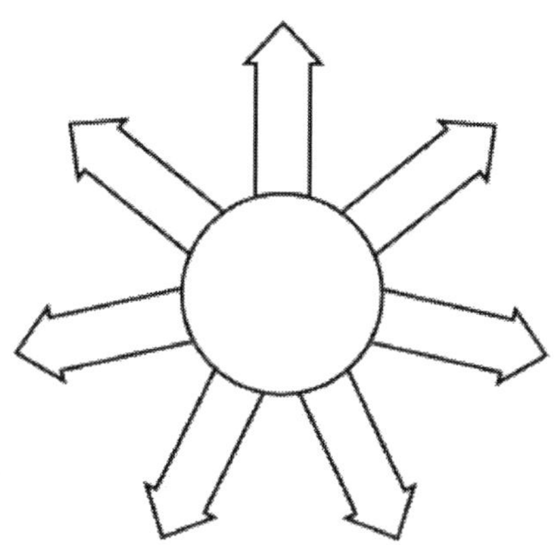

The Diverging Radial layout uses a central figure as a focus, with various elements flowing out of or away from the central figure. Among other purposes, it can be used to show how one person or resource is being pulled in many directions or answering to many masters. Where the Converging Radial layout tends to show pressure from many incoming factors, the Diverging Radial layout works better to indicate a variety of disparate demands or responsibilities.

How to draw the "Diverging Radial" Layout

Diagrammer

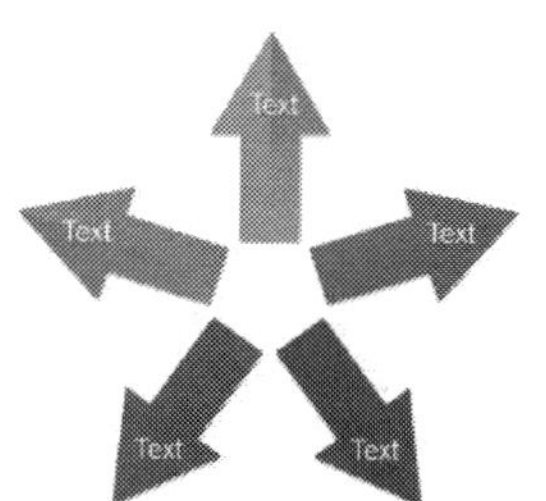

www.Diagrammer.com
Flow, Merge/Divide, 5 Nodes, 2D
Angled, Flow Merge and Divide 474

PowerFrameworks

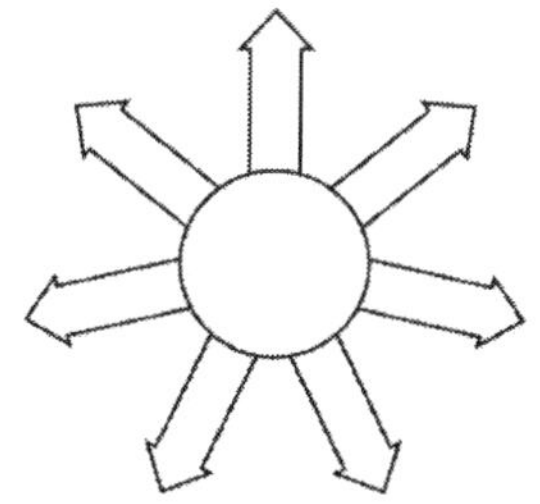

www.PowerFrameworks.com
Keyword Search "FR005", "FR005-0700"

SmartArt

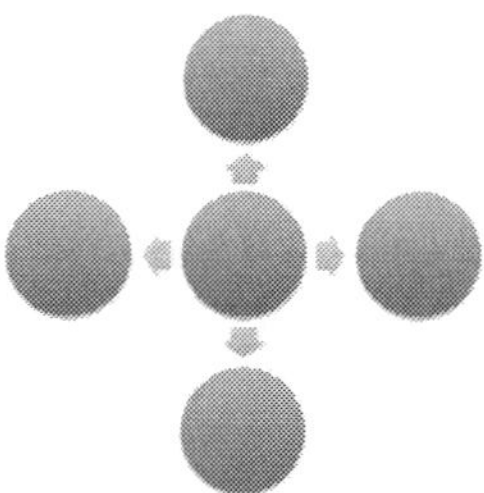

PowerPoint SmartArt
Cycle, Diverging Radial

Slide: "Competing for Mindshare"

On the left, this slide shows the Diverging Radial layout with one function (Research) at the center, and arrows radiating outwards towards six other functions. Each function is depicted by a label and the icon of a person. Unlike the Converging Radial layout, which implies stress from many factors impinging upon the central figure, here the central figure has responsibility towards at least six functions and is being overstretched.

To further illustrate this quandary, the circle drawn outside of those six functional representatives depicts a barrier beyond which the central figure, "Research," has no control: these six representatives receive information and perspectives from alternative information sources, sources with which the research figure has no contact.

On the right side of the slide, the pie graph shows that almost half of the other functions—the researchers' line partners—do not look to the Research function as their first source for customer insight, and the quotation in the lower right gives one company's solution to that challenge.

Competing for Mindshare

As research constituencies expand, along with the information sources available to them...

Network of Research Constituents and Their Alternate Information Sources

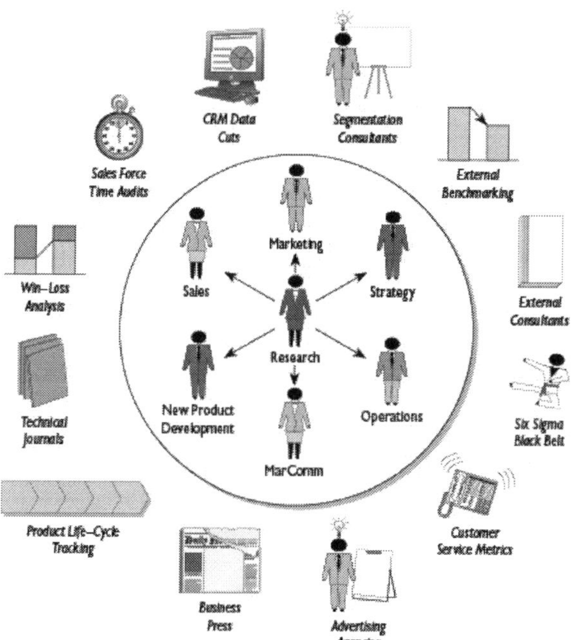

...many decision makers look beyond Research for their customer understanding

Line Partners' Primary Source of Customer Insight

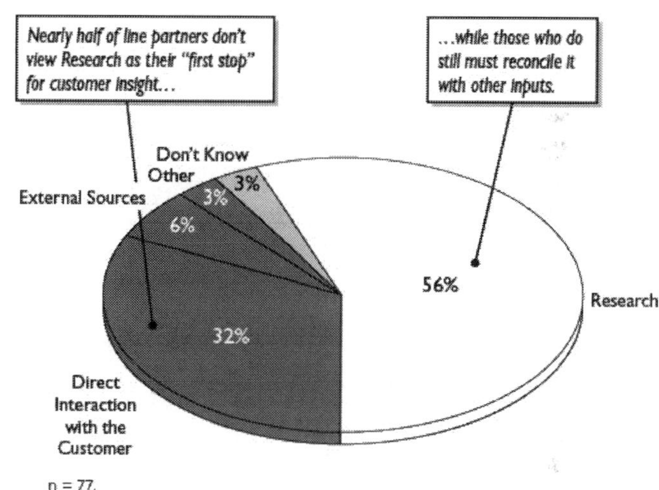

n = 77.

Paving the Way

"We must act as a filter to understanding as opposed to the sole generator. Our objective is to ensure that people can interpret what we find and build on it as opposed to trying to build the perfect answer for them."

Director, Research and Planning
Financial Services Company

Source: CEB Business Alignment Tool Survey; CEB research.

CHAPTER 18: "DOWNWARD SPIRAL" LAYOUT

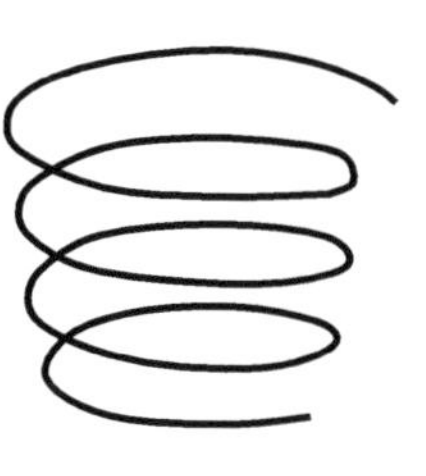

The Downward Spiral layout works well to demonstrate how a serious initial problem becomes grave. This layout quickly communicates to the audience that there is a difficult situation, and that it can or will get worse if nothing is done to prevent the descent or to address the problem. Often, many factors contribute to the problem, and the Downward Spiral layout enables the presenter to show not only the factors themselves but also their relation to each other.

How to draw the "Downward Spiral" Layout

Charteo

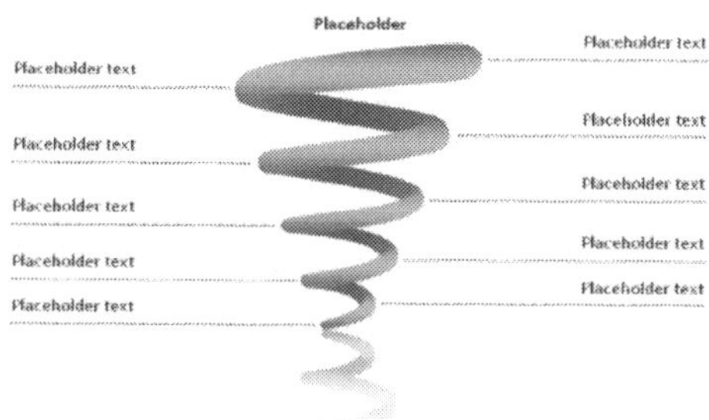

www.Charteo.com
Graphics and Metaphors, Spiral, 3D Spiral Chart 8

Slide: "The Vicious Circle"

This version of the Downward Spiral layout shows at a glance that a problem is going from bad to worse: the downward spiral in the center is flanked on the left by three categories (Individual Level, Project Level, and Portfolio Level) and on the right by a list of eight factors that all build up—or rather break down—to the final disastrous outcome. The three individual level problems listed at upper right cause the situation to deteriorate by impeding success at the project level in the middle, where three more factors (once again listed on the right) cascade into even greater problems at the overall portfolio level. The dashed lines across the page offer a helpful visual divider between the three sections.

The Vicious Circle

A suboptimal mix of internal and external resources rapidly spirals into lost productivity

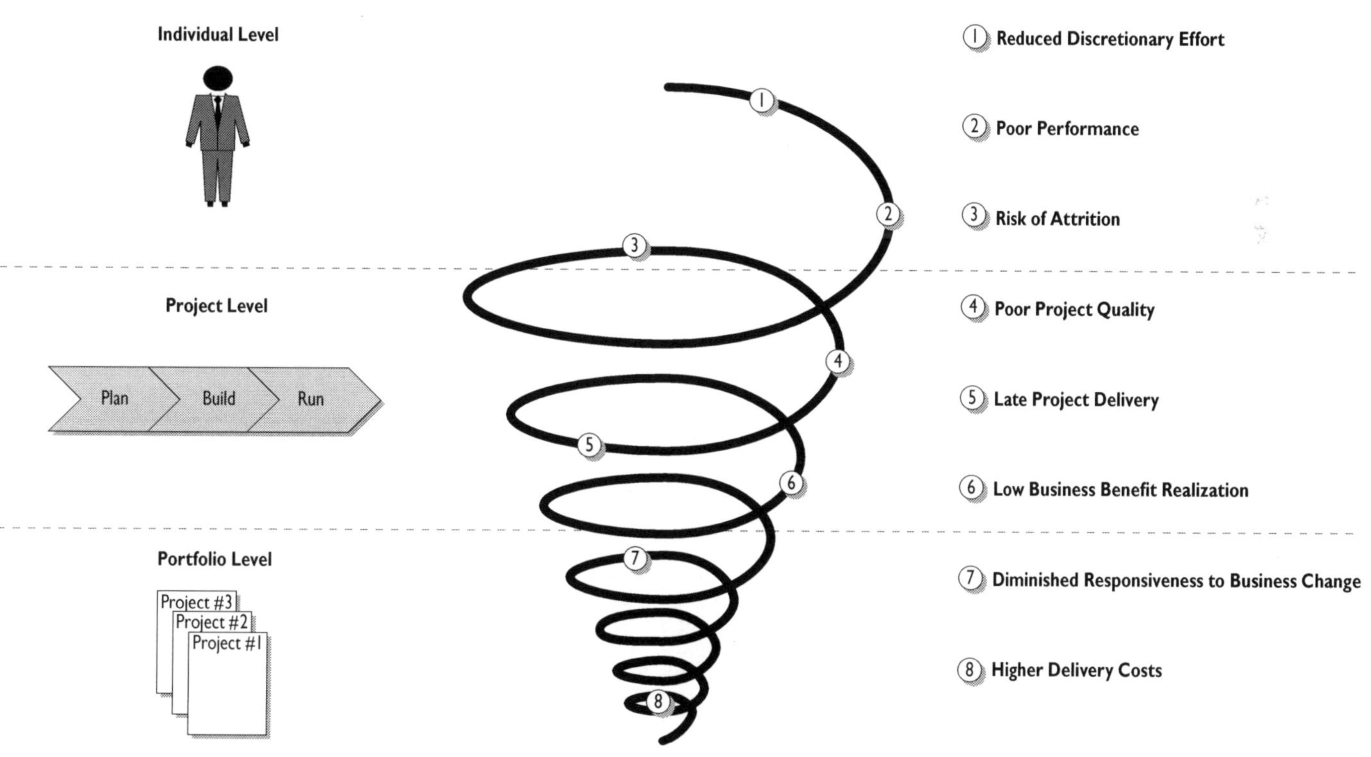

AEC1A5FB69

Source: CEB research.

CHAPTER 19: "FLOWCHART" LAYOUT

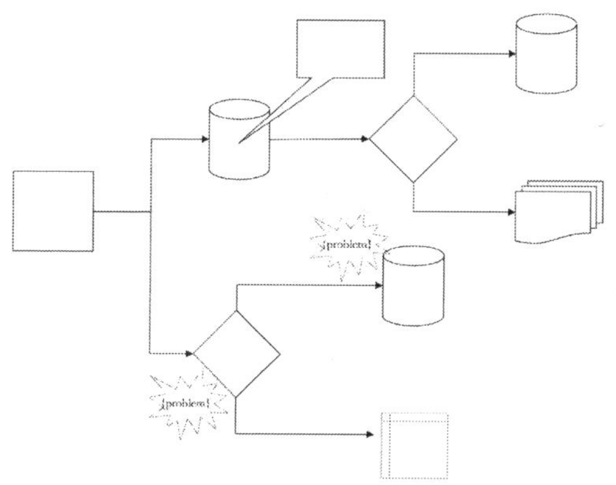

The Flowchart layout is used when the presenter needs to show a complex process with various paths and possibilities. The process could involve manufacturing, customer service, IT planning, or many other processes. The power of this layout lies in its visual portrayal of complexity, which is much more succinct and instantly comprehensible than a text-based description of the same complexity could ever be. Variation in the shape of each node or the style of each arrow provides a further tool for communicating detailed information.

How to draw the "Flowchart" Layout

Charteo

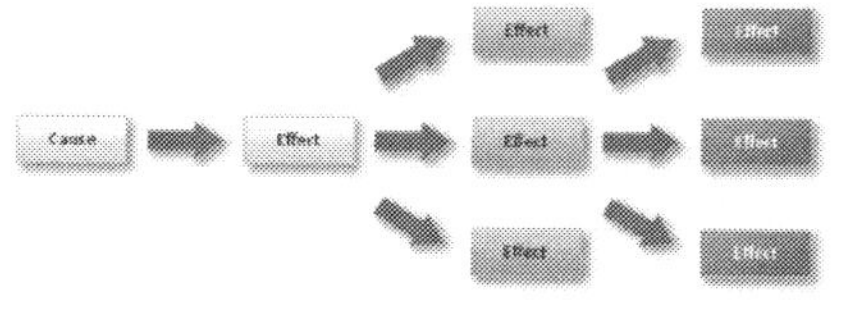

www.Charteo.com
Processes and Flows, Cause and Effect, Cause and Effect Chart 1

SmartArt

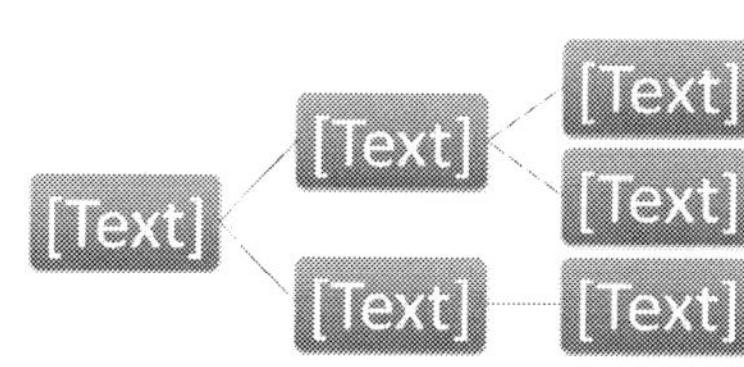

PowerPoint SmartArt
Hierarchy, Horizontal Hierarchy

Slide: "Flowchart of Patient Path"

This Flowchart layout describes a patient's path through a doctor's office. It proceeds from the upper left to the lower right. The legend in the lower left provides the key to the different shapes on the diagram: processes (rectangles) or decisions (diamonds) along the path from the start to the end (oblongs). At each point along the path arrows direct the audience to the next appropriate box, based on the decision made at that particular point.

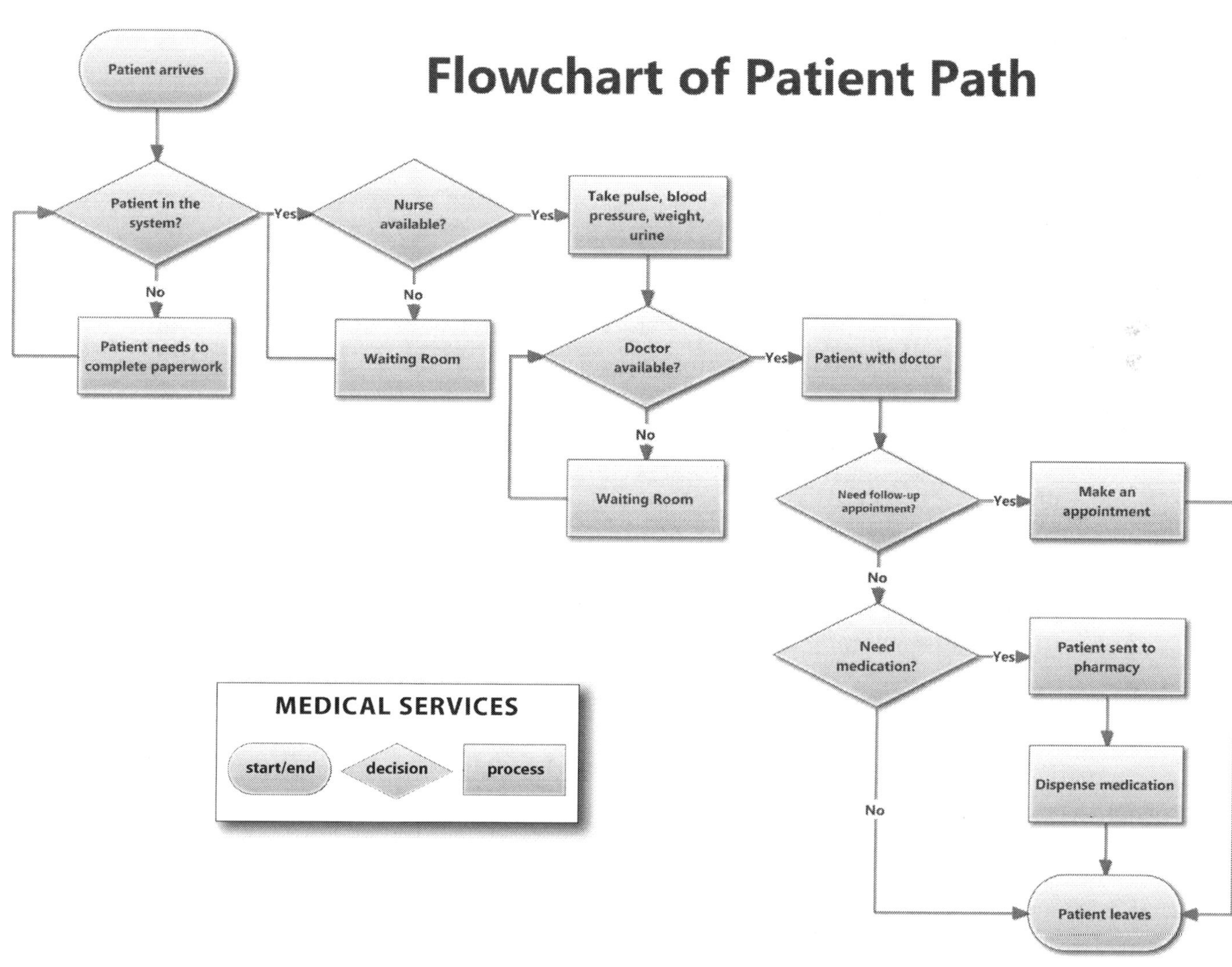
Flowchart of Patient Path
Patient arrives
Patient in the system?
Yes
No
Patient needs to complete paperwork
Nurse available?
Yes
No
Waiting Room
Take pulse, blood pressure, weight, urine
Doctor available?
Yes
No
Waiting Room
Patient with doctor
Need follow-up appointment?
Yes
No
Make an appointment
Need medication?
Yes
No
Patient sent to pharmacy
Dispense medication
Patient leaves
MEDICAL SERVICES
start/end
decision
process

Slide: "Sequence Diagram: Shopping Cart"

This example of the Flowchart layout depicts the various steps that occur during a computer program for an online shopping cart experience. The four key elements are the customer on the left, the shopping cart, the order itself, and the item being purchased. The arrows and text beneath those four main elements map out the sequence in which the program obtains the price for an item and calculates the total cost for the shopping cart. The layout first flows from left to right, beginning when the customer places something in a shopping cart and continuing across as the program requests a total by querying item price; then the flow reverses as the item price is used to calculate the total price and return that value to the shopping cart.

The vertical dashed lines and shaded rectangles act as visual placeholders beneath the elements at the top, and allow the presenter to anchor the arrows at both ends, showing what happens between each step. Notice also the use of solid arrows and dashed arrows to distinguish between functions calling for data and the value resulting from the function.

Sequence Diagram: Shopping Cart

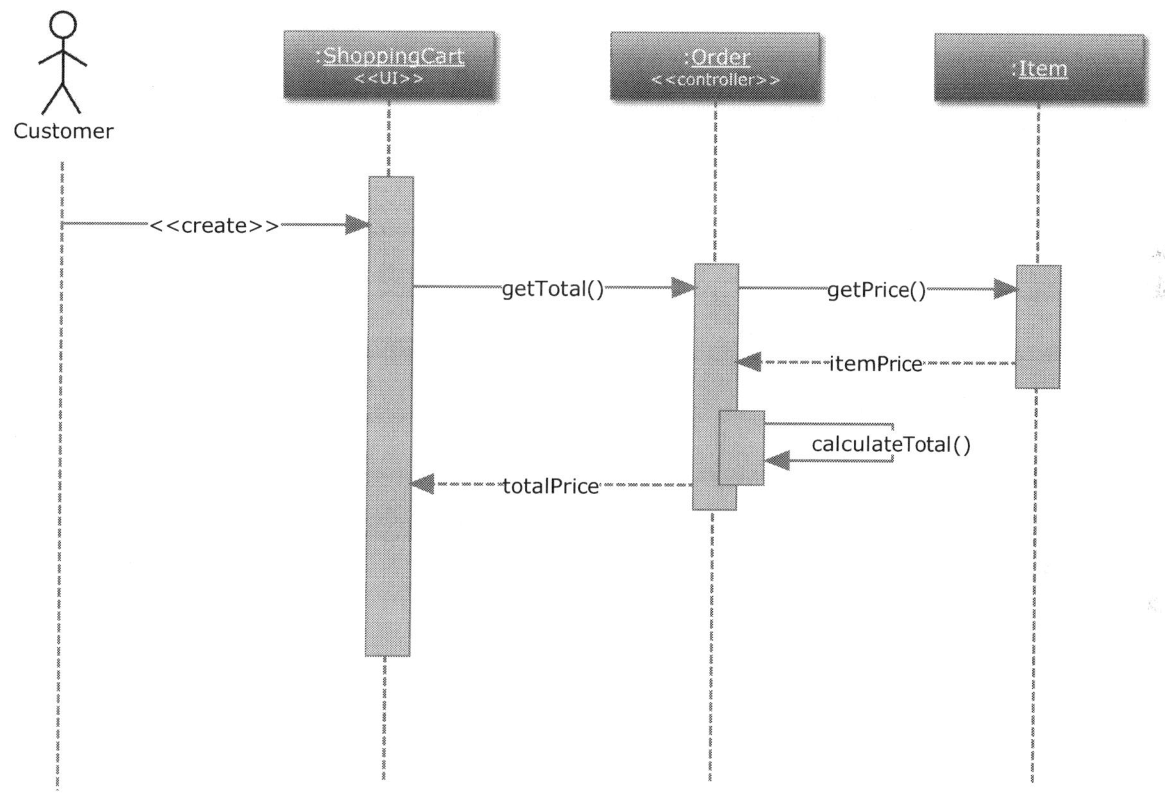

Slide: "Flowchart – Value Stream Map"

This example of the Flowchart layout adds some nonlinear complexity in mapping a production and shipping plan. The audience's attention is initially drawn to the top center of the slide by the visual weight of the dark rectangle around "Production Control." The flow of the slide proceeds counter-clockwise, through an annual production plan, to the suppliers on the upper left. The chart then flows left to right across the bottom, through a four-step milling process to the two customers on the upper right, where it is completed in a market forecast, which returns to Production Control.

There are three features to note here. First, each node or arrow involves an icon with embedded text, rather than icons accompanying text as in other examples. Second, the two exceptions to the overall counter-clockwise flow occur in the feedback loops of the milling process and in the long arrow from the lower left to the top center. Finally, by drawing the four stages in the milling process horizontally, the presenter contrasts the time each stage takes and the time between stages: although the total lead time is 68 days, the total value-added time is only 15 minutes. These details can lead to a very rich discussion about the root causes (and "route" causes) of such delays—and help identify process improvements.

Flowchart - Value Stream Map

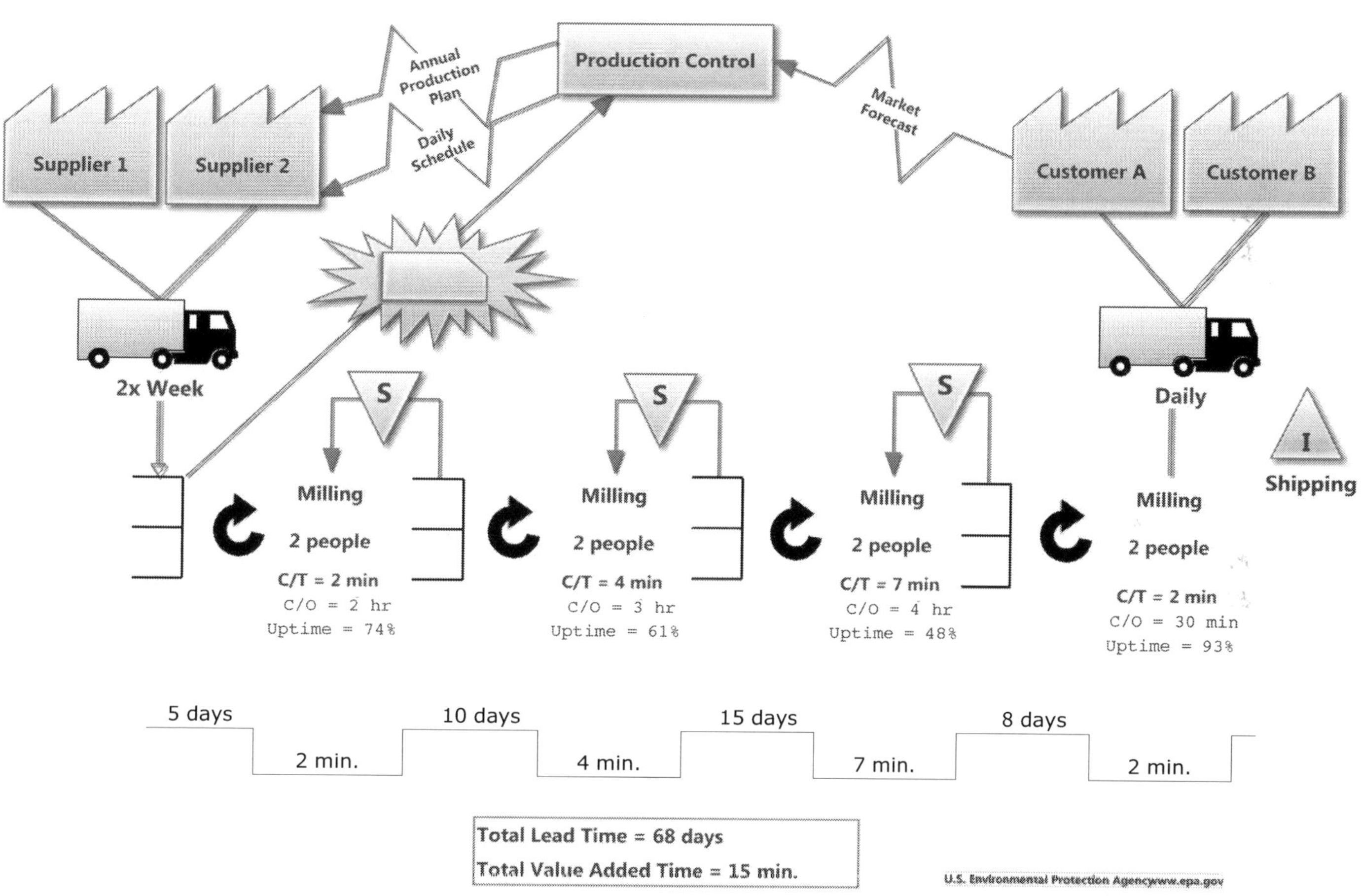

Slide: "The Probate Process"

The overall top-down flow of this Flowchart layout combines with a left to right flow, portraying four distinct steps of the probate process, and a number of sub-steps. The upper portion of the chart shows the first two main steps, each of which has three sub-steps, which altogether take four to six weeks. The lower middle portion of the chart shows two main steps (each with an additional sub-step) that can take four months to one year. The final stage, depicted in the bottom portion of the chart, can take four to six weeks.

Note how effectively this chart combines words and icons: each node has a relevant symbol, accompanied by descriptive text. For example, the courthouse symbol appears each time there is a court hearing, and the paper "Notice" symbol with its envelope icon appears each time notice must be mailed to specified parties.

The Probate Process

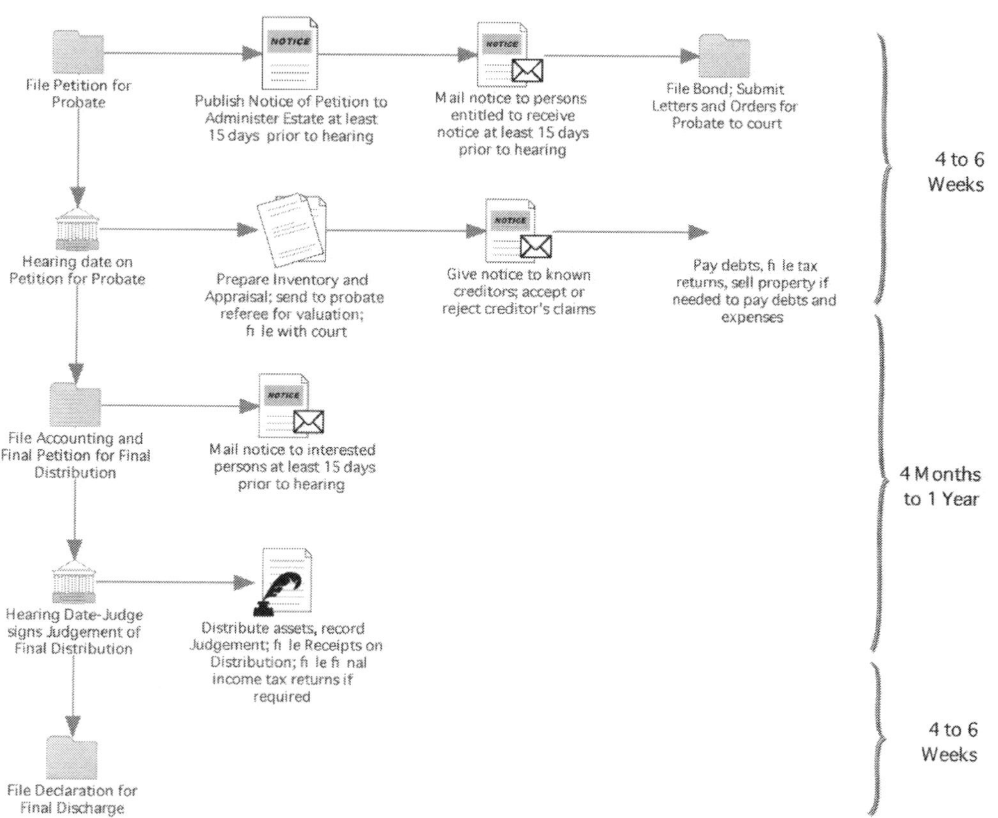

Slide: "Defining the Nebulous"

This Flowchart layout describes the flow of a new business idea, highlighting the importance of a "Discovery Process" for more nebulous ideas. It inserts some complexity into what is overall a simple design. A new idea can take two paths in traveling from the cross-functional Business Opportunities discussion at the top center of the slide, to the Attractiveness-Fit Matrix at the bottom. Well-defined opportunities—those that include a good understanding of customer needs and market dynamics—take the simple path on the right. More nebulous opportunities follow a detailed three-step process on the left, involving an Innovation Charter, an initial Attractiveness-Fit matrix, and a Discovery Process that "converts nebulous, cross-silo opportunities into testable concepts" through a more rigorous analysis of customer needs and market dynamics. The nodes in this diagram are symbolic icons with accompanying descriptive text.

To emphasize the importance of the Discovery Process, the presenter gray-shades the arrows in its icon, describes the process in the center of the slide, and makes reference to the process in the slide's subtitle.

Defining the Nebulous

Opportunities Are Triaged Based on Their Level of Definition, with the Most Nebulous Opportunities Going Through the New Discovery Process

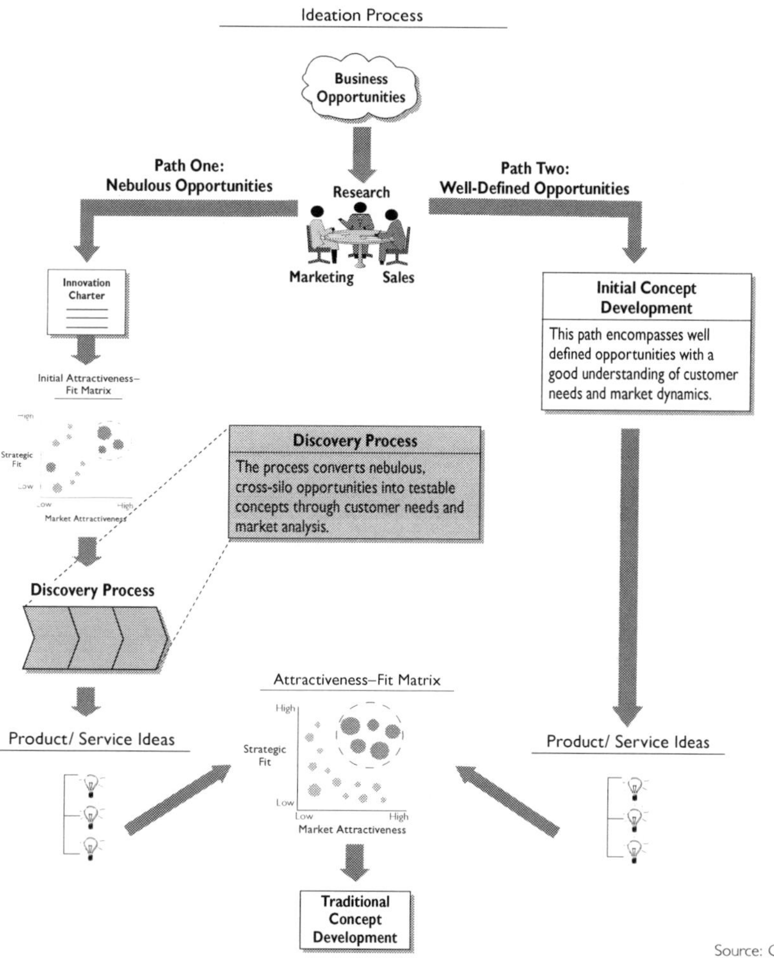

Source: CEB research.

Slide: "Even simple technology can have high impact if used innovatively"

This Flowchart example illustrates how automation simplifies an equities trade entry process. The equities trade flow begins at the left, when the client calls in an order. The text-filled chevrons at the top of the chart show two main categories for the process ("Sales/trading" and "Exchange floor"), which are subdivided into five further categories that act as column-headers, structuring the layout of the 22 steps in the process. Dashed-line arrows indicate alternative sub-paths, as the order proceeds from sales/trading to the exchange floor. The annotations at the bottom of the chart further clarify the systems and the people responsible for each phase in the process.

Within the main part of the slide, note how the legend in the upper right clarifies the nature of the 22 steps: the presenter draws the audience's attention to the shaded boxes, which indicate 17 manual steps. The technology being described automates nine of those steps (the ones labeled by a circled A) and eliminates five others (the ones crossed off with an "X"), thus reducing the number of manual steps from 17 to three.

The text in the right bar of the slide describes the financial impact of the technology and the areas of opportunity for automation.

EVEN SIMPLE TECHNOLOGY CAN HAVE HIGH IMPACT IF USED INNOVATIVELY

EQUITIES TRADE ENTRY-AUTOMATION EXAMPLE

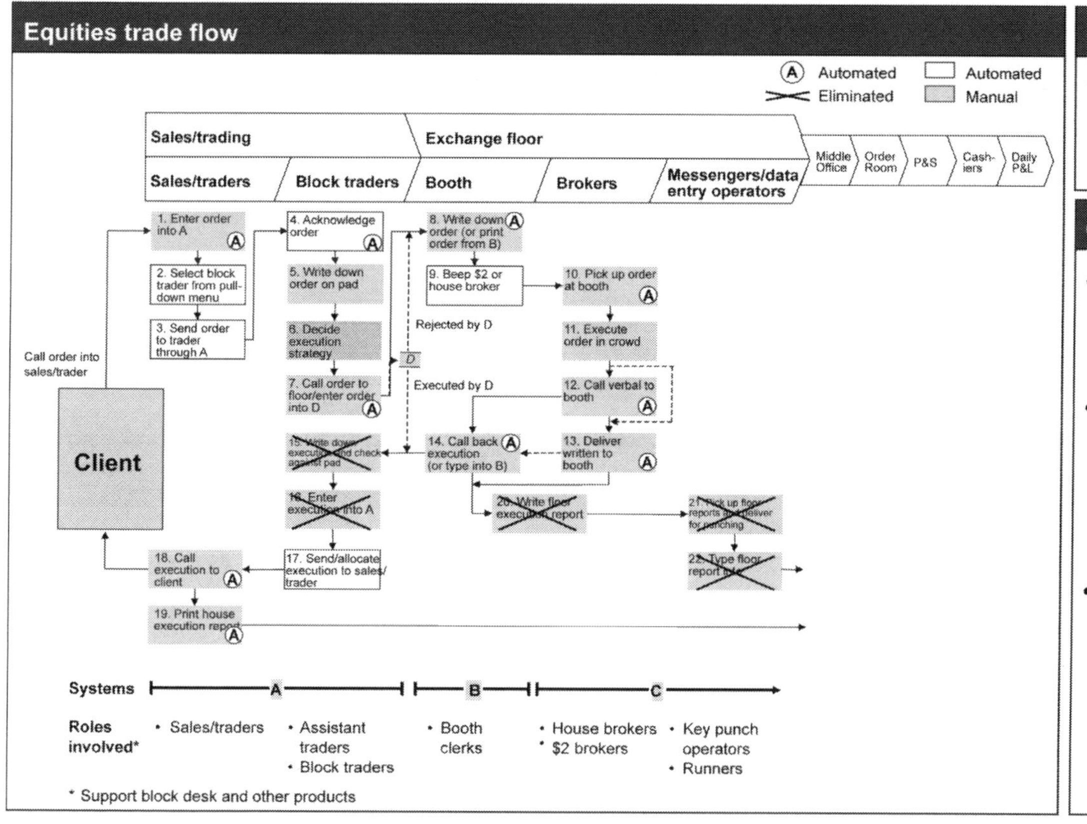

Impact

- USD 3-4 million in additional capacity created in sales, trader, and block trader groups

Opportunity areas

- Automating order execution and handoff between client and block desk
- Automating the exchange floor process (e.g., handoff between block trader and floor, handhelds for floor brokers)
- Automating the middle office (e.g., house execution report between the block desk and order room, electronic allocation entry directly by clients)

Slide: "Finding the (Right) Way"

This Flowchart layout describes a process taken by marketers to envision the next generation for their function. It proceeds from four entry points on the left, through a process in the middle, to three outcomes on the right. Each node in the flowchart contains a descriptive title and an icon that visually depicts what the process entails. For example, the node titled "Horizon Scanning" shows a telescope, while "Input Review and Analysis" shows a boiling cauldron—implying that the various options are boiled down to a single vision. This unified "Vision of the Future," depicted in the middle-right, is the chart's only non-oval-shaped node: embedding it in a star marks it as the key point of the slide, the goal to which the process leads. This vision is developed into a reality through the three types of initiatives depicted on the right.

The five numbered callout boxes give the audience a clear roadmap to follow from the beginning to the end of the flowchart; the roadmap's unity is strengthened by the ellipses, which tie the callout texts into one narrative sentence.

Finding the (Right) Way

Marketers Take a Methodical Approach to Determining "What They Want to Be"

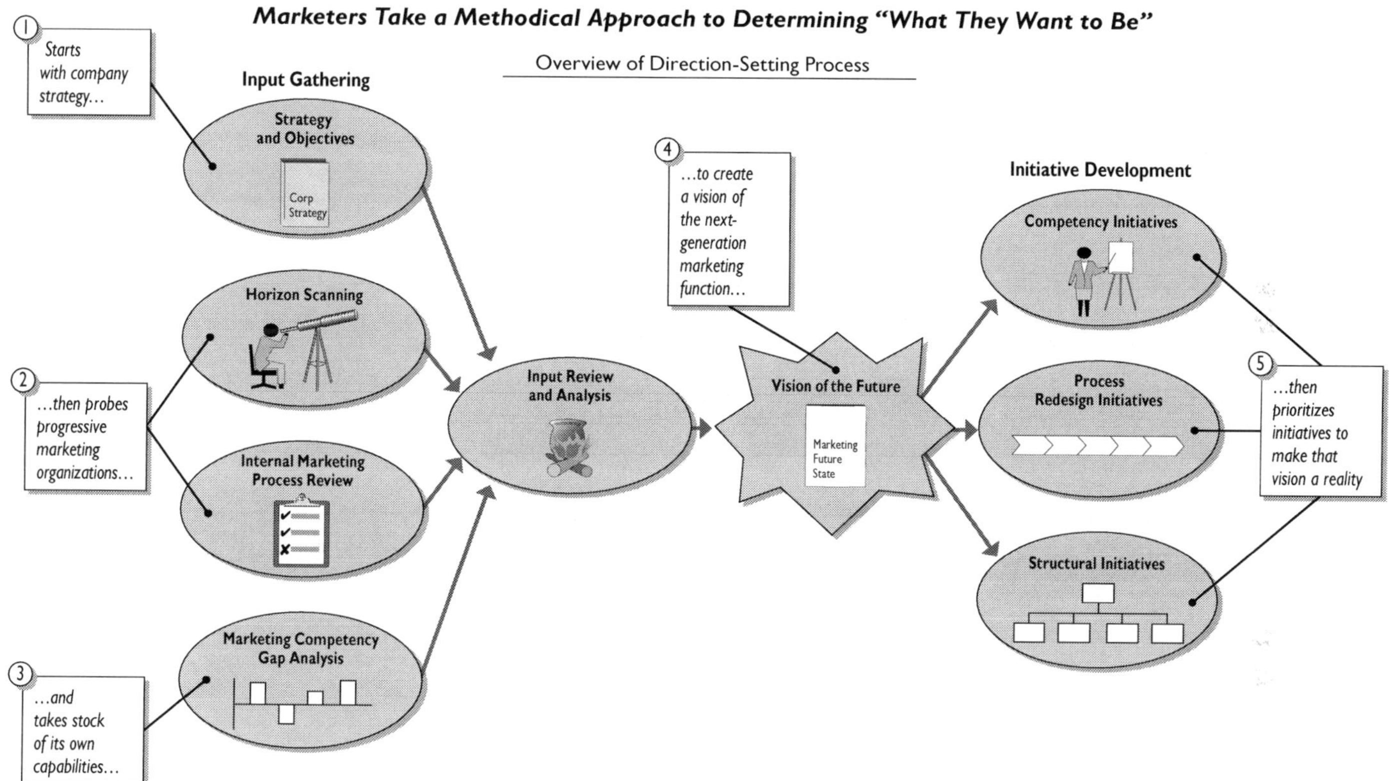

Source: CEB research.

Slide: "My digital life 2.0"

This Flowchart layout maps a consumer's digital life through various spheres of experience, centered on devices linked in a multitude of ways. The Phone Experience resides within the Audio Experience, which in turn overlaps with the Computing and the Video Experiences, while the Computing Experience overlaps with the Mobile Experience and the Photo Experience. The lines connecting devices show both the means of connection (wireless, Firewire, USB, etc.) and the frequency of connection (solid lines signal constant connection; dashed lines, occasional).

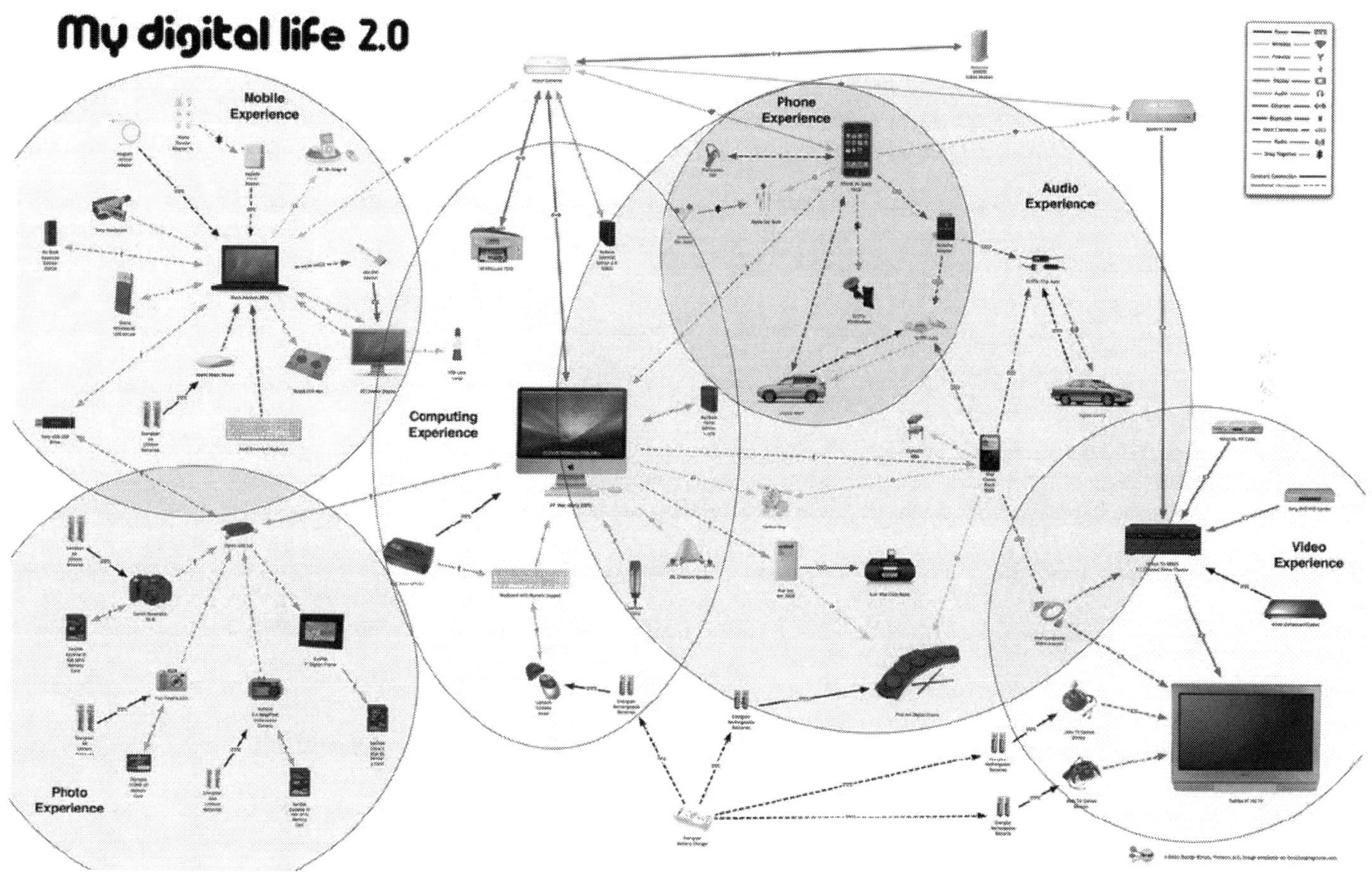
My digital life 2.0
Mobile Experience
Phone Experience
Audio Experience
Computing Experience
Video Experience
Photo Experience

CHAPTER 20: "FROM-TO" LAYOUT

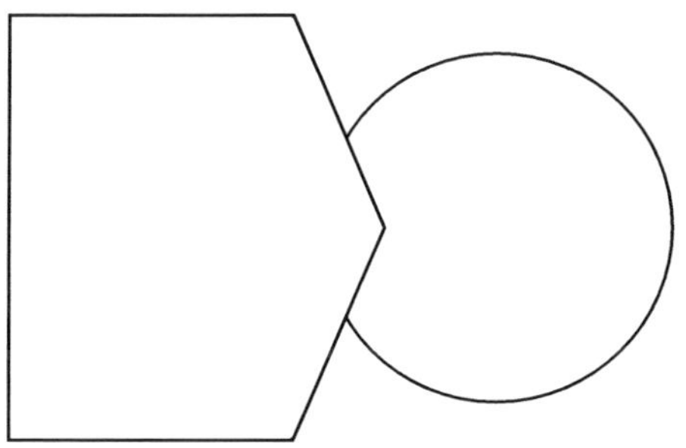

The popular From-To layout enables the presenter to contrast and relate two concepts. The concepts can be related as cause to effect, general to particular, or an unsatisfactory state to a more desirable state (for example, current to future). The examples in this chapter portray these various options.

How to draw the "From-To" Layout

Charteo

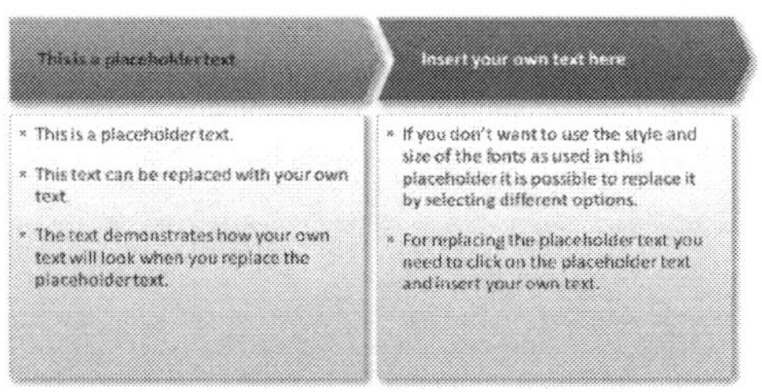

www.Charteo.com
Processes and Flows, Process-Linear, Text Arrows 1

Diagrammer

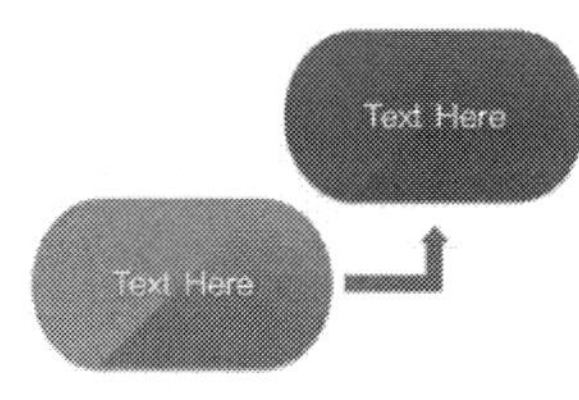

www.Diagrammer.com
Flow, Linear, 2 Nodes, 2D Mixed, Flow Linear 1450

Slide: "Employee motivation drives retention and performance"

In this version of the From-To layout, the "From" arrow on the left lists a series of key questions for discussion, and points to the "To" box on the right, which lists a series of best-practice examples. Each of the five questions on the left corresponds to one of the five examples on the right. The arrow shape indicates the flow of the slide, while the darker background of the box provides visual weight and draws the audience's attention, as to a conclusion or case in point.

EMPLOYEE MOTIVATION DRIVES RETENTION AND PERFORMANCE

Key questions for discussion

- How does the bank actively improve job designs (e.g., reduce waste, ensure growth opportunity) to increase motivation?
- What incentives are most effective to create enthusiasm in the organization?
- How can staff get involved (e.g., by sharing improvement ideas and knowledge)?
- How does the bank offer non-formal rewards (e.g., celebration of successes)?
- How does the bank measure employee satisfaction? How does the bank take action to address areas of improvement?

Best practice examples

- Build employee engagement to drive productivity (e.g., through lean programs and performance transformations)
- Run employee motivation surveys regularly – and act on the results
- Leverage non-financial rewards and incentives systematically
- Celebrate successes, even small ones, if needed (e.g., for project milestones)
- Build an employee network

Slide: "Media Concept Test"

This From-To layout utilizes the standard elements, but with a twist—here the right side of the slide is an arrow, indicating that the proposed objective, the "To," is itself an action step rather than an end state. As in the previous example, the "From" side lists a series of questions; but here they do not map to examples on the right. Instead, the right side details the research survey that will be used to answer the initial questions. As noted above, the arrow shape of the "To" figure indicates that the work described in the slide is incomplete until the listed steps are fulfilled.

Media Concept Test

Several critical marketing decisions that would benefit from quantitative consumer research:

1. What price should we set?
2. Which consumer segments should we focus on?
3. What is the most compelling and comprehensible language for describing the service?
4. Which features should we emphasize most?

Recommendation: run a concept test (consumer survey to assess interest in alternative product "concepts")

- Service described in a series of alternative "concepts" (one page of text and illustration); each concept represents a different combination of price points, language, and features
- Concepts subjected to preliminary testing/refinement in two focus groups, to ensure consumer comprehension
- 4,000 respondents surveyed to compare levels of interest in each concept (each respondent views only one concept)
- Total cost for the research approximately $xxK
- Time from approval of concept to top-line results is six weeks

Expected results from survey

- Level of consumer interest in each of the alternative concepts
- Estimate of % of households nationally, and by demographic segment and price-point, who would be interested in the service.

Next steps

- Develop concepts and survey questionnaire
- Field research

Slide: "If HSAs are accepted, total asset accumulations ..."

This example of the From-To layout embeds complexity while retaining overall simplicity of design. The arrow on the left contains a considerable amount of information, including a table at its base. The arrow points to the right, where a detailed chart shows the annually estimated number of HSA accounts as well as predictions of total HSA assets/spending, both of which are increasing substantially. The box below that chart lists the slide's key take-aways, shading them for emphasis.

IF HSAs ARE WIDELY ACCEPTED, TOTAL ASSET ACCUMULATIONS AND THE AMOUNT OF CONSUMER SPENDING COULD BE SIZABLE

ILLUSTRATIVE

Potential scenario

Product:
- Single person HSA with catastrophic coverage
- $2,500 deductible
- 20% co-insurance after deductible
- $5,000 maximum out-of-pocket

Funding:
- On average funded with $2,000 annually
- Unused, accumulated assets grow at 7% annually

Enrollment:
- ~25 million accounts by 2013

Distribution of medical expenses for commercially insured population*

Portion of population %	Estimated 2004 medical claims $
30	24
30	496
20	1,452
16	5,324
4	28,556

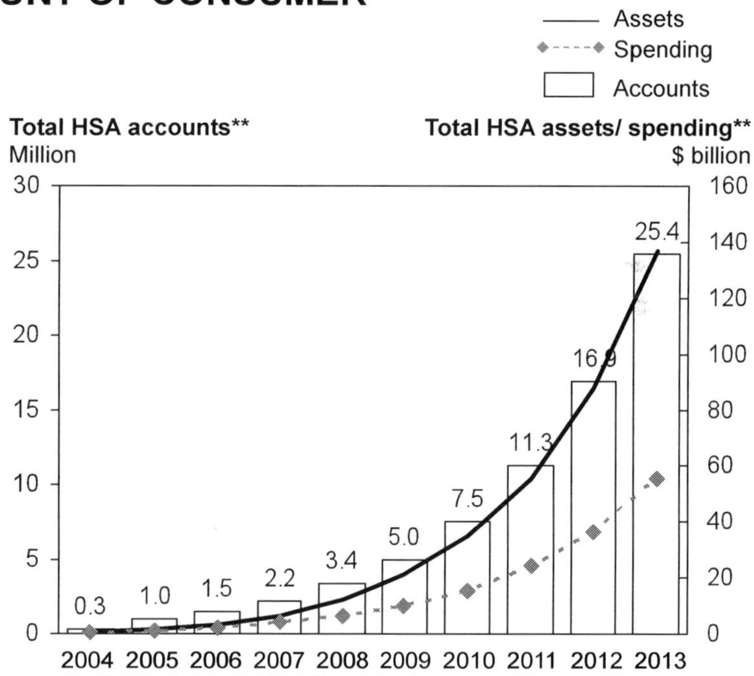

By 2013 there could be . . .
- 25 million HSA accounts
- $125 billion-$150 billion in accumulated assets, of which $60 billion-$65 billion could be in liquid accounts***
- $50 billion spent through HSA accounts

* Figures used to predict the probability of an individual's level of medical expense in any given year
** Based on a simulation of 1,000 typical consumers
*** Assumes regulations require a minimum of the annual deductible to be available in a liquid account
Sources: Milliman USA; Health Affairs

Slide: "Problems of our own making"

This From-To layout shows the causes of increased occurrence of financial crises, in a left to right flow depicting cause-and-effect. Within the middle-left "cause" column, two charts show how over time national economies have become more interdependent and more countries have attained a high degree of capital mobility. The arrow indenting the border between the columns (along with the explanatory text on the far left) suggests the causal relationship between the data contained in the first two charts and the data in the chart on the right. This chart of effects indicates that the number of financial crises in developed countries has doubled. The main point of the page is summarized in the upper-left corner.

Our interdependent financial systems amplify—not insulate—economic blows.

- Executives and managers need to boost their ability to manage alongside uncertainty, not least because it is likely to become more prevalent.
- The heightened interdependence of national economies and markets appears to amplify, not insulate, shocks beginning in one part of the international financial system.
- Increased capital mobility and financial exposure to foreign economies, for example, may have helped double the number of financial crises in developed countries since the immediate post-war period.

PROBLEMS OF OUR OWN MAKING

Cross-Border Asset Ownership
1980–2007

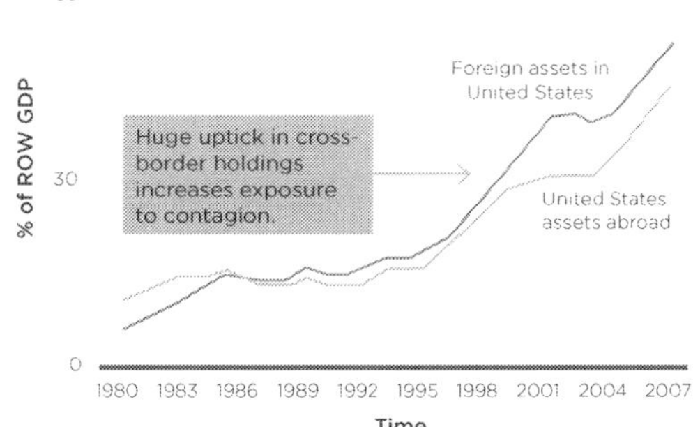

SOURCE: Krugman, Paul. "The International Finance Multiplier," October 2008.

Degree of Capital Mobility of 163 Countries
1970 Versus 2000

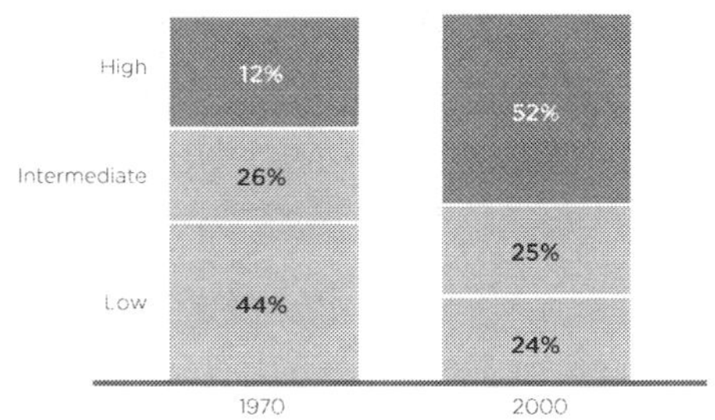

SOURCE: Edwards, S., Capital Controls, Sudden Stops and Current Account Reversals, NBER, March 2005.

Frequency of Occurrence of Financial Crises
Industrialized Countries, 1945–1971 Versus 1973–1997

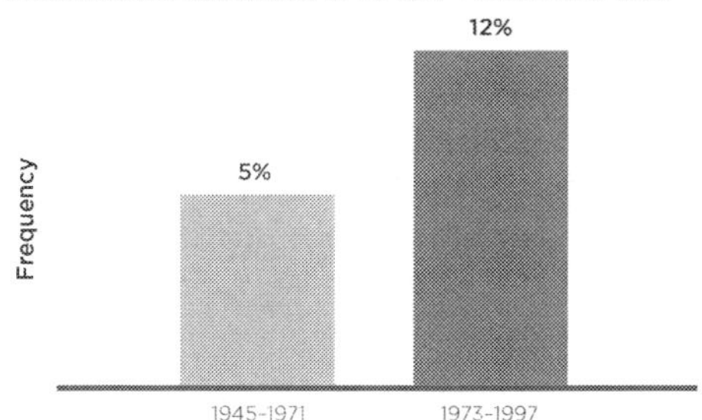

SOURCE: Bordo et al. "Is the Crisis Problem Growing More Severe?" 2000.

Slide: "Now That's a Growth Environment"

This version of the From-To layout is not simply past-to-present or cause-to-effect but general-to-specific. The slide identifies an organization's four key growth attributes, listed on the left and heading each row. Following the growth attribute heading, each row contains a box which shows (both graphically and textually) a firmwide manifestation of the attribute. Finally, an arrow points from each attribute manifestation box to the corresponding box in the right column, showing how the attributes manifest in the Research Function—a fact which is once again portrayed both graphically and textually.

In the first row, for example, the firmwide manifestation of the Risk-Reward Culture is represented by a balance icon, indicating the fairness of the culture, and on the right side its research manifestation is represented by a To Do list, indicating entrepreneurial elements in the day-to-day job of the researcher.

Now That's a Growth Environment

Attributes of Growth-Oriented Organization

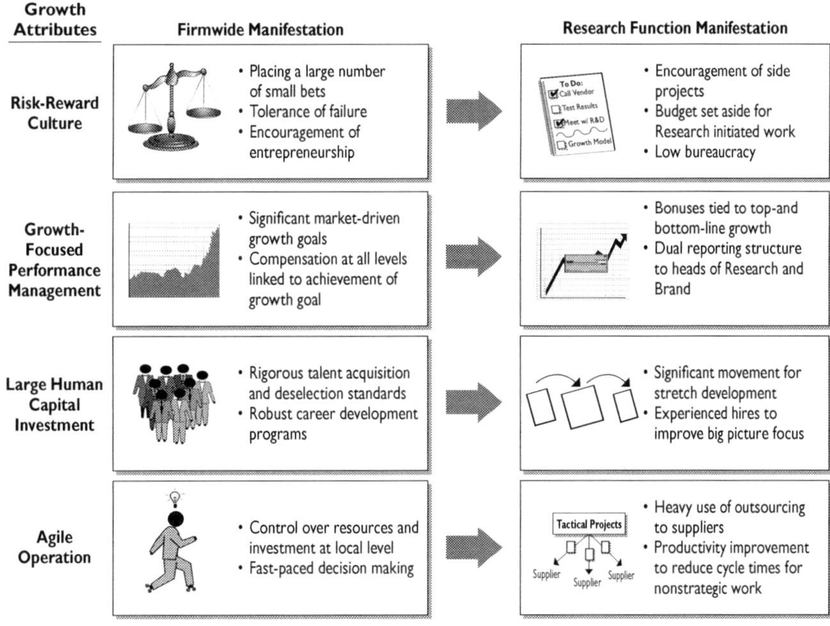

A Different World

"I've worked at other companies that thought they were focused on growth, but when I got to Frito-Lay, I realized what an organization built around growth really feels like."

Group Manager, Consumer Strategy & Insight

Source: CEB research.

Slide: "'Insurance-Tinted' Glasses Obscure Market Reality"

In this interesting twist on the From-To layout, the progression is not before-to-after but from a narrow focus to a broader view. On the left, the two-dimensional segmentation shows that a majority of life insurance companies, confident in the degree to which they are differentiated by their strategies, have clustered in the customer-focused and proprietary region. But this perspective, based on the point of view of the companies themselves, is limited; and on the right the slide shifts the frame of reference to the customers' perspective, which allows the audience to step back, view the data from a broader perspective, and come to the insight which the layout reveals.

This is an excellent example of the importance of setting the frame, whether that involves determining the scope of a two-dimensional data set, or deciding the overall question of what goes on a slide. Just as the photographer chooses the lens angle or scope for a photograph, so too the presenter chooses whether to use a narrow lens on the data set (as on the left of this slide) or to use a wide angle lens (as on the right of this slide).

"Insurance-Tinted" Glasses Obscure Market Reality

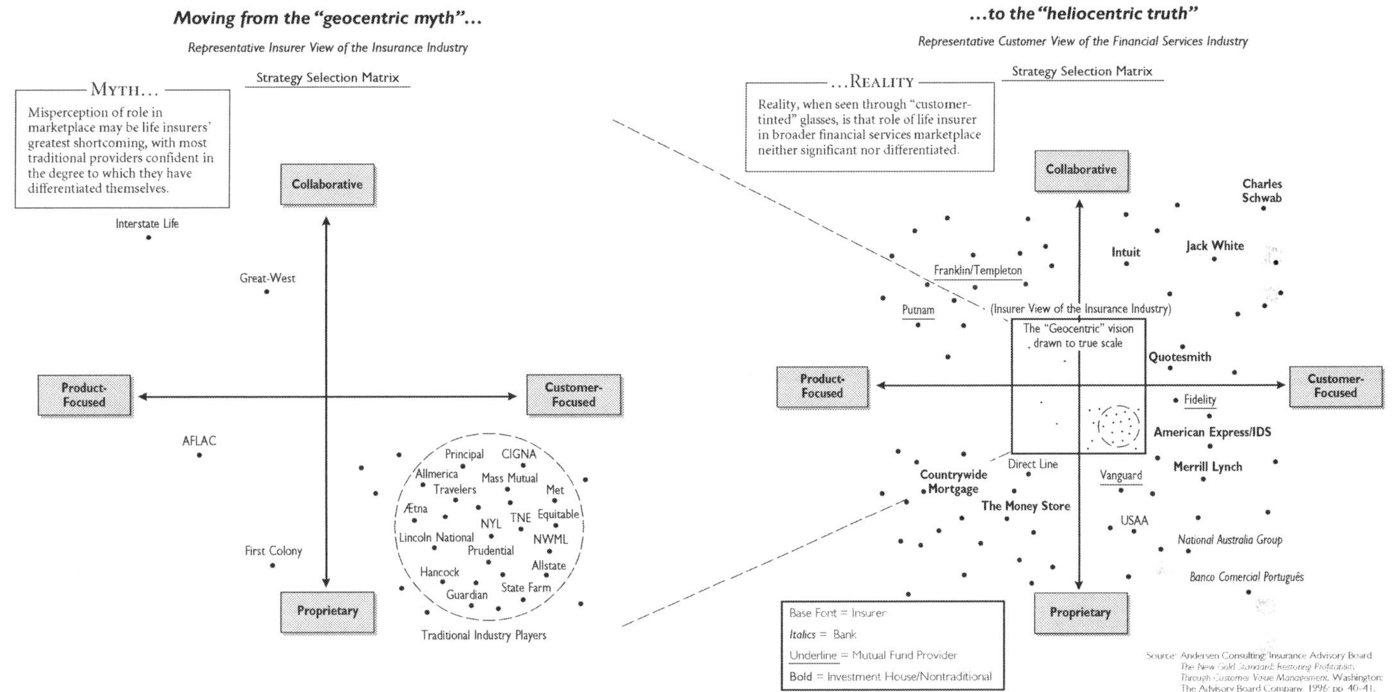

Source: Andersen Consulting/Insurance Advisory Board. *The New Gold Standard: Restoring Profitability Through Customer Value Management.* Washington: The Advisory Board Company, 1996: pp. 40–41.

CHAPTER 21: "FROM-TO PROCESS" LAYOUT

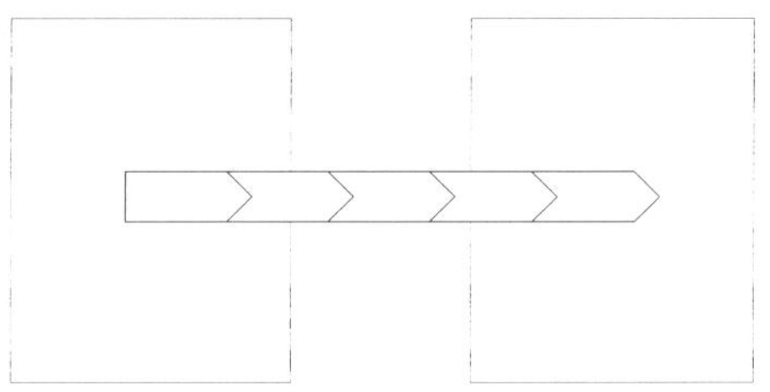

The From-To Process layout adds an important detail to the From-To layout, in the form of a process to move between the "From" and "To" states. It is ideal for comparing a current state of affairs with a desired state, and how to get from one to the other.

How to draw the "From-To Process" Layout

Charteo

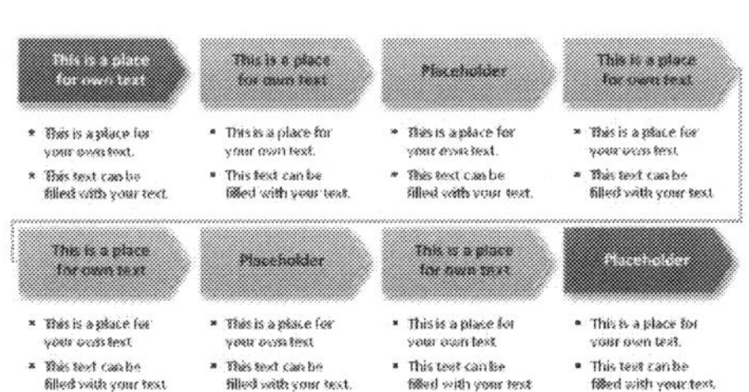

www.Charteo.com
Processes and Flows, Process-Linear, Text Arrows 71

Diagrammer

www.Diagrammer.com
Flow, Linear, 3 Nodes, 2D Mixed, Flow Linear 198

Slide: "Framework for Breaking Down 'A to B'"

This slide utilizes the From-To Process layout, to show a complex procedure through which a company can shift internal stakeholders' beliefs in order to establish a new shared understanding of how the company will succeed. The overall left to right flow of the slide shows the process through which the stakeholders advance in understanding. This flow is undergirded at the bottom of the slide by a description of the nonlinear procedure through which the consultative team develops the overall process. They begin on the far right at #1, with the goal of determining the supporting rationale for the end-state "B"—the desired internal understanding. They proceed to the lower left at #2, identifying the beliefs underlying the current understanding. Finally, at #3 in the bottom center, they deduce the specific evidence required to change those beliefs.

The overarching message of the slide appears in the upper left, followed by four key points that summarize the details of the process.

Company maps out the shift in internal beliefs required to embed Foundational Knowledge.

- A logical framework helps identify the specific evidence required to change internal stakeholders' beliefs.
- First, construct the supporting rational ("desired beliefs") for "B"—typically spelled out in the Foundational Knowledge platform.
- Second, investigate what alternative rationale ("current beliefs") underlies "A."
- Finally, identify "evidence required": specific data and anecdotes that would debunk current beliefs in favor of desired beliefs.

FRAMEWORK FOR BREAKING DOWN "A TO B"

Illustrative Deconstruction

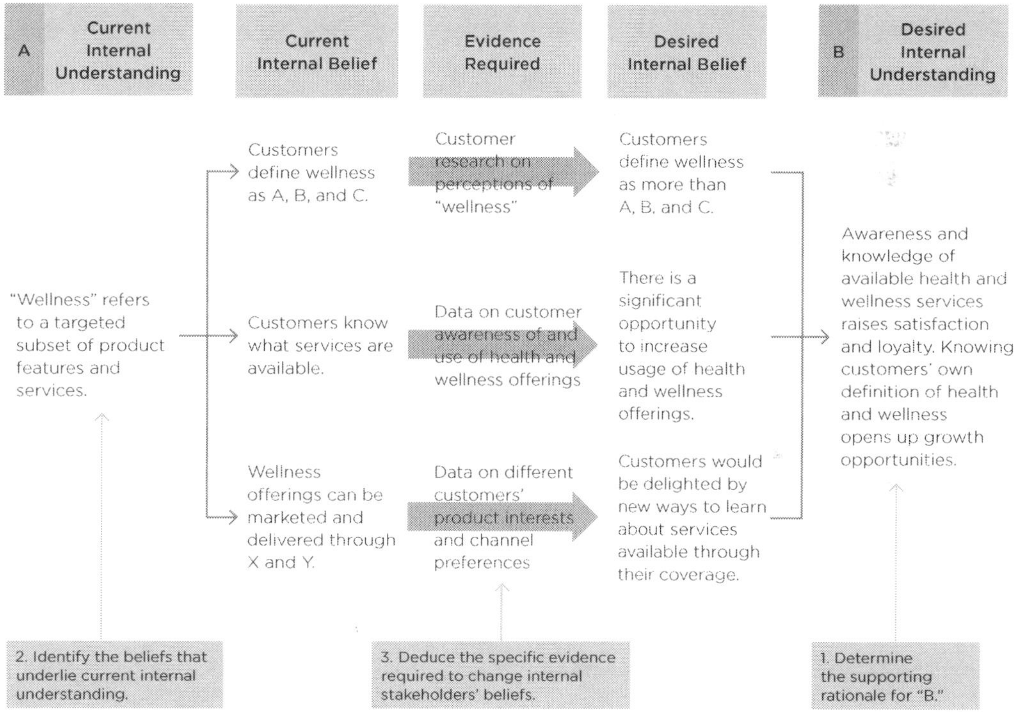

A Current Internal Understanding	Current Internal Belief	Evidence Required	Desired Internal Belief	B Desired Internal Understanding
"Wellness" refers to a targeted subset of product features and services.	Customers define wellness as A, B, and C.	Customer research on perceptions of "wellness"	Customers define wellness as more than A, B, and C.	Awareness and knowledge of available health and wellness services raises satisfaction and loyalty. Knowing customers' own definition of health and wellness opens up growth opportunities.
	Customers know what services are available.	Data on customer awareness of and use of health and wellness offerings	There is a significant opportunity to increase usage of health and wellness offerings.	
	Wellness offerings can be marketed and delivered through X and Y.	Data on different customers' product interests and channel preferences	Customers would be delighted by new ways to learn about services available through their coverage.	

2. Identify the beliefs that underlie current internal understanding.

3. Deduce the specific evidence required to change internal stakeholders' beliefs.

1. Determine the supporting rationale for "B."

CHAPTER 22: "GAMEBOARD" LAYOUT

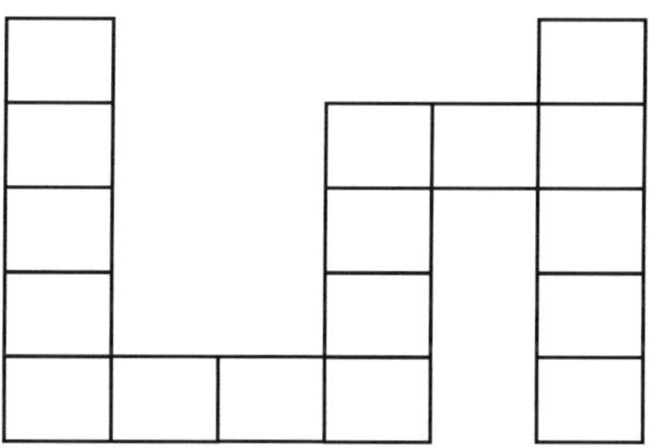

The Gameboard layout depicts a process displaying a series of steps, some of which may be grouped into subcategories. It is particularly suited to describing processes where each step includes many details, and also when the process being described presents different options or decisions, as opposed to being more straightforward and linear. The Gameboard layout can imply playfulness, competition, or celebration, although these undertones are not necessary.

How to draw the "Gameboard" Layout

Charteo

Process Chart – Rectangle (8 Steps)

Enter your subheadline here

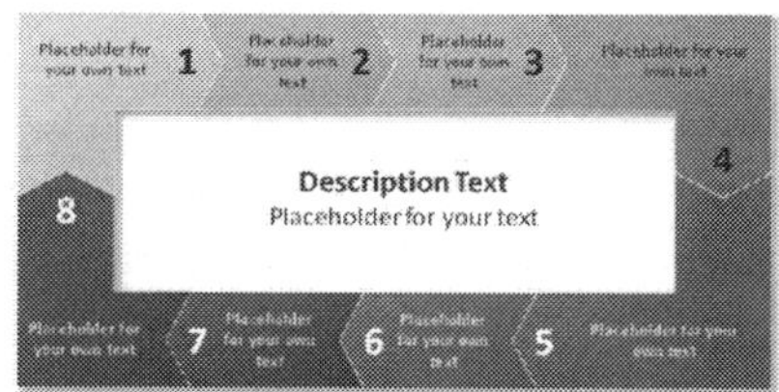

www.Charteo.com
Processes and Flows, Process-Rectangular, Rectangle 10

Slide: "The Long Road to a Firm-Changing Insight"

This first example of the Gameboard layout details five steps in a case study of gaining firmwide impact for a specific market research insight. Each square in the gameboard contains a descriptive title, a pictorial icon, and summary text. The gray arrows around the outside of the board reinforce the clock-wise flow (along with the numbering of squares 1 through 5) and present the timing of each step. The emphasis is on each step's details and the overall elapsed time (18 months). If the presenter wished to emphasize each step's relative length or the time between the steps, then a Timeline layout would be more appropriate (see the Timeline Chapter).

The verbal anecdote quoted below the gameboard provides a concrete summary of the process outcome.

The Long Road to a Firm-Changing Insight

A Robust Idea Selection and Research Process Ensures That Eventual Growth Recommendations Are CEO-Worthy

Case Example: Portfolio Growth Drivers Model

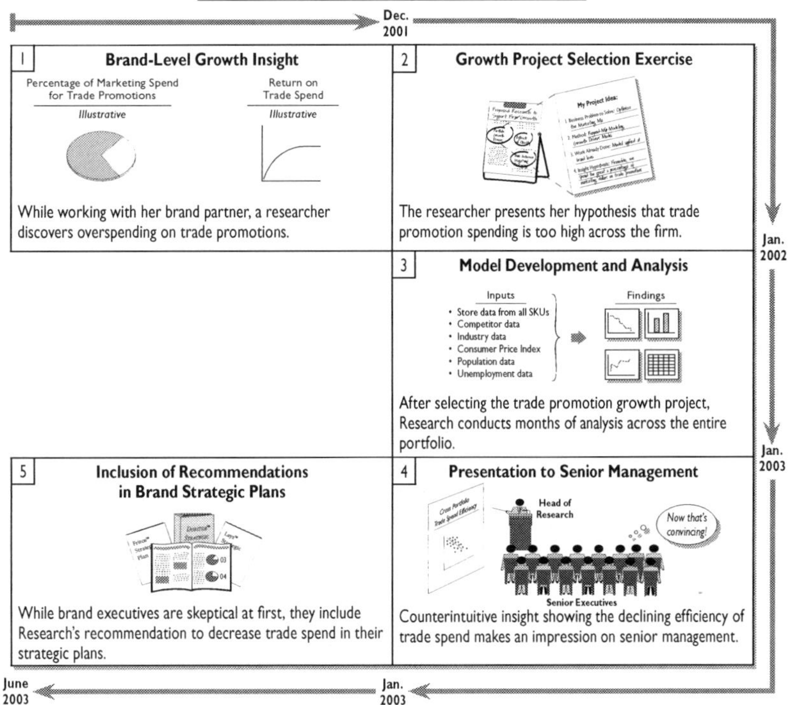

Wake Up Call

"Research had been sending reports on declining effectiveness of trade spend up the flagpole for some time, but it took seeing it in the actual sales numbers to wake everyone up."

Group Manager, Consumer Strategy & Insight

Source: CEB research.

Slide: "Guiding Light"

This example, describing changes to a sales process, is a variation on the previous example, containing more steps, some of which are highlighted. The gray shading used to highlight the later gameboard squares shows that those steps are led by the sales representative rather than by the system. Each square includes a title describing the action, a graphic image depicting the step, and explanatory text. Many of the squares in this example also have complex graphics; steps 5 and 6, for example, each illustrate a supporting process by embedding a mini-gameboard within the overall Gameboard layout. Step 5 is even more complex, ending in a puzzle graphic, which suggests that the proposed solution is comprised of various customized parts (see the Puzzle Pieces chapter for using a puzzle graphic as an overall slide layout).

Guiding Light

Redesigned Needs-Identification and Fulfillment Process

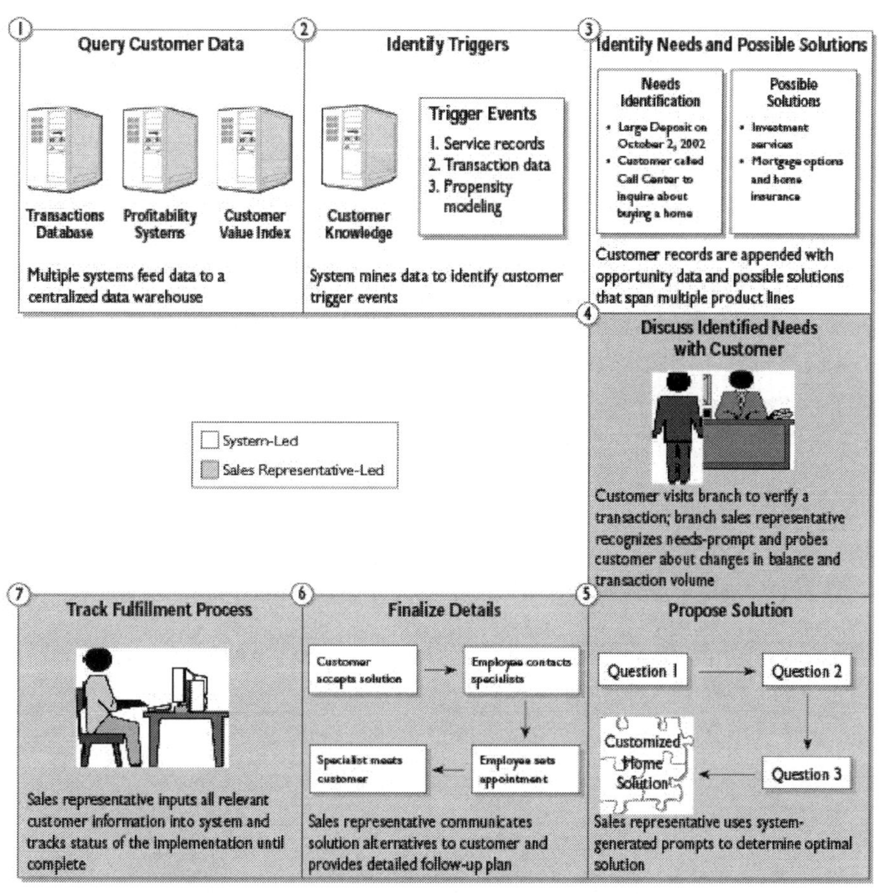

Slide: "Competition in the Name of Learning"

This Gameboard layout describes a training game to teach "solutions selling." The layout combines visual and timeline features from the previous examples and also includes two new elements: a pre-game preparation (described in the bulleted text before the first square), and two graphics in the center of the board that exemplify the overall process. Although the icons in each square are less detailed than those of the previous examples, the title for each square is more concrete, and the accompanying text gives more narrative. The surrounding arrows show the exact timing of the nine events, which occur across the span of four days.

This example shows how the Gameboard layout adapts well to the addition of graphics in the middle and the side. The layout in the upper left shows how the participants in the "game" receive the case study before the process even begins. The space in the middle is occupied by two illustrative graphics: a detailed list of the various executives who judge the competition, and a funneling image that shows how the number of contestants decreases with each round of the selection process. The addition of the gray arrow in the background of the funnel suggests the winning team "rises to the top."

Competition in the Name of Learning

Solutions-Selling Simulation Exercise

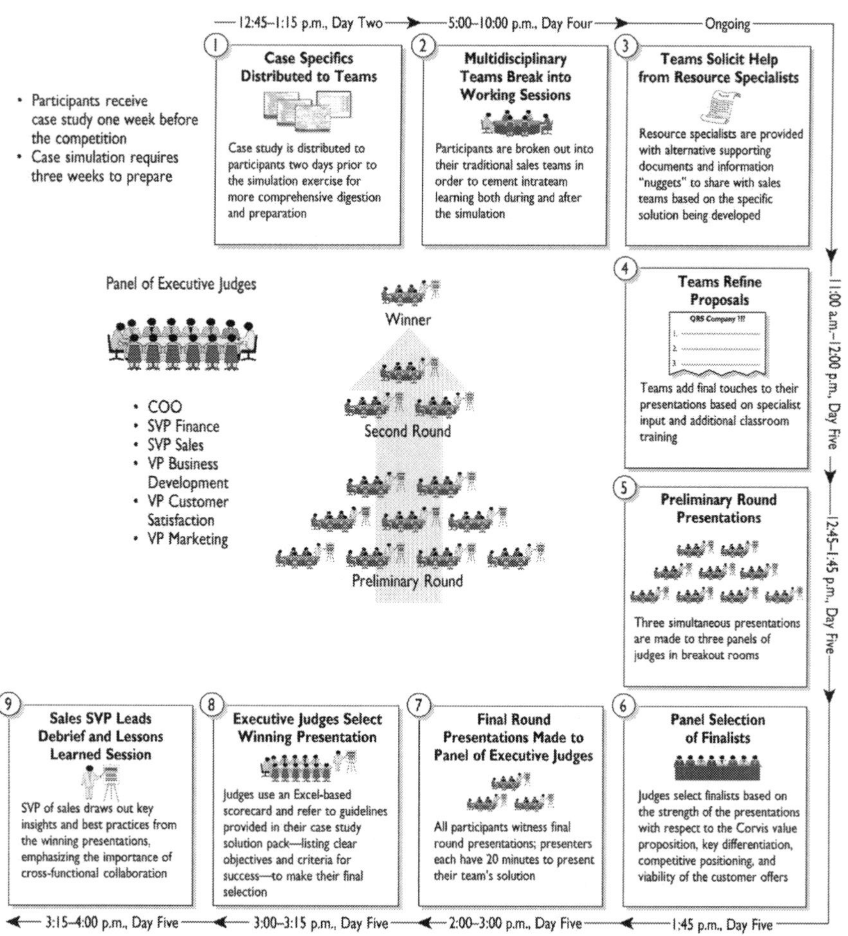

Source: Corvis Corporation; CEB research.

Slide: "Review Process Reinforces Comprehensive Approach"

This final Gameboard layout presents a process for developing a consensus risk assessment. It includes more steps than the previous examples and groups them into four categories: Reviewing Previous Quarter, Examining Trends, Developing Scenarios, and Establishing Warning Signs. The flow of the page, which is indicated by both the numbered squares and the arrows around the outside, begins in the upper left, proceeds across the top to the upper right, goes down to the lower right, and then continues across the bottom to the lower left. Each square of the gameboard has a descriptive title, brief explanatory text, and an icon or image illustrating what happens at that stage in the process. Finally, the supporting text placed in the middle of the gameboard comprehensively reviews the details of the Quarterly Economic Review and Tripwire Analysis.

This layout was originally designed to display across two portrait-oriented pages, and has been reduced to fit this page, which is why it has a white "gutter" down the middle of the page, and why its type size is so small.

Review Process Reinforces Comprehensive Approach

Twelve-Step Process from Initial Review to Tripwire Development

Reviewing Previous Quarter

1 Meeting Kickoff
- Committee begins with review of previous quarter's outlook

2 Critical Development Review
- Critical developments occurring since previous meeting reviewed
- Implications for consensus view discussed

3 Major Economic Forecasts
- Review of alternate scenarios for global economy over next two years
- Scenarios include forecasts for underlying economic indicators

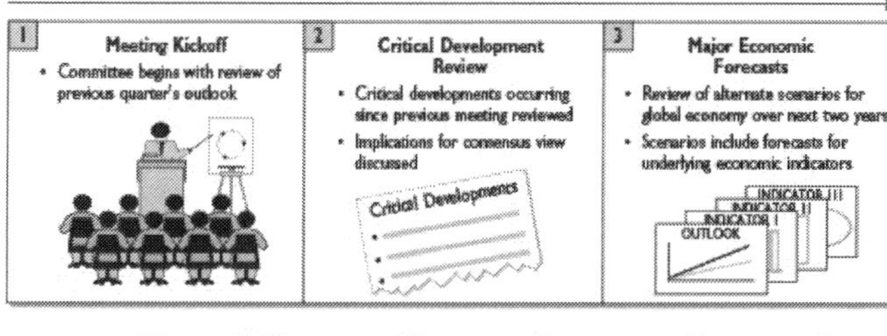

Examining Trends

4 Country/Region Reviews
- Review of country- and region-specific positions, forecasts
- Graphical analyses track key indicators

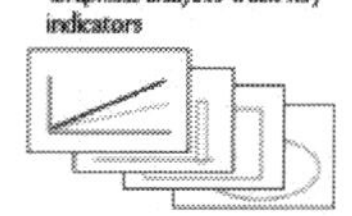

5 "12 Industry" Outlook
- Examination of 12 global industries over next 12–18 months
- Drawn primarily from senior lending officers

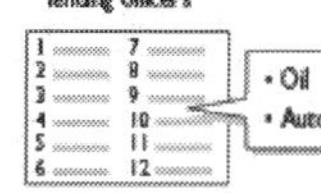

6 Reviewing Uncertainties
- Team considers implications of forecasts, market reviews
- Goal is to understand key influences on external environment

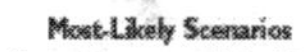

Developing Scenarios

7 Most-Likely Scenarios
- Expected outcomes defined for country, regional economics
- For more important countries, expected geopolitical situation is also defined

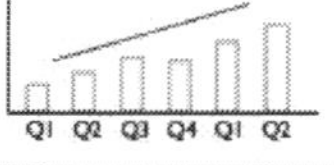

Components #2 and #3: Quarterly Economic Review and Tripwires Analysis

This "gameboard" documents components #2 and #3 of the review process. Armed with data, committee convenes each quarter to review global external environment, reviewing economic forecasts, alternate scenario, and prior committee outlook; committee spends considerable time debating implications for company's most important geographic markets and customer segments. Based on review, committee members define possible economic and geopolitical scenarios for next two years, each with a set of "tripwires" that could signal its occurrence; set of scenarios includes both probable critical events and less likely but highly unfavorable "what if" scenarios. "Tripwires" are explained in greater depth on page 131.

8 Worst-Case Scenarios
- "What ifs" depict possible, highly unfavorable economic or geopolitical developments
- Timeframe is next two years

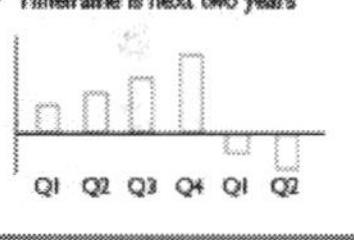

Warning Signs

9 Critical Events
- For each most-likely scenario, committee determines critical events necessary for it to occur
- Timeframe: next 3–18 months

Brazil: Critical Events
- Recapitalization Complete
- New Treasury Chief
- Phone Co. Meets Earnings

10 "Key Watch Dates"
- Committee defines dates that critical events are expected to occur by or on
- If critical events do not occur, committee may revisit outlook

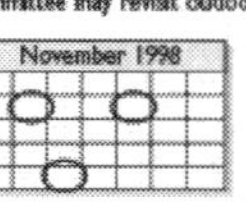

Establishing

11 Signposts
- Committee develops key indicators or signposts for each "what if" scenario

"Thailand Meltdown" Signposts

12 "Tripwires"
- Threshold levels for each signpost set in advance
- Tripwire system "sounds alarm" if crossed

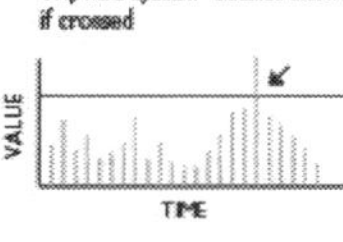

Consensus Outlook

Result of all analysis is consolidated into consensus view

Source: Company reports; CEB research.

CHAPTER 23: "GANTT CHART" LAYOUT

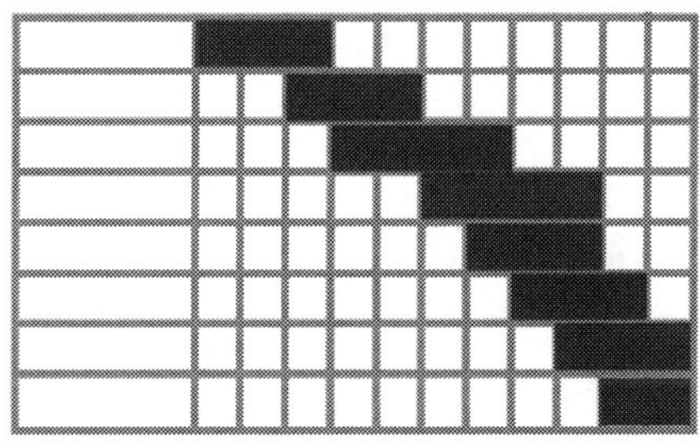

A Gantt Chart is used to show a project timeline, with various tasks and sub-tasks, as well as major project milestones and interim deadlines. This layout organizes large amounts of information related to managing a project, conveying what is happening, when it needs to happen, and how the tasks are related. It is distinct from the RASCI layout, which focuses primarily on who is responsible for each task.

How to draw the "Gantt Chart" Layout

Charteo

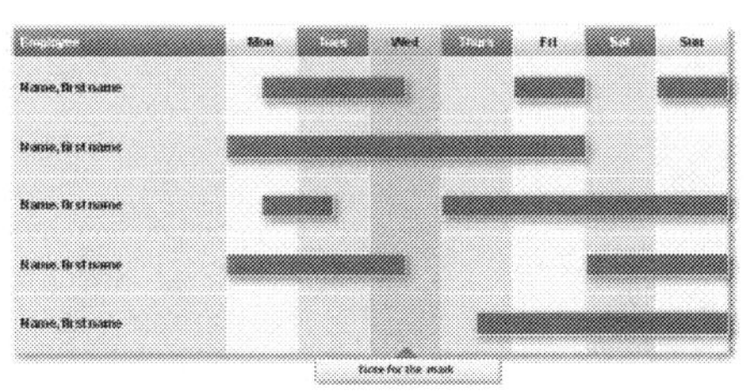

www.Charteo.com
Time/Planning, Gantt Charts/Project Plans, Gantt Chart 1

PowerFrameworks

2 weeks, 7-day week

www.PowerFrameworks.com
Keyword Search "TT012," "TT012-tt012_week"

Slide: "Lock-Step Order"

This Gantt Chart layout shows the activities of three different groups, listed down the left side of the slide: Executive Committee, Call Center Value Chain Team, and Change Management Team, as they play out across a timeline displayed along the top of the slide. Within the resulting grid, the two different graphical shapes signify two different types of activities: the small triangles indicate specific meetings whereas the continuous arrows along the bottom represent the ongoing implementation activities of the Change Management Team.

A glance at the upper portion of the chart reveals that the Executive Management Committee meets only twice during the month, but the Value Chain Management Team meets more frequently, at least once a week. The long chevrons at the bottom are designed to show the start and end dates of a project, and indicate whether it is still ongoing. The callout boxes on the right side highlight the key takeaways the presenter wants to communicate to the audience—notice how they are sequenced numerically and also linked by the ellipses.

Lock-Step Order

Value Chain Management Schedule

Call Center Example

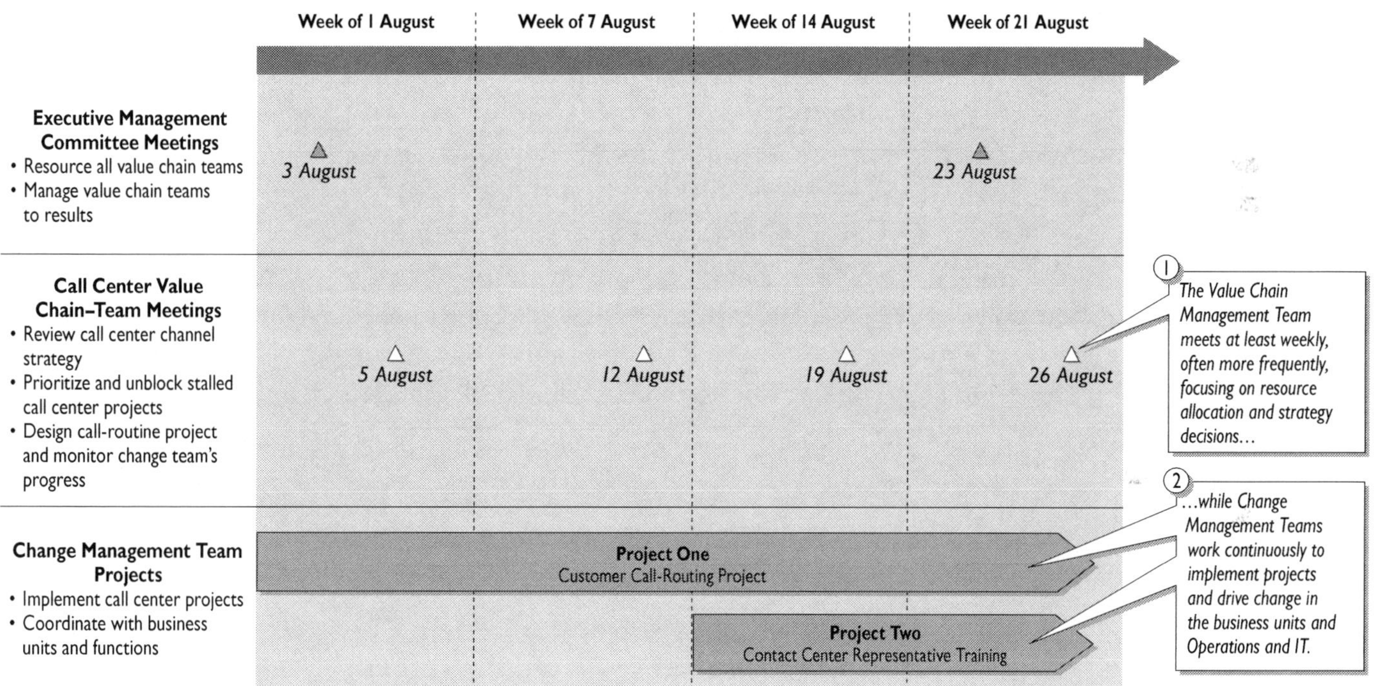

* Pseudonym.

Source: Koolhaas*; CEB research.

Slide: "IT Skills Forecast"

This more complex version of the Gantt Chart layout shows the life cycle of eight different enterprise applications over the course of 11 years. The columns on the left name the application, list the technical skills it requires, and indicate the relevant resources. Along the upper right side of the slide, the 11 years are listed, and under this timeline the life cycle of each application is portrayed. The legend in the lower right corner of the layout provides the various shapes in each timeline: a large triangle means a Major Upgrade, an octagonal stop sign means a System Retirement, etc. Within each life cycle, the audience can see very clearly which years a system will receive an upgrade or be replaced. Whenever a system is replaced, a second horizontal line appears just below the retiring system's lifecycle line, showing when the new system is implemented.

IT Skills Forecast

Application	Technical Skills	Current Resources	Application Life Cycle										
			2000	2001	2002	2003	2004	2005	2006	2007	2008	2009	2010
Vehicle Pricing System	ERP	1 App Manager (M. Elliott) 2 Senior Programmers (H. Smith, K. Jones)											
Sales Planning System	Programming Language #1	1 Senior Programmer (J. Fiske) 1 Junior Programmer (M. Bhinge)											
Marketing Reporting	ERP	2 Senior Programmers (K. Mishra, C. Axarlis)											
Shipping Schedule System	Programming Language #2	1 Junior Programmer (D. Stanciu)											
Parts Purchase System	Programming Language #1	1 Senior Programmer (L. Foster)											
Transport Dispatch System	Programming Language #2	1 App Manager (M. Grimes) 1 Junior Programmer (M. Davenport)											
Warranty System	Programming Language #1	1 Junior Programmer (M. McWha)											
Customer Relations System	Programming Language #1	1 Senior Programmer (V. Balasubra)											

Legend	
Major Upgrade	▼
Minor Upgrade	▽
System Retirement	⬣
Replacement System	■

Note: The trends listed on this page are hypothetical and do not necessarily reflect elements of Toyota Motor Sales' corporate or IT strategy.

Source: Toyota Motor Sales, U.S.A.; CEB research.

CHAPTER 24: "GROWTH OPPORTUNITY" LAYOUT

The increasing dimensions of the circles in the Growth Opportunity layout convey the idea of expansion, with a present state growing into and being encompassed by a much larger future state. The layout can be drawn with full circles, in which case the image of growth is best communicated by aligning their bases. It can also be drawn with quarter or half circles, the centers of which are aligned. The Growth Opportunity layout is suited to showing qualitative growth (e.g., an increase in the types of customers served—from just adult females to all adults, and from just all adults to both adults and teenagers). Quantitative growth is better indicated by a column chart.

How to draw the "Growth Opportunity" Layout

PowerFrameworks

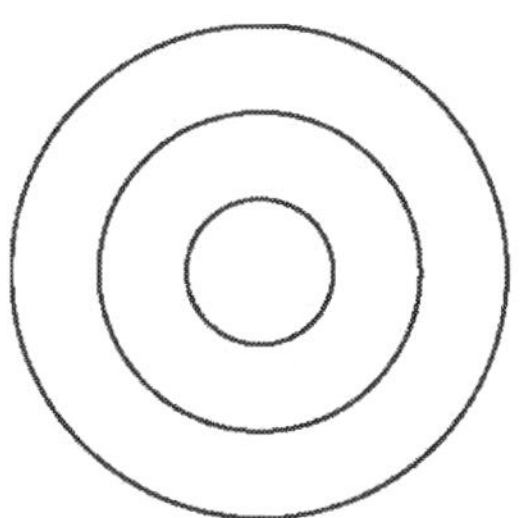

www.PowerFrameworks.com
Keyword Search "SG002", SG002-0200

SmartArt

PowerPoint SmartArt
Relationship, Stacked Venn

Slide: "Built for Another Purpose"

The upper part of this slide shows a Growth Opportunity layout executed in quarter-circles. Note that each arc represents a discrete, qualitatively unique aspect. The smallest quarter circle represents the scope and posture of the typical current market research department: the department focuses on product research (scope) and reacts to incoming research requests (posture). The medium arc represents an expansion in terms of both scope and posture: the department now works on entire product portfolios, and partners with clients to plan research, as opposed to merely reacting to requests. The outside arc takes the expansion further, until the market research department initiates research with a company- or enterprise-wide scope.

In this layout, quartering the circle provides two axes, allowing representation of simultaneous growth in two different dimensions. When growth in two dimensions occurs at differing rates, the Matrix layout is more appropriate. Growth on a single dimension is better represented by the full-circle form of the Growth Opportunity layout.

The layout at the bottom of the slide contrasts the characteristics of the current market research department with the characteristics required to achieve the proactive, enterprise-wide posture indicated in the upper layout.

Built for Another Purpose

Research (understandably) focuses on reactive project work...

Expanding Research's Role to Support Growth

Illustrative Representation of Research's Activities

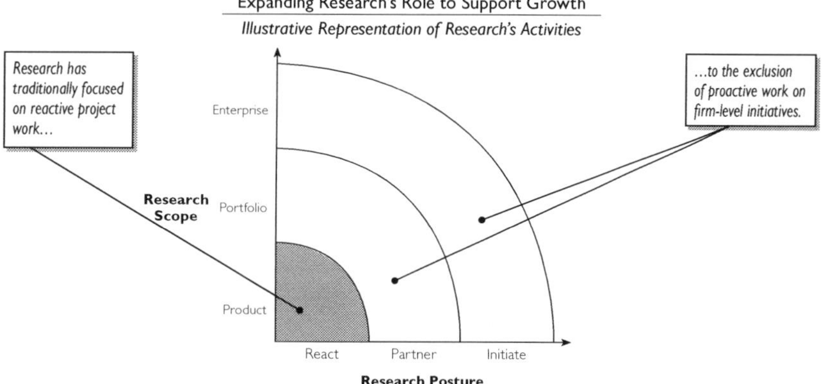

...but is not balancing its tactical work with a larger growth mission

Spectrum of Market Research Function Attributes

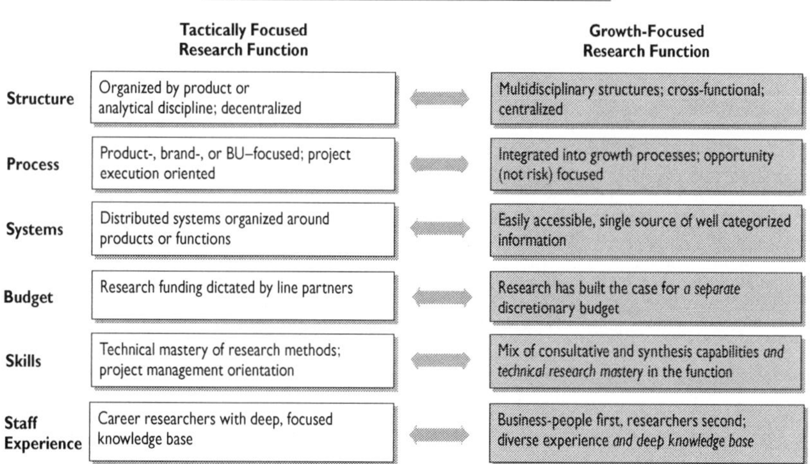

	Tactically Focused Research Function		Growth-Focused Research Function
Structure	Organized by product or analytical discipline; decentralized	⟷	Multidisciplinary structures; cross-functional; centralized
Process	Product-, brand-, or BU–focused; project execution oriented	⟷	Integrated into growth processes; opportunity (not risk) focused
Systems	Distributed systems organized around products or functions	⟷	Easily accessible, single source of well categorized information
Budget	Research funding dictated by line partners	⟷	Research has built the case for *a separate* discretionary budget
Skills	Technical mastery of research methods; project management orientation	⟷	Mix of consultative and synthesis capabilities *and technical research mastery* in the function
Staff Experience	Career researchers with deep, focused knowledge base	⟷	Business-people first, researchers second; diverse experience *and deep knowledge base*

Source: CEB research.

CHAPTER 25: "IMPROVEMENT STEPS" LAYOUT

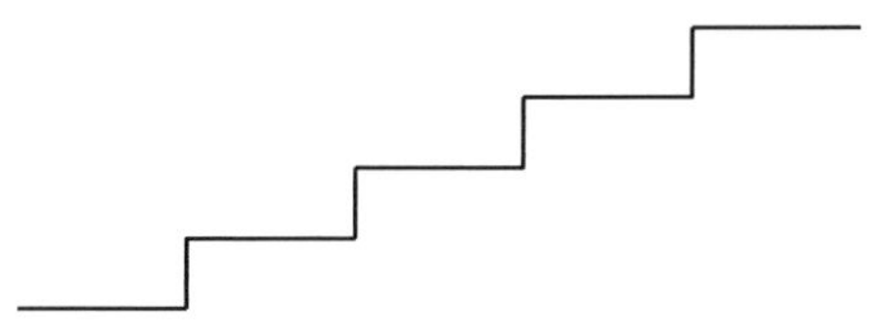

The idea of a series of steps leading to improvement can be communicated by two fundamental symbols: staircases and arrows. The generic form presented here is of a staircase; the image makes the idea of discrete improvement steps immediately evident. A similar effect can be achieved using arrows (either a single arrow, or multiple arrows in sequence) pointing diagonally upwards. The "how to" examples below show a mixture of staircases and arrows; most instances of the Improvement Steps layout use both.

How to draw the "Improvement Steps" Layout

Charteo

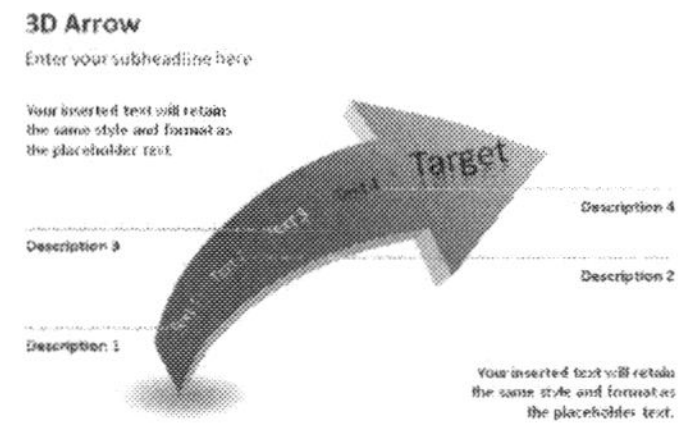

www.Charteo.com
Concept Charts, Arrows, 3D Arrows 28

Diagrammer

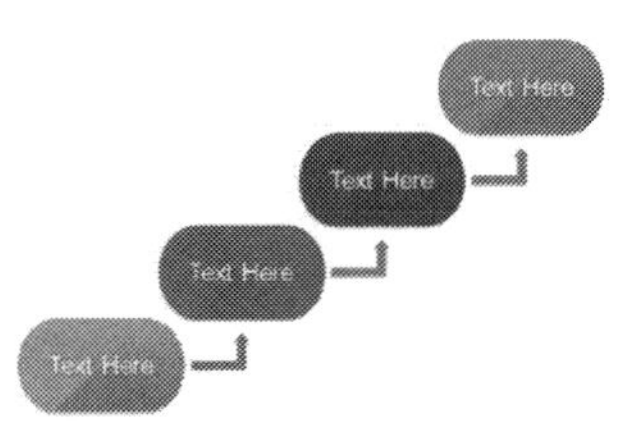

www.Diagrammer.com
Flow, Linear, 4 Nodes, 2D Mixed, Flow Linear 1452

PowerFrameworks

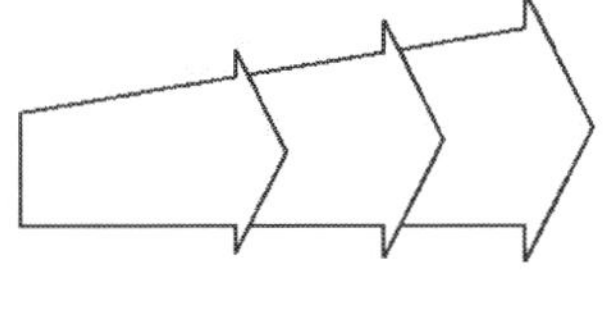

www.PowerFrameworks.com
Keyword Search "AV010", "AV010-0300"

SmartArt

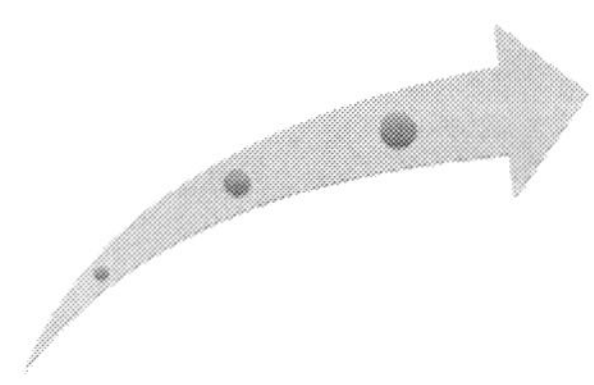

PowerPoint SmartArt
Process/Upward Arrow

Slide: "Bank of America leveraged new research techniques ..."

The idea of a staircase to improvement is illustrated with great clarity in this slide, which explains the steps taken in developing of Bank of America's successful "Keep the Change" product innovation. The steps in the process are unmistakably depicted as actual steps of a staircase; what differentiates the Improvement Steps layout from the Linear Process layout is the clear signal of improvement provided by the upward flow of the stairs.

The staircase graphic leaves a large amount of space below each step, allowing the presenter to include sufficient detail on each, as well as detail about the end result on the right of the staircase.

This arrangement allows the slide to exemplify simplicity of design and complexity of detail. The layout design is very simple, immediately evident: it's a staircase. At the same time, it provides details that engage the audience: the kind of research done, the insights gathered, the people involved, the number of concepts generated, and the content of the winning idea.

Bank of America leveraged new research techniques to develop "Keep the Change" product

Research
- Observed clients and interviewed them in the street
- Looked at how people balance their checkbooks at home
- Watched mothers shop, eat out, and make bank deposits

Insights
- People rounded checkbooks to the nearest dollar (quicker and more convenient)
- Many "boomer" women could not save (not enough money and cannot control impulse buying)

Ideation
- Insights fed into 20 brainstorming sessions with
  - Product managers
  - Finance experts
  - Software engineers
  - Operations experts

Concept development
- 80 concepts boiled down to 12; one favorite prototyped
- Woman buys a coffee in a store for $1.50; rounds up to $2.00; change put into a savings account

- **'Keep the Change' launched 2005**
  - **700,000 new checking accounts**
  - **1mn new saving accounts**
- **99% of people who signed up have stayed with it**

A whole new kind
of change jar.
Keep the Change™
We'll match 100% of your Keep the Change™ savings
for the first 3 months.

Source: *Business Week*

Slide: "5 steps to improving marketing ROI"

The use of the alternative symbol for the Improvement Steps layout, the arrow, is illustrated here. In this case a single arrow pointing diagonally upwards shows the five-step trajectory towards improving return on investment in marketing.

Arrows are preferable to staircases when, as in this example, there is the possibility of overlap between steps. For instance, step 3, "Optimize marketing execution," need not be entirely complete before the beginning of step 4, "Ensure lean purchasing and non-working spend." By contrast, in the example on the preceding page, a company will not move from "Ideation" to "Concept development" until the former step is complete.

5 steps to improving marketing ROI

5 Sustain ROI

- Organizational capabilities, processes, and governance to continuously improve marketing ROI

4 Ensure lean purchasing and non-working spend

- Reduced non-working spend
- Vendor management and consolidated buying
- Reduced wasteful and duplicative spend

3 Optimize marketing execution

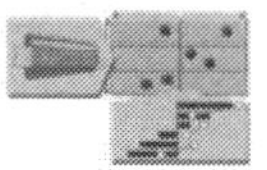

- Tailored messaging for target segments
- Increased promotion effectiveness through test and learn
- Lead generation and management

2 Optimize vehicle mix

- Optimal vehicle mix
- Balance of 'push' vs. 'pull' spending

1 Align spend with market oppt. and business priorities

- Business objectives
- Comprehensive view of spend
- Priority segments
- Focus and allocate spend on right products and markets

CHAPTER 26: "INPUTS TO OUTPUT" LAYOUT

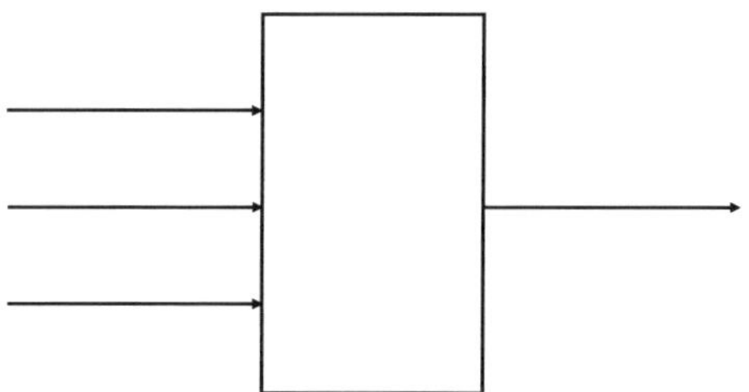

The Inputs to Output layout shows a set of inputs in left to right trajectory flowing into some process or analysis and flowing out as some useful result. Typically the leftmost third of the slide lists the inputs, the center third describes what happens to them, and the rightmost third presents the results. Arrows are used to reinforce the left to right flow. The Inputs to Output layout is appropriate when the process that produces results from the inputs can be described either in a single step or in multiple parallel steps. When multiple, sequential steps must be described, the From-To Process layout is more appropriate.

How to draw the "Inputs to Output" Layout

Charteo

Cause and Effect Chain – Problem Analysis:

Identify problems by constructing a problem chain that shows causes and effects

www.Charteo.com
Processes and Flows, Cause and Effect Diagrams, Cause and Effect Diagrams 23

Slide: "Proactive Succession Planning Ensures ..."

Here the elements of succession planning are communicated using an Inputs to Output layout. Three discrete types of inputs (talent review results, requirement profiles, and development/career planning) are presented on the left in three separate chevrons. To their right and in the middle, one large chevron lists the succession planning activities, which involve analysis of those inputs. Note that these activities occur contemporaneously; if they were sequential, a From-To Process layout would be a more appropriate layout choice.

The outputs are presented in two levels. First, the actual planning outcomes are identified in the two rectangles to the right of the succession planning chevron. Note that the upper rectangle, since it illustrates multiple similar outputs, is actually depicted by multiple superimposed rectangles. To the right of these primary planning outcomes, the second, higher level outcome—the benefit (namely, that newly opened "positions are filled rapidly and with qualified candidates")—is highlighted in a circle.

The left to right trajectory is emphasized by the three chevrons on the left of the slide, the large chevron in the middle, and the thin arrowhead indicating the higher level outcome on the right.

PROACTIVE SUCCESSION PLANNING ENSURES THAT POSITIONS ARE FILLED RAPIDLY AND OPTIMALLY

Sample design of succession planning

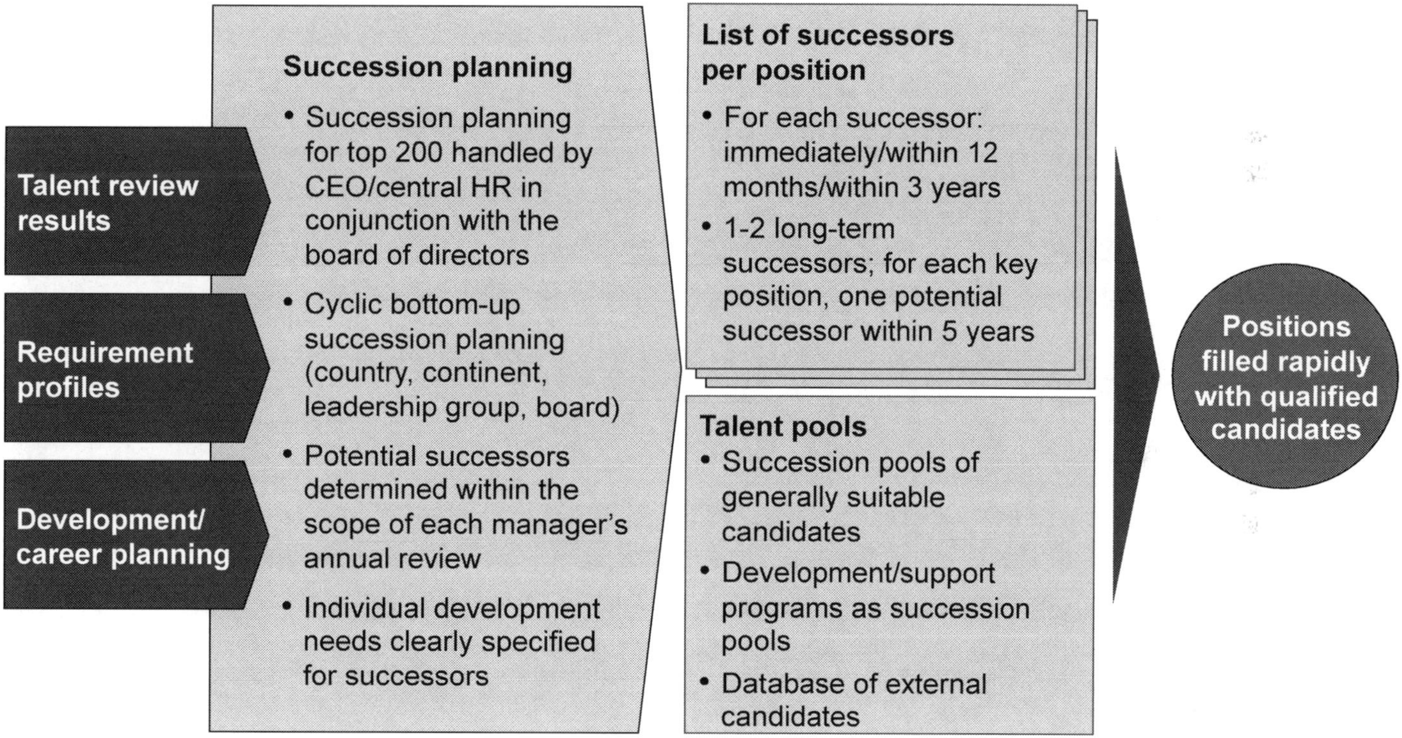

Talent review results

Requirement profiles

Development/ career planning

Succession planning

- Succession planning for top 200 handled by CEO/central HR in conjunction with the board of directors
- Cyclic bottom-up succession planning (country, continent, leadership group, board)
- Potential successors determined within the scope of each manager's annual review
- Individual development needs clearly specified for successors

List of successors per position

- For each successor: immediately/within 12 months/within 3 years
- 1-2 long-term successors; for each key position, one potential successor within 5 years

Talent pools

- Succession pools of generally suitable candidates
- Development/support programs as succession pools
- Database of external candidates

Positions filled rapidly with qualified candidates

Sources: interviews

CHAPTER 27: "LINEAR PROCESS" LAYOUT

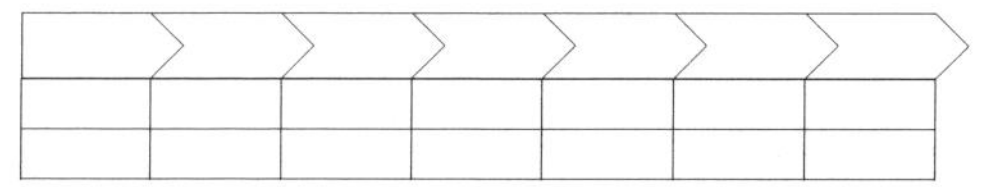

The variety of this book's examples of the Linear Process layout suggests, correctly, that it is the most popular slide layout in use. The reason behind this is simple. Presentations are made to foster collaboration with others and collaboration frequently occurs within a planned process. It is the steps, sequence, and details of such processes that this layout communicates.

The Linear Process layout can convey up to about eight stages comfortably. (For more than eight stages, consider the Gameboard layout.) The benefit of being able to show the entire process on one page cannot be overstated. Discussion is far more effective when an audience can see the whole process in a glance, and research suggests that ideas are communicated more effectively when multiple steps are shown together.

How to draw the "Linear Process" Layout

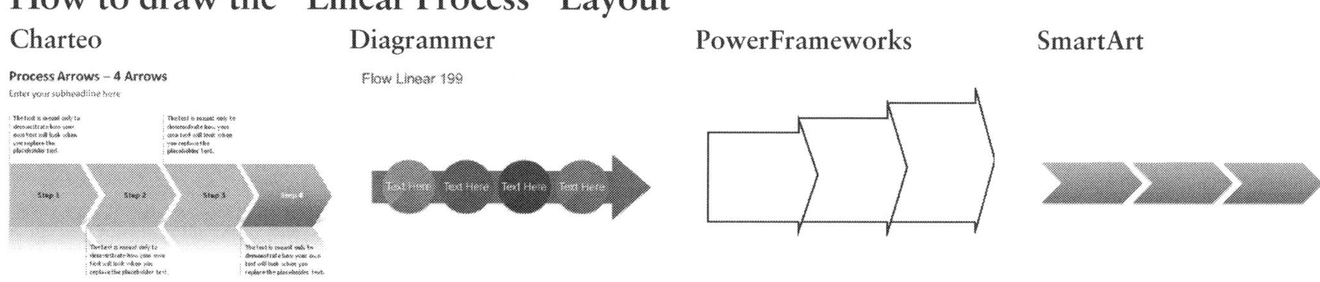

www.Charteo.com
Processes and Flows, Process-Linear, Process Arrows 3

www.Diagrammer.com
Flow, Linear, 4 Nodes, 2D Mixed, Flow Linear 199

www.PowerFrameworks.com
Keyword Search "AV012", AV012-0300

PowerPoint SmartArt
Process/Basic Chevron Process

Slide: "Process Improvement"

Our first example of the Linear Process layout describes, appropriately, a process for improving processes. The activity that occurs before the process begins—in this case the selection of which process to improve—is identified within the circle on the upper left of the slide. The five generic stages of process improvement (define, measure, analyze, improve, and control) are contained within five chevrons that run sequentially across the top of the page. Beneath each chevron lies a brief synopsis of what occurs during that stage, with the actual details underneath.

Process Improvement

How to change and improve process performance

Select process to improve → Define → Measure → Analyse → Improve → Control

Define

Scoping and Target Setting

- Confirm project charter
- Understand critical success factors
- Map the existing process
- Understand Issues & create Hypothesis Trees
- Establish baseline on performance

Measure

Understand current Process performance

- Measure current performance against success factors
- Determine process stability and capacity
- Identify issues and risk
- Solution generation, evaluation & prioritisation

Analyse

Idea generation and solution establishment

- Undertake root cause and confirm with data
- Verify impact through quantification
- Design Future State
- Create Solution implementation Plan

Improve

Pilot implementation & solution iteration

- Pilot and implement solution
- Assess performance and adjust
- Ensure scalability of solution
- Create detailed rollout plan

Control

Scale rollout and continuous improvement

- Scale up and roll out plan
- Adjust and improve based on outcomes of rollout

Slide: "Targeted improvement: Test-and-learn example"

This essentially straightforward three-step process describing a twelve-week performance improvement program is refined by an additional feature. In contrast to the previous example, which presented each stage's descriptive content in a single bullet list, this example divides each stage's content by type (time, activities, and deliverables) and separates each type into a different row. The content is thus divided not only by its stage within the process, but also by its informational character. Since the more important divisions in the Linear Process layout are vertical (i.e., between stages) the rows are divided unobtrusively by thin dotted lines, so as not to overemphasize the horizontal divisions.

Targeted improvement: Test-and-learn example

	Design test-and-learn pilot program	Prepare for test-and-learn pilot launches	Operate pilots & define measurement program
Timeline	Weeks 1-3	Week 4-6	Weeks 7-12
Key activities	▪ Identify potential test program goals through interviews & best practice case studies ▪ Prioritize & select country(ies) for pilots ▪ Develop high-level pilot design	▪ Prepare detailed design for pilots ▪ Conduct workshop(s) with key stakeholders ▪ Gain necessary sign-offs to launch pilots	▪ Launch & operate pilots (e.g., including mid-course correction) ▪ Evaluate & synthesize findings ▪ Define recommendations for measurement program
Key deliverables	▪ Recommendation on test program objectives ▪ Pilot program design – Target users – Country selection – Key test variables – Measures of success	▪ Detailed pilot design (hypotheses, test plan, communications plan, contingency plans) ▪ Train key participants in pilot to ensure launch readiness	▪ Pilot execution with key stakeholders ▪ Synthesis of pilot findings ▪ Recommendations on: – Measurement program design – Rollout/scaling plan

Slide: "Technology Provides Opportunities to Understand Customer Needs and Price Sensitivity"

Including explanatory graphics within or below the chevrons in a Linear Process layout can help clarify a complex procedure. This example describes a three-stage process for growing a bank's mortgage business using database analysis. For the first step, "client segmentation," the image of a typical CRM (Customer Relationship Management) analysis is provided. The image shows a matrix with customer segments down the left side, combinations of parameters across the top, and, in the individual cells of the matrix, the expected lifetime value of the customer for each set of parameters in each segment. The actual words and numbers within the matrix are almost illegible, because it is the idea of analysis, not the details of this particular analysis, that is presented in this stage. The graphics in the second and third stages illustrate the test parameters and measures used, and the evaluation of single and combined factors, respectively. Simplicity of design is retained despite the layers of content: the three-part nature of the process is clearly evident, and the complexity of detail is conveyed through the bulleted lists below each chevron.

Technology Provides Opportunities to Understand Customer Needs and Price Sensitivity

MORTGAGE EXAMPLE

Phase 1: Client segmentation

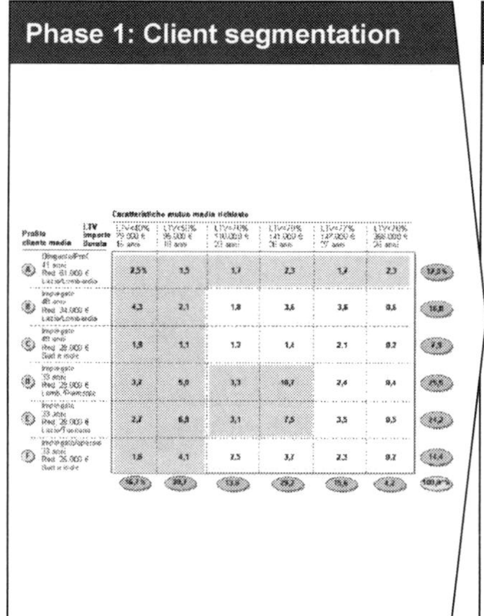

Phase 2: Design and test

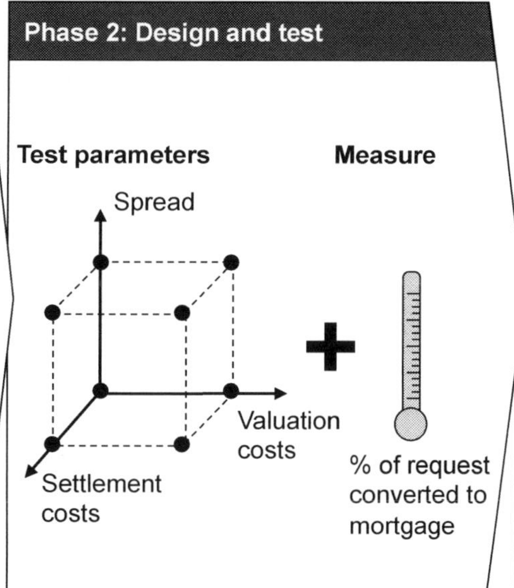

Phase 3: Analysis of results

Evaluation weight of single factors
Conversion rate of applications

⊖ **Spread** ⊕

⊖ **Valuation costs** ⊕

Evaluation weight of combined factors
Conversion rate of applications

Val. costs

⊖ **Spread** ⊕

- Client segmentation by client profile and mortgage features
- Identification of clusters of client/product to be addressed by new pricing strategy

- Definition of modifiable parameters in the offer (spread, valuation costs, settlement costs)
- Design of experimental tests using DOE* methodologies from Six Sigma to minimize tests and optimize analyses

- Definition of weight of single factors and identification of key levers
- Analysis of mutual interaction among factors
- Definition of optimal values

* DOE (Design of Experiment): methodology stemming from manufacturing industry and applied in R&D for defining optimal features for a product

Slide: "Two Sides of the Same Coin"

This slide describes a sales organization's evolution from product selling to solution selling. This process is markedly different from the ones considered earlier, given the evolutionary and therefore overlapping nature of the stages. This is conveyed graphically by partially overlaying each circle (representing a stage in the process) with the next. The evolutionary aspect is also indicated by the fact that, while there are six stages identified in the depiction of the process above, the details below describe only four distinct organizational states. The absence of a one-to-one correspondence between the different stages in the upper process and the states described in the table below suggests the fluid nature of the organizational evolution.

The richness of detail here is worthy of note. This single slide describes the development of a sales organization through four distinct states in multiple terms: nature of the customer-supplier relationship, level of access to customer, type of information exchange, discussion focus, structure of relationship, time horizon, and measure of success. The slide provides a comprehensive and meticulous account of the evolution towards solutions selling.

Two Sides of the Same Coin

Relationship Considerations for the Sales Organization Across the Product–Solutions Spectrum

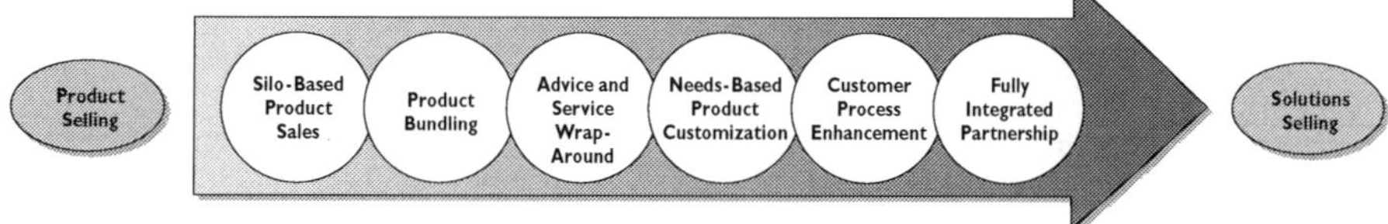

Nature of Relationship	Supplier reacts to customer purchase orders	Based on segment-level needs, supplier develops a package of products and services	Supplier customizes products and services according to customer's specific need; may collaborate with customer in design process	Supplier is customer's trusted advisor; customer asks supplier's advice on addressing general business needs; supplier has right of first refusal
Level of Access to Customer	Purchasing manager; single customer point of contact	Head of purchasing and business unit management; contacts at more than one level of customer organization	Business unit management and functional leadership; access to key decision makers at select customer locations	Executive committee and board; unlimited access to web of decision influencers and decision makers at multiple customer locations
Information Exchange	Limited to customer's immediate product/service needs	Customer communicates short-term product/service needs to supplier on a "need-to-know" basis	Customer regularly volunteers information concerning long-term product/service needs and short-term business strategy	Customer and supplier financials, long-term business strategy, and competitive positioning are communicated openly on an ongoing basis
Focus of Discussions	Price of products/services	Price of products/services and availability of special features	Customer process enhancement; customer risk sharing	Mutual customer and supplier value growth; gainsharing
Supplier Relationship Structure	Salesperson assigned to customer territory; no executive involvement	Account manager assigned to one or more accounts; minimal executive involvement	Sales team (perhaps cross-functional) appointed; executives are regularly involved with accounts	Dedicated account teams with relationship steward assigned; executives are assigned to and responsible for specific account results
Relationship Time Horizon	This month (current sales opportunity)	This year (anticipated upcoming sales opportunities)	Multiple years	Long-term; weathers economic downturns
Measure of Success	Sales volume (revenue)	Customer satisfaction with supplier products and services; volume (revenue) and profitability; cross-sales	Customer loyalty; customer's financial/business performance (revenue, profitability)	Mutual value creation for both customer and supplier beyond commercially available choices

Source: CEB research.

Slide: "Allocated Staged Investment to Build Familiarity ..."

Another variation on the Linear Process framework is introduced with this example, in which the rising height of each stage communicates a stage-by-stage increase—in this case, an increase in amount invested. The slide's main point is that each stage of the process requires an increase in the investment of the previous stage, with the "go" / "no go" decision taken in Stage 4.

Each stage has a title describing that stage's activity (Search, Design, Prototype, Commit/Abandon) and a subtitle that provides a straightforward characterization of the size of the investment ("Seed capital," Small bet, Medium bet, and Large bet). The details of each stage are embedded within each column, and the percentage of the total investment is given above each stage: 10% for the first stage, 20% for the second, and so on. Thus the increase in investment is communicated in three ways: visually, by the rising height of each stage; numerically, by the percentage of investment indicated; and verbally, by the subtitle of each stage ("Small," "Medium," etc.).

Note that this layout is not a column chart—although the bars increase in size, they are not drawn to scale (Stage 2 at 20% is not twice the height of Stage 1 at 10%, for example). Instead, the increasing height of the bars shows conceptually that the investment increases as the process continues.

Allocated Staged Investment to Build Familiarity and Create Option Value With Minimal Risk

Staged investment process

Stage 1: Search — 10% of total estimated investment

'Seed capital'

- Articulate assumptions and identify key uncertainties
- Design and test offering in the market
- Evaluate go/no-go for next phase

Stage 2: Design — 20% of total estimated investment

Small bet

- Incorporate initial learnings
- Revise assumptions and formulate new approach
- Redesign and retest offering in the market
- Evaluate go/no-go for next phase

Stage 3: Prototype — 30% of total estimated investment

Medium bet

- Incorporate new learnings
- Solidify assumptions and revise approach
- Refine and retest offering in the market
- Evaluate go/no-go for next phase

Stage 4: Commit/ abandon — 40% of total estimated investment

Large bet

- Formulate explicit strategy and either
  - Commit resources and take residual risks
    OR
  - Put on hold/retain familiarity
    OR
  - Let option expire

Decreasing uncertainty, increasing investment

Slide: "Result of Energy Inspection of city heat supply systems"

This layout combines a fairly simple process along the bottom with a visually rich and detailed flow diagram along the top. The five stages along the bottom of the slide describe the various steps in an energy audit, and the flow diagram along the top shows the conclusion yielded by the audit: 51% of the energy generated is lost and not usable.

The power of the upper diagram lies in the way it shows the three different sources of loss: their relative size is portrayed graphically by the size of the streams diverging from the lighter-colored usable energy on top, and this graphic portrayal of their size is reinforced at each branch where the numerical value of the loss is given. In the top center of the layout, the usable energy likewise splits into three different areas: Commercial, Population, and Budget; and here too the relative size of the branches indicates the magnitude of the portion for each area. By giving the Loss section of the flow a darker shade, and also by reuniting the three streams of loss, this layout effectively draws the audience's attention to the conclusion in the bottom right of the flow diagram—that 51% of the energy goes to waste.

The text in the upper right of the slide describes the purpose of the Energy Audit, and also reveals the 25% return on investment for pursuing an audit, and the sizable losses that may result if nothing is done.

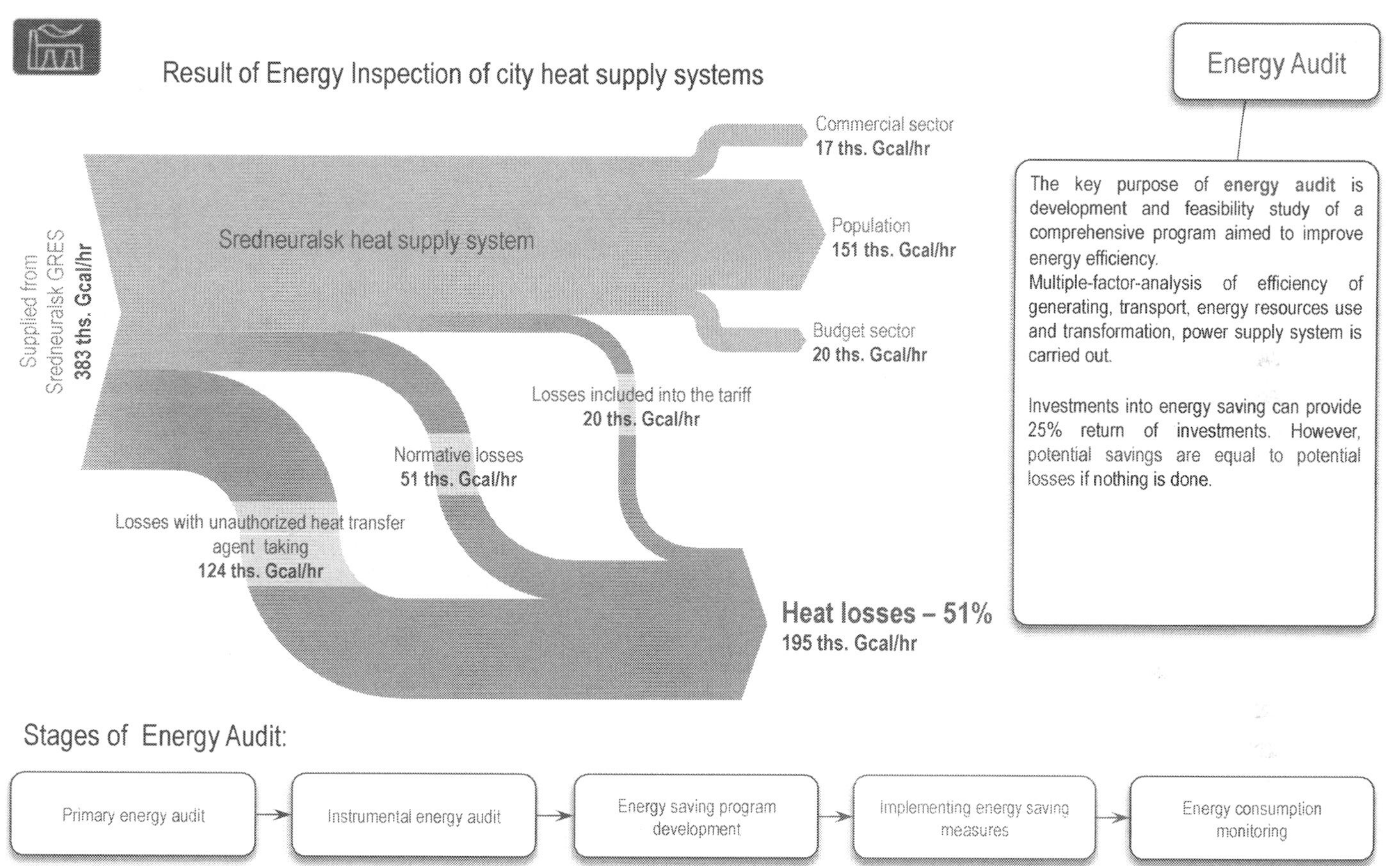

Energy saving starts with energy audit

1

Slide: "Innovation Process Fraught with Failure Points"

This final example of a Linear Process demonstrates just how much detail can fit on a slide without its becoming an eyesore. The slide passes the squint test—it is clearly a six-stage process—and the extensive detail fits carefully within that process, which is why it does not overwhelm.

The slide shows the six stages in the product development process, the types of growth stalls that can be triggered in each stage, and case examples—each with an iconic illustration—of such stalls.

To be fair, this layout was designed to be printed on two vertical pages, rather than as the single horizontal slide we have reproduced here (a fact which accounts for the large gutter between the third and fourth stages). The type size of the font of the single-page version is too small to be read with anything less than 20/20 vision. It is not a good idea to use any font size smaller than what is conventionally used in a newspaper, i.e. nine point; and while raising this slide's type size to nine point would make the slide somewhat more dense, it should still work. As always, combining complexity of detail with simplicity of design conveys all the information a presenter needs without overwhelming the slide—or the audience.

Innovation Process Fraught with Failure Points

Companies make mistakes in defining basic dynamics of R&D... ***...and in moving products (or businesses) through the development process***

The Innovation Management Process

	Organizing Research and Development	Determining Appropriate R&D Funding Levels	Establishing and Managing Development Cycle Times	Commercializing New Technologies	Organizing New Business Ventures	Setting Technology Standards
Sample Problems	• Over-decentralization of R&D creates narrow focus on close-in, low-risk product categories • Geographic isolation of R&D from sales force, corporate headquarters results in strategic isolation as well	• Cutting R&D dollars to boost earnings or to fund expensive marketing campaign risks long-term viability of product portfolio • Concluding (falsely) that potential for R&D-based innovation no longer exists dashes best hope for renewable competitive advantage	• "Over-engineering" helps create image of "perfected" products, but cedes first-mover advantage to rivals • Elaborate, systematized approval process slows entire product cycle despite intent to improve hit rate	• Company rejects next-generation technology, viewing it as "inferior" relative to dominant technology • Company invents competence-based new product, but concludes that product is too far removed from current offerings to introduce	• Company hobbles promising new substitute product by siting it under umbrella of existing technology • Competing teams chartered to develop same new product slow time to market despite intent to reduce risk in product development	• Company lacking market power to establish new product as standard gets trapped in technology "cul-de-sac" • Business units free to reject standards proposed by sister division often deliver coup de grace to innovation

Case Examples

Xerox

Well-documented failure of Xerox to commercialize invention of distributed personal computing in mid-1970s partly attributable to isolation of Palo Alto Research Center (PARC) from organization at large

RCA

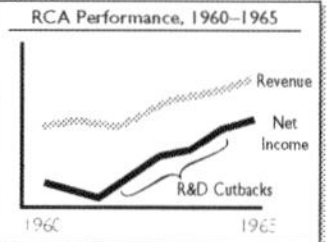

Facing slower top-line growth and shrinking profits as color TV reached saturation, RCA pulls the plug on many R&D investments to show improved bottom-line results

Apple Computer

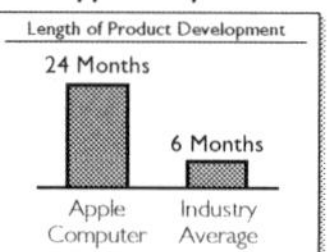

Apple Computer's repeated attempts to shorten new product development cycle thwarted in part due to culture that over-engineered its products

Eastman Kodak

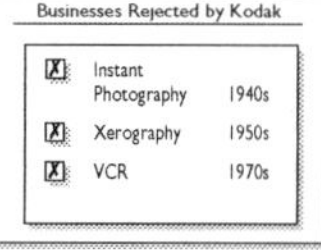

Kodak turns down offer to finance Polaroid, rejects option to acquire original xerography patents; internally developed VCR "mothballed" when management concludes consumers would not pay $500 for it

Digital

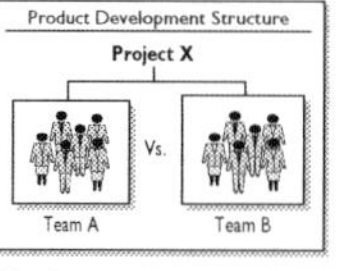

Digital pits competing teams against each other to develop new products; system is designed to reduce risks (and avoid costly mistakes) but slows overall process

BFGoodrich

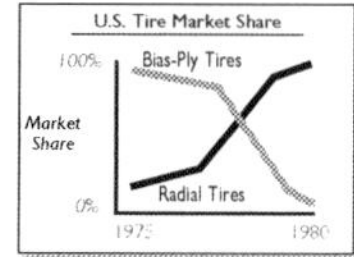

BFGoodrich attempts to launch the "radial age" in 1960s, but market leaders Goodyear and Firestone refuse to make costly conversion; auto manufacturers, unwilling to source radials only from Goodrich, refuse to convert

Source: Foster, Richard F., *Innovation: The Attacker's Advantage*. New York: Summit Books, 1986; CEB research and analysis.

CHAPTER 28: "MAP" LAYOUT

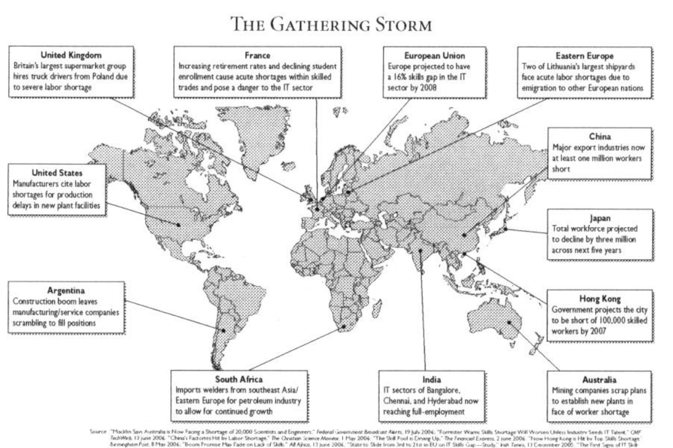

Source: "Macklin Says Australia is Now Facing a Shortage of 20,000 Scientists and Engineers," *Federal Government Broadcast Alerts*, 19 July 2006; "Forrester Warns Skills Shortage Will Worsen Unless Industry Seeds IT Talent," *CMP TechWeb*, 13 June 2006; "China's Factories Hit by Labor Shortage," *The Christian Science Monitor*, 1 May 2006; "The Skill Pool is Drying Up," *The Financial Express*, 2 June 2006; "Now Hong Kong is Hit by Top Skills Shortage," *Birmingham Post*, 8 May 2006; "Boom Promise May Fade on Lack of Skills," *All Africa*, 13 June 2006; "State to Slide from 3rd to 21st in EU on IT Skills Gap—Study," *Irish Times*, 13 December 2005; "The First Signs of IT Skills Shortages Emerge in France," *Forrester.com*, 28 February 2006; *Manpower Global Survey*, January 2006; "Labor Shortage Grows Acute in Lithuania—Daily," *Baltic Business Daily*, 17 October 2005; CEB research.

The Map layout is used to communicate data where the geographical dimension is the most important. Besides showing actual locations, maps can also be used to communicate how particular data varies by location, and (more conceptually) to signify the geographical reach of a particular enterprise or project.

How to draw the "Map" Layout

Charteo

Vereinigte Staaten von Amerika
Bundesstaaten

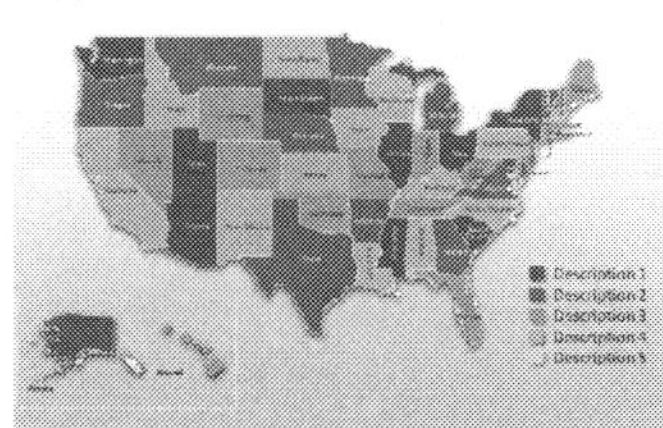

www.Charteo.com
Maps, Country Maps, America, Federal States 7

PowerFrameworks

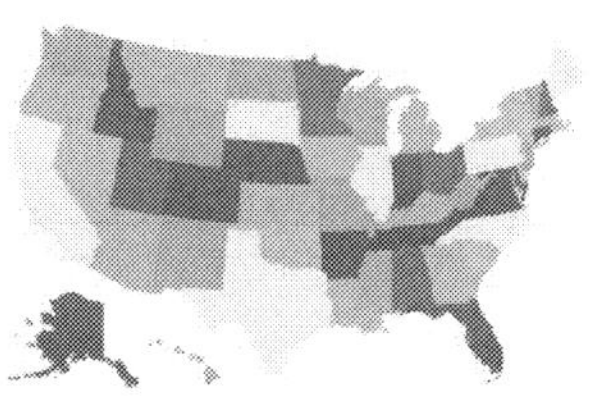

www.PowerFrameworks.com
Keyword Search "MP009","mp009_colored_states_without_lakes"

Slide: "The Gathering Storm"

This Map layout with specific callouts from multiple places around the world is designed to demonstrate a global consensus on the issue being discussed—in this case, labor shortages. A number of examples from a variety of regions are presented, all indicating a similar conclusion, that labor markets are intensifying around the globe. The image of the world map makes it easy to anchor each callout in its region of origin, as well as emphasize the near-universal nature of the consensus. Each callout lists the location where the example comes from, and shares the data point relevant to labor markets.

The Gathering Storm

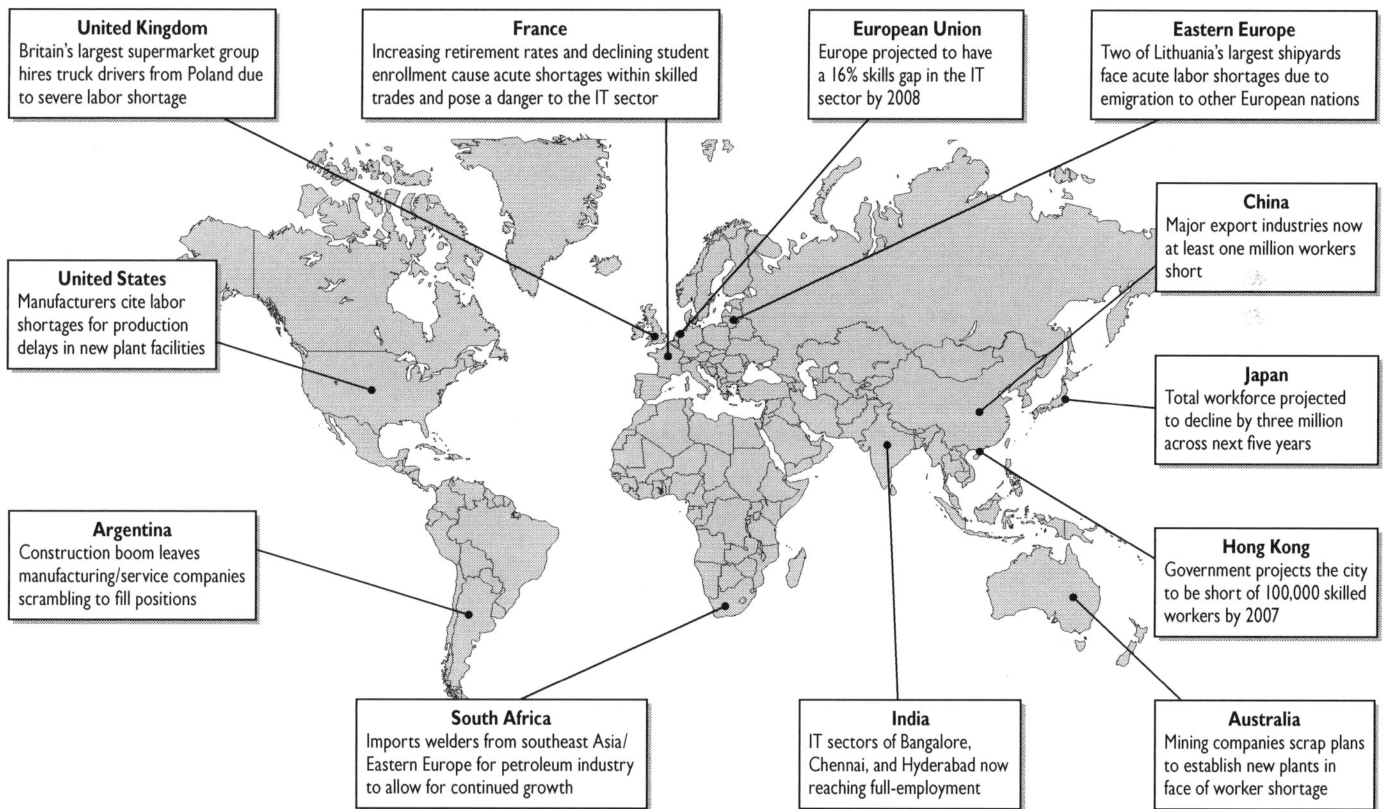

Source: "Macklin Says Australia is Now Facing a Shortage of 20,000 Scientists and Engineers," *Federal Government Broadcast Alerts*, 19 July 2006; "Forrester Warns Skills Shortage Will Worsen Unless Industry Seeds IT Talent," *CMP TechWeb*, 13 June 2006; "China's Factories Hit by Labor Shortage," *The Christian Science Monitor*, 1 May 2006; "The Skill Pool is Drying Up," *The Financial Express*, 2 June 2006; "Now Hong Kong is Hit by Top Skills Shortage," *Birmingham Post*, 8 May 2006; "Boom Promise May Fade on Lack of Skills," *All Africa*, 13 June 2006; "State to Slide from 3rd to 21st in EU on IT Skills Gap—Study," *Irish Times*, 13 December 2005; "The First Signs of IT Skills Shortages Emerge in France," *Forrester.com*, 28 February 2006; *Manpower Global Survey*, January 2006; "Labor Shortage Grows Acute in Lithuania—Daily," *Baltic Business Daily*, 17 October 2005; CEB research.

Slide: "There Are Significant Differences..."

This slide compares geographical areas on two data points: total savings in 529 College Savings Plans, and average account size. The more shaded states have higher average account sizes while the less shaded ones have average account sizes that are lower. The number listed in each state shows the total assets under management in millions of dollars.

There are Significant Differences in Total 529 Savings and Average Account Size by State

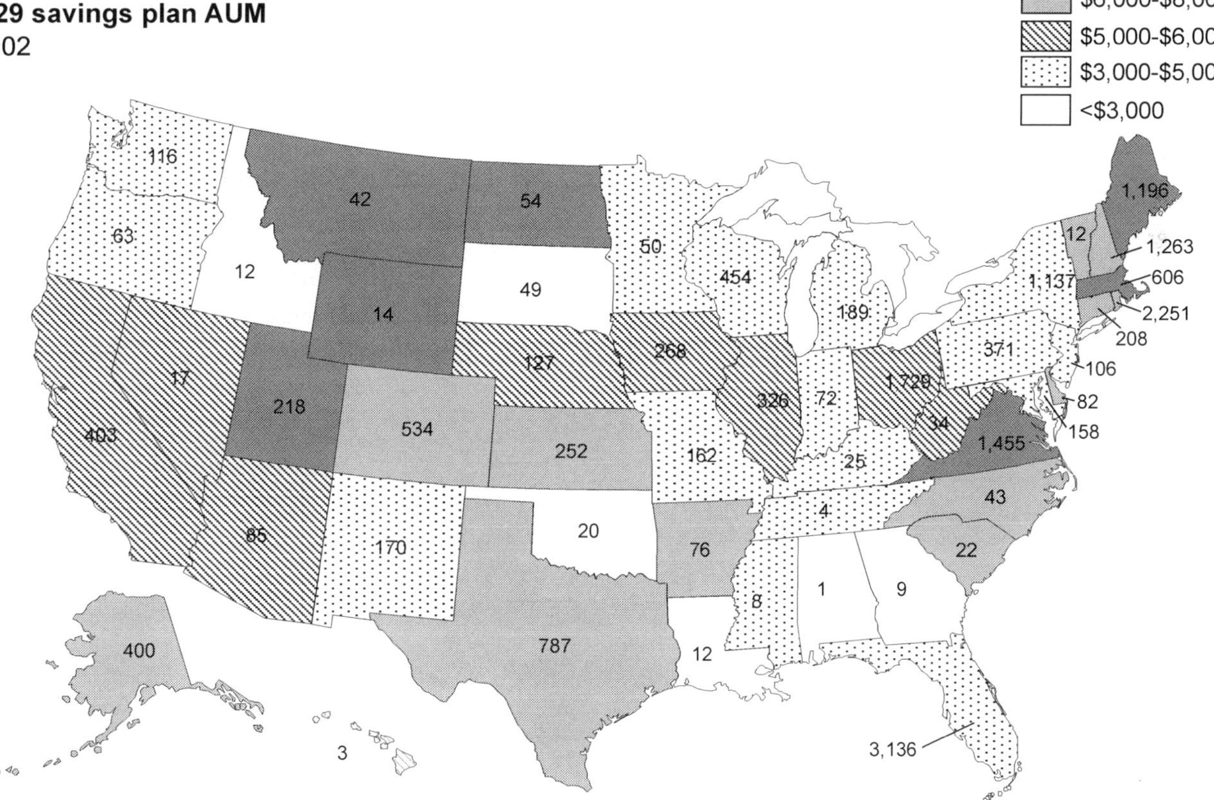

Source: College Savings Plan Network

CHAPTER 29: "MATRIX" LAYOUT

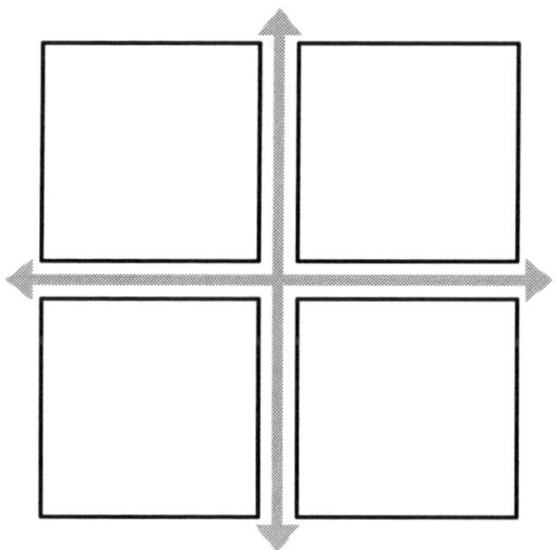

Use the Matrix layout when you need to show information laid out along two dimensions or axes. Each axis is divided into two or more qualitative subsets, and the intersection of those axial divisions yields boxes or cells. This enables the presenter to outline the topic quickly by means of four or more separate cells, and discuss the attributes of each.

How to draw the "Matrix" Layout

Charteo

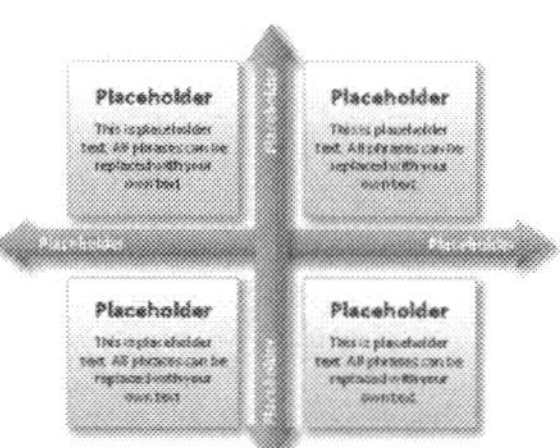

www.Charteo.com
Matrix Charts, Basic Matrix Layouts, Basic Matrix 10

PowerFrameworks

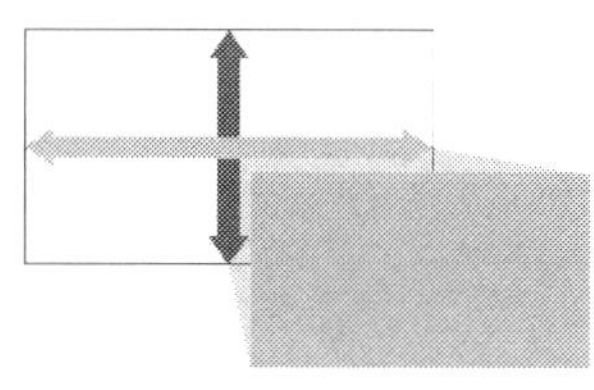

www.PowerFrameworks.com
Keyword Search "RE027", RE027-re027_matrices-Matrix

SmartArt

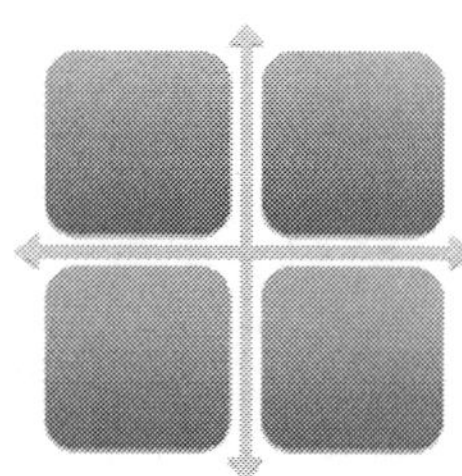

PowerPoint SmartArt
Matrix, Grid Matrix

Slide: "Executing targeted improvements requires strong management and governance …"

This paradigmatic example of the Matrix layout highlights the importance of management strength in Information Technology (IT) deployment. Both the vertical and the horizontal axes are split into High and Low—in this instance, top quartile and bottom quartile. The vertical axis shows the management practice score, and the horizontal axis shows the intensity of IT deployment. This shows clearly that it is necessary to have both of those dimensions together in order to achieve a substantial increase in overall productivity (upper right box), because one dimension without the other yields only mediocre results (upper left and lower right boxes). These numerical and graphical findings are reiterated in the text at the bottom.

Executing targeted improvements requires strong management and governance …

Increase in total factor productivity, Percent

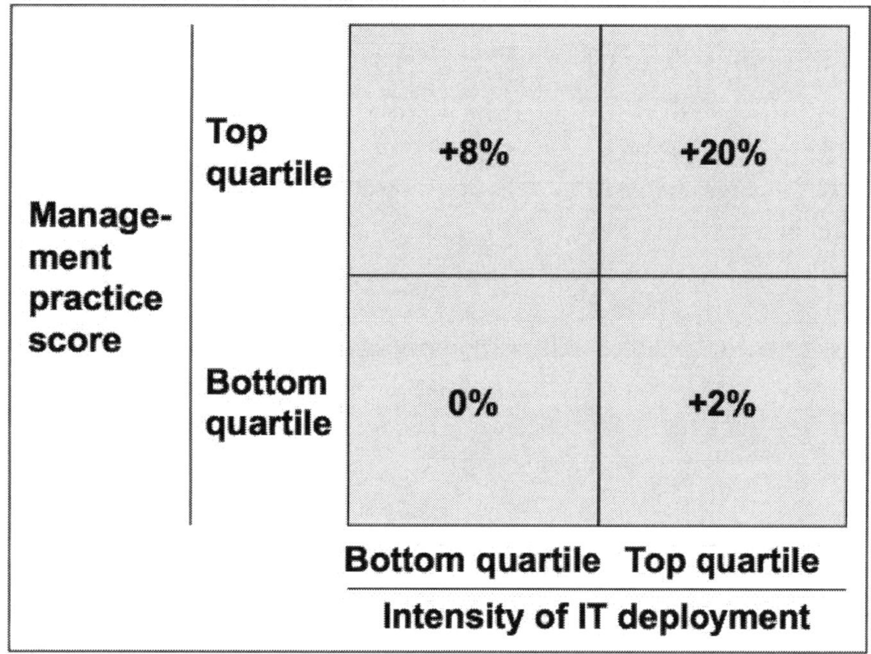

Management matters

- Investing in IT has low impact if companies are poorly managed
- Corporations must have the right management practices to get the most out of IT investments

SOURCE: LSE

Slide: "One Way to Look at Things"

This example embeds the two dimensions in the middle of the graphic, around the axial arrows. The vertical dimension shows time—how long an economic downturn will last—and the horizontal dimension shows customer behavior—whether they like or dislike economizing. The resulting four segments are named and discussed; in the upper right quadrant, for example, "Cool to be frugal" customers are those who embrace economizing in an extended recession. Each segment has four or five characteristics that accompany and define that scenario.

Notice that the whole point of the slide is to show scenarios—different versions of what the future might hold—and the Matrix layout helps the presenter clarify these possibilities, ultimately helping decision makers in the audience become more comfortable with uncertainty.

Note also that the axes are conceptual and not to scale: the top of the vertical axis covers 18-24 months, but the bottom deals with a period of 5+ years. The point is not to provide a timeline for particular events but to divide and thus highlight attributes of the time periods involved.

Scenarios can help decision makers get comfortable with uncertainty.

- The full treatment yields four possible scenarios, each with a number of unique characteristics, but potentially a few common ones, too.
- This output can be used in a number of ways beyond pushing managers' thinking:
  - A common understanding of (and vocabulary for) what the near future might look like;
  - A "wind tunnel" to stress-test pending decisions;
  - A guide to selecting leading indicators for making course corrections.

ONE WAY TO LOOK AT THINGS

Potential Scenarios

Developed Economies, 2009–2014

Bad: Extended Recession (18–24 Months)

Suspended Animation

- Conditions seen as temporary setback for existing expectations.
- Weak brand allegiances broken.
- Most nice-to-haves forgone (but not forgotten).
- Small luxuries selectively protected.
- Companies struggle to sustain SKUs, invest in lesser brands.

Cool to Be Frugal

- Early adopters, media, and influencers reinforce low-cost mind-set and lifestyle.
- Low-cost product lines grow in fad-like boom.
- Impressionable segments retain frugal behaviors for life; most others revert.
- Companies struggle to differentiate in rush to "me too" value positioning.

Customers Frustrated by Economizing ⟷ Customers Embrace Economizing

Bitter Denial

- Frustration breeds pessimistic outlook in general.
- Supplier loyalties severely eroded.
- Customers persistently dissatisfied as they can't afford what they want.
- Companies struggle to keep customer trust.

The Great Temperance

- Thrifty mind-set becomes dominant across sectors and categories.
- Private labels/value brands prevail.
- Net, permanent shift in savings/consumption levels.
- Companies struggle to innovate products and categories.

Worse: "Contained Depression" (5+ Years of Low Growth)

Source: CEB research.

Slide: "Forewarned Is Forearmed"

This version of the Matrix layout works similarly to the previous slide, with two key differences: the axes here are more explicitly a gradual continuum, and two types of information—characteristics, and reaction when stressed—are added for each of the four quadrants. In this model of Social Styles, the vertical axis shows the continuum of emotional responsiveness, and the horizontal axis shows the continuum of assertiveness. Each quadrant has both a qualitative name (e.g., "Analytic") as well as a title that describes that style functionally (e.g., "Process-Oriented"). By positioning the key takeaway points on the left, the presenter can summarize the model's important conclusions without detracting from the clarity provided by the layout's overall four-fold segmentation.

> **Technique #1: Sensitize for a small set of warning signals that indicate you are going too far.**

- The Social Styles matrix clusters people into four quadrants representing broad personality types—Amiables, Expressives, Drivers, and Analytics.
- Using the assertiveness and responsiveness continuums, along with the defining characteristics for each personality type, you can make an educated guess regarding where to place a customer.
- Once you know a customer's social style, you can sense when customer boundaries are threatened by looking for probable stress signals—when pushed too hard, Drivers become autocratic, Expressives attack, Amiables acquiesce, and Analytics avoid.

FOREWARNED IS FOREARMED

Social Styles Model

Less Emotionally Responsive (Task-Oriented)

"Analytic"

Process-Oriented	
Characteristics to Look For: ▪ Logical ▪ Thorough ▪ Serious ▪ Systematic ▪ Prudent	When Stressed, Analytics *Avoid* Early signals: ▪ Detachment ▪ Silence

"Driver"

Results-Oriented	
Characteristics to Look For: ▪ Independent ▪ Candid ▪ Decisive ▪ Pragmatic ▪ Efficient	When Stressed, Drivers *Become Autocratic* Early signals: ▪ Pushiness ▪ Intense or cold ▪ Use of imperatives

Less Assertive (Ask-Oriented) ⟷ More Assertive (Tell-Oriented)

"Amiable"

Feeling-Oriented	
Characteristics to Look For: ▪ Cooperative ▪ Supportive ▪ Diplomatic ▪ Patient ▪ Loyal	When Stressed, Amiables *Acquiesce* Early signals: ▪ Passive-aggressive acceptance ▪ Extreme reluctance to move forward

"Expressive"

Social-Oriented	
Characteristics to Look For: ▪ Outgoing ▪ Enthusiastic ▪ Persuasive ▪ Fun-loving ▪ Spontaneous	When Stressed, Expressives *Attack* Early signals: ▪ Loud language ▪ Emphatic gestures

More Emotionally Responsive (Relationship-Oriented)

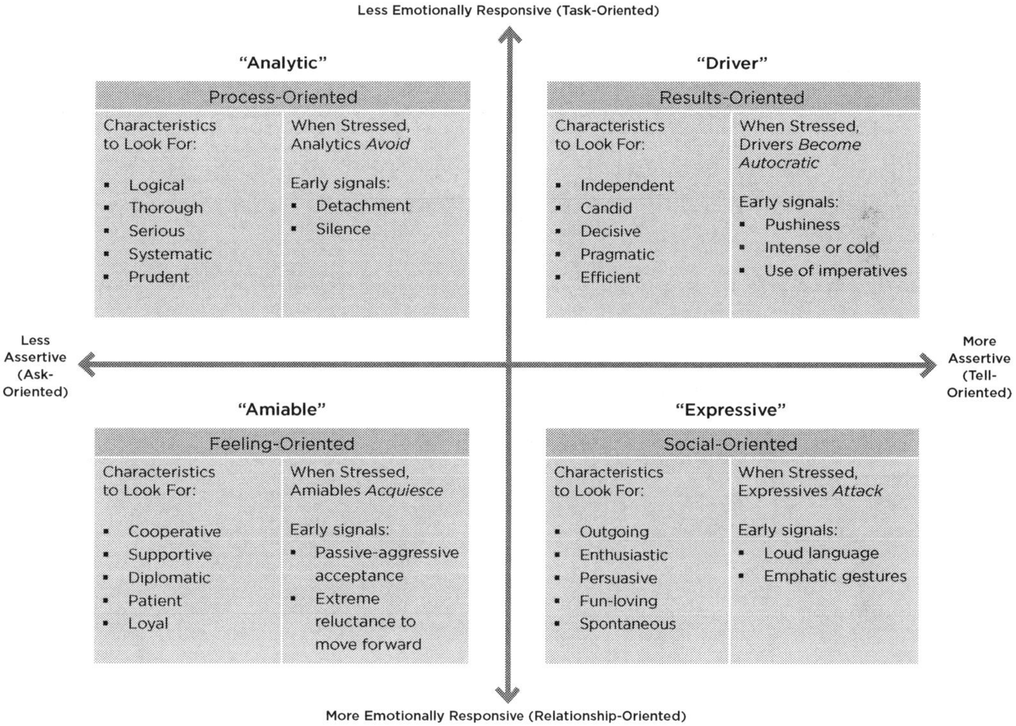

Source: Robert and Dorothy Bolton, Social Style/Management Style, 1984.

Slide: "Experience from a Distance"

This simple but elegant layout takes the Matrix to another level. It incorporates the standard, qualitative features on the axes (e.g., partner vs. own, on the horizontal; and service vs. product, on the vertical), but it also features a mini-case example, complete with relevant detail, in each of the four segments. The call-out boxes annotate key points, and the gray back arrow emphasizes the ascendancy illustrated by the slide: the greater risks—and rewards—as businesses proceed to the model depicted in the upper right.

Experience from a Distance

Indirect companies pushing the limits of marketing expertise and business model innovation in pursuit of the benefits of experience

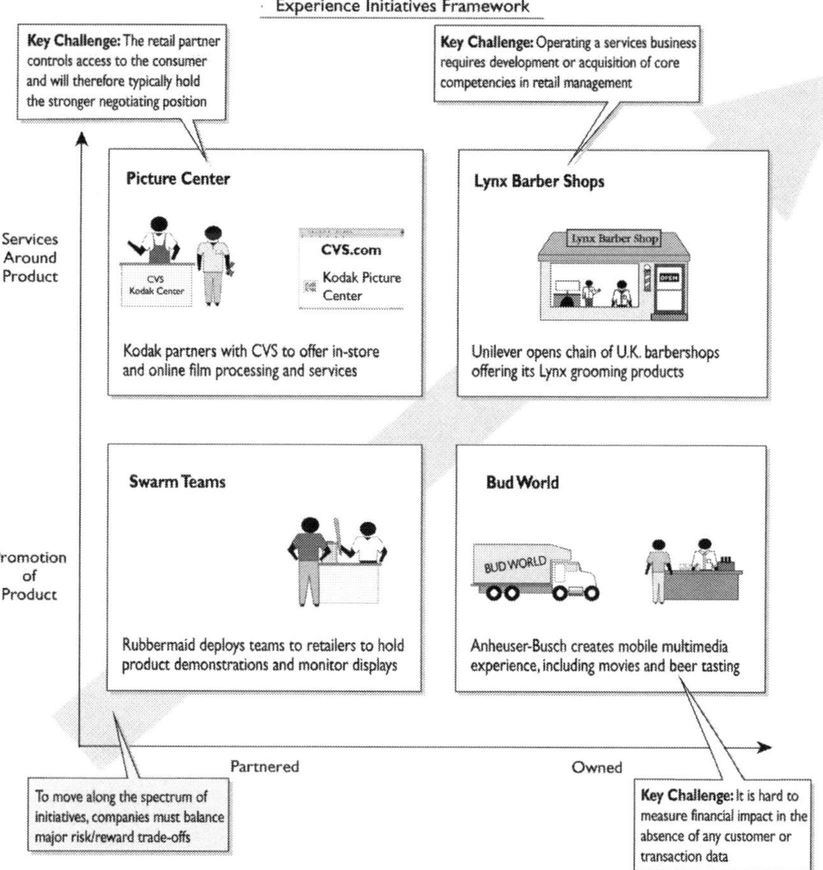

Source: CEB research.

CHAPTER 30: "MAZE" LAYOUT

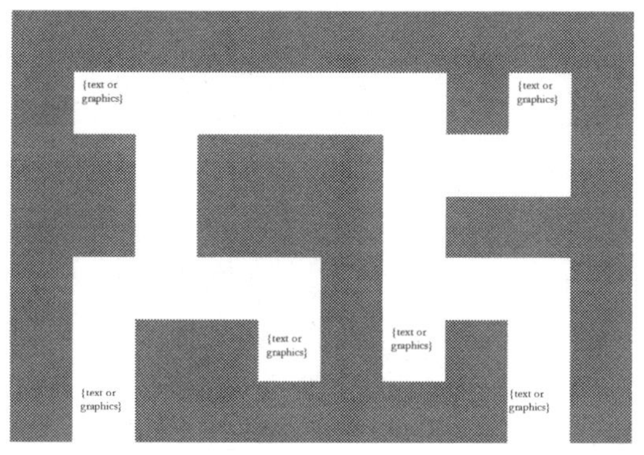

The Maze layout is effective when the presenter needs to show a complicated or confusing process that can involve various paths and some dead ends. The image of the maze implies the difficulty of navigating through the nonlinear process to the designated goal, and suggests that help may be needed to do so.

How to draw the "Maze" Layout

Charteo

Labyrinth

Enter your subheadline here

www.Charteo.com
Graphics and Metaphors, Labyrinths, Labyrinth Chart 13

PowerFrameworks

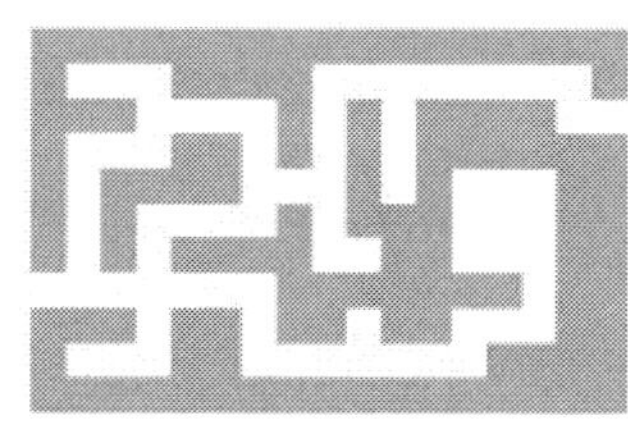

www.PowerFrameworks.com
Keyword Search "CN044","CN044-cn044_v2"

Slide: "Costly Mistakes"

This version of the Maze layout places the maze on the left of the slide and shows a client in the maze's center. Faced with the company's many service options, the client does not know which way to turn with his needs. Without any guidance from the company, the self-managed client is likely to wander; and his or her experience—and the company's profits—will not be optimized. This likelihood is further illustrated by the chart on the slide's right. The chart depicts the large share of wallet that a company achieves in the long term by guiding and optimally placing the client at the beginning of the customer relationship; conversely, a misplaced client yields a very low share of wallet.

Costly Mistakes

Clients often self-manage into the wrong business line...

...leaving them poorly served and the institution ill-positioned to capture additional share of wallet

Clients' Self-Navigation of the Institution

Illustrative

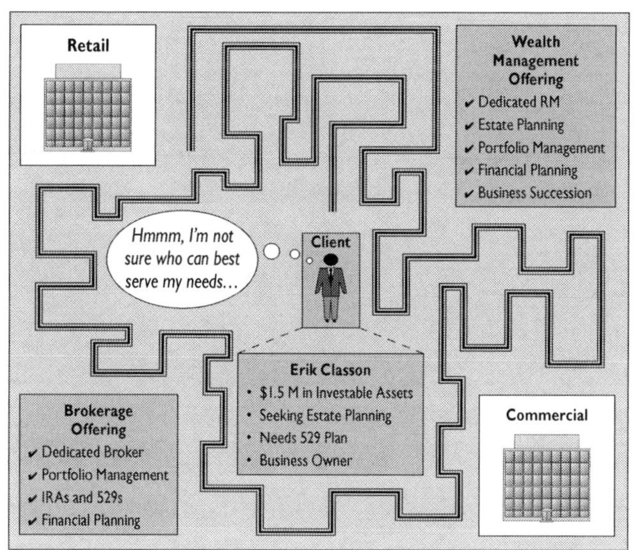

Share of Wallet of Optimally Placed Versus Misplaced Client

Illustrative

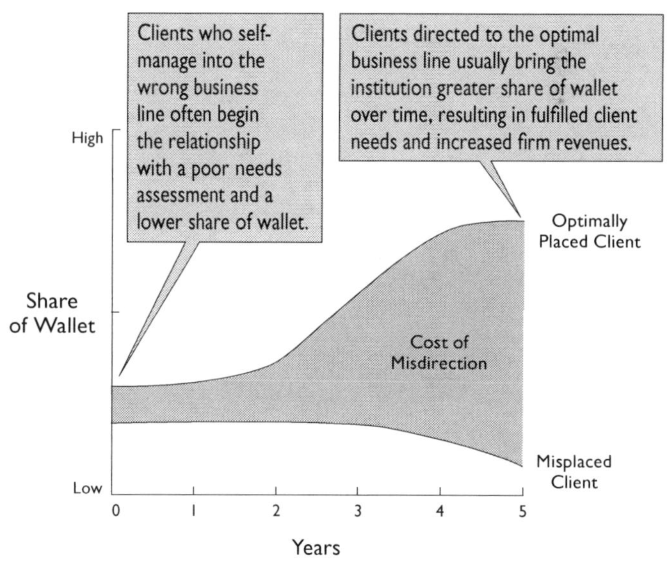

Source: CEB research.

CHAPTER 31: "METAPHOR" LAYOUT

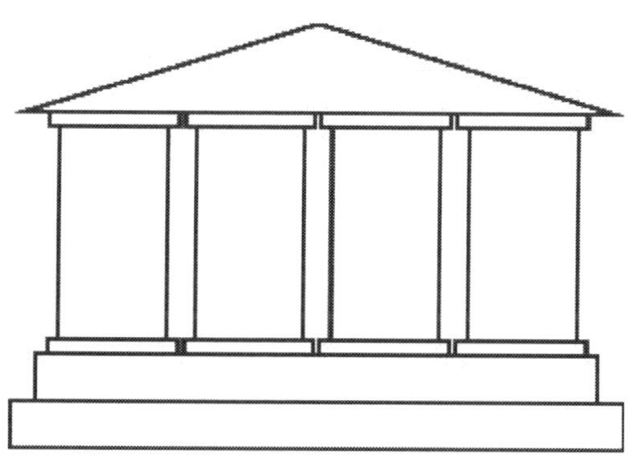

There are many metaphors that serve well as layouts. Among the most common are buildings, tables, bridges, and ladders. Some individual metaphors are so popular that they have separate chapters in this book, including Tip of the Iceberg, Gameboard, and Balance/Out-of-Balance.

How to draw the "Metaphor" Layout

Charteo

House Chart – 4 Columns

Enter your subheadline here

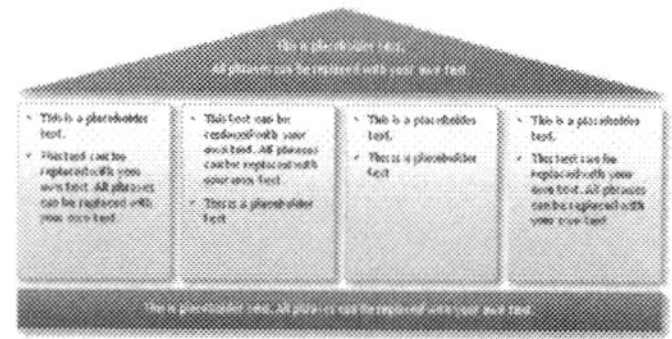

www.Charteo.com
Concept Charts, Templates, Houses, House Chart 5

Diagrammer

Text Here
Text Here
Text Here
Text Here

www.Diagrammer.com
Stack, Vertical, 4 Nodes, 2D Angled, Stack Vertical 44

PowerFrameworks

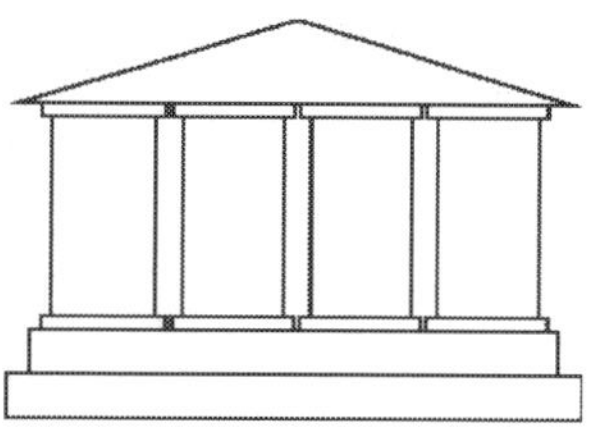

www.PowerFrameworks.com
Keyword Search "HI001", HI001-0402

Slide: "Pillars of Insight"

This slide uses the metaphor of a building with four supporting pillars to portray the necessity of certain elements for the integrity of an overall structure. In this case the structure is a research organization, and the pillars identify organizational conditions or environmental factors that tend to support the creation of insight. These factors are recognition of insight as a top priority, reward for risk taking, fairness and accuracy of informal feedback, and employee satisfaction regarding compensation.

The layout allows important details to be communicated with each pillar. In addition to the name of the pillar (at the top) and an explanation of why the pillar is important (at the bottom), each pillar also includes a chart showing the actual survey results from which these conclusions were drawn. In each case, the difference in scores reported by researchers rated less or more insightful by their managers is shown as a column chart. Maintaining a consistent vertical axis across all four charts allows comparison across the four pillars.

The inclusion of quantitative details such as these makes the slide more convincing than if it contained only assertion and qualitative anecdote.

Pillars of Insight

Four Environmental Factors Drive Insight Productivity

Pillar #1: Clarity of the Insight Mandate

Insight Is a Top Priority

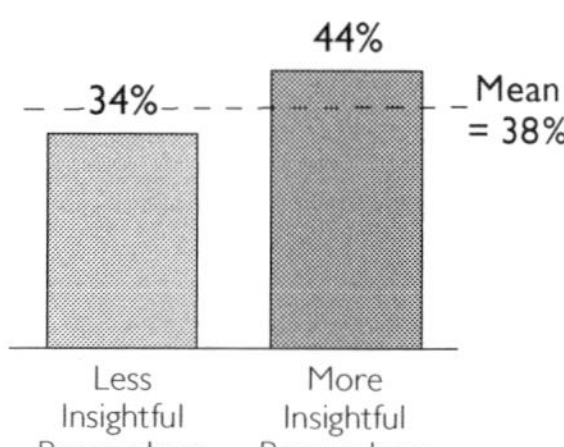

Clarifying insight generation—often an amorphous and overused concept—makes the activity accessible to the whole team.

Pillar #2: Level of Team Support for Risk Taking and Creativity

Team Rewards Risk Taking

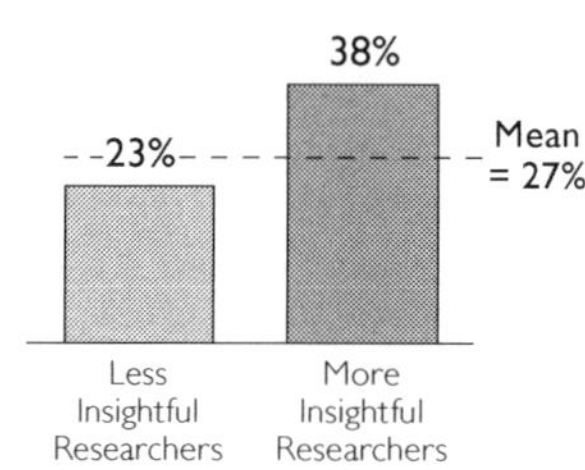

Researchers who see their immediate peers taking risks and developing creative ideas—critical components of insight generation—are inspired and empowered to do the same.

Pillar #3: Manager's Fairness, Integrity, and Openness

Informal Feedback Is Fair and Accurate

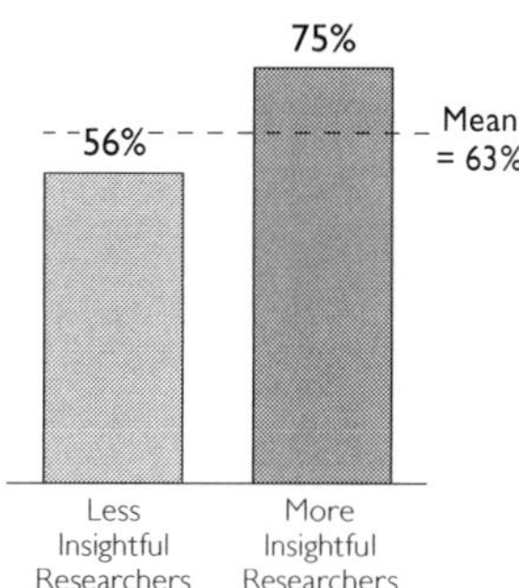

Direct managers are the most critical drivers of staff willingness to "go the extra mile," therefore moving from analysis or understanding to true insight.

Pillar #4: Satisfaction with Compensation

Overall Satisfaction with Total Compensation

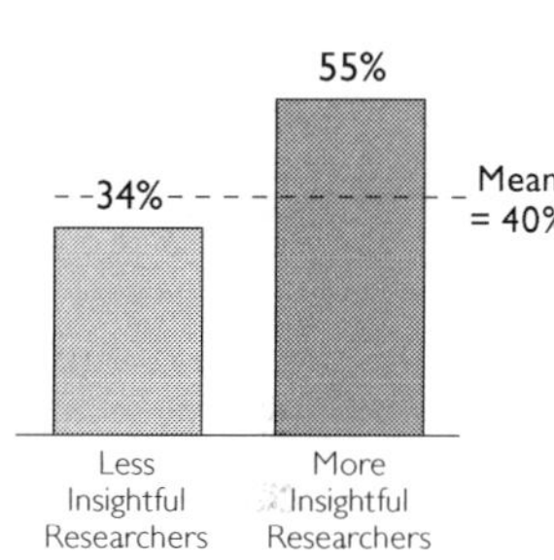

Satisfaction with Research's job offer drives not only staff willingness to "go the extra mile" but also the function's ability to attract and retain key talent.

Note: Percentage of more or less insightful researchers either agreeing or strongly agreeing (6 and 7 in 1–7 scale).
Variables represent most significant element of index. "More insightful" researchers rated 8–9. "Less insightful" researchers rated 1–5.

Source: MREB Employee Survey, 2007; CEB research.

Slide: "Speaking Their Language"

When discussing roles and relationships, the visual metaphor of a table is a useful alternative to the Organization Chart layout. This example explains how a Chief Marketing Officer can secure the collaboration of other senior executives by explaining how their particular positions benefit from improvements in marketing, and by describing the specific contributions required from them in order to achieve these improvements.

The table is centered on the slide, and selected senior executive positions have their relevant benefits and requirements highlighted. In contrast to the hierarchy conveyed by an Organizational chart's structure, this table Metaphor layout instead emphasizes collaboration among peers.

Speaking Their Language

CMOs need to show peers "what's in it for them" to generate and sustain support

The Internal Exchange for Securing Buy-In to Customer-Focused Investments

Benefits to CEO
- New avenues for company growth
- Differentiation of company's proposition

Requirements from CEO
- Executive support for customer initiatives
- Approval of resource reallocation

Benefits to CFO
- Reduced volatility of cash flows (due to increased customer loyalty)
- Sustained premium pricing (due to differentiation)
- Greater leverage in marketing investments through concentration on key segments

Requirements from CFO
- Funding for customer-focused investments
- Collaboration with marketing to model and prioritize most promising investments
- Sensitivity to adverse customer (and ultimately cash-flow) impact of cost-cutting measures

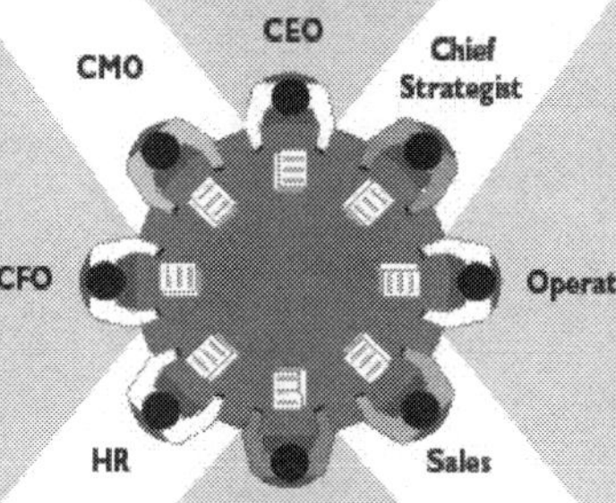

Benefits to Operations
- Clarity of executable priorities based on customer values
- Principled SKU reduction (through better understanding of consumer preferences)

Requirements from Operations
- Consistent frontline execution in keeping with customer values
- Support for investments in physical plant to improve the customer experience
- Tolerance for changes in processes to accommodate customer needs

Benefits to BU heads
- Identification of new sales growth opportunities
- Shared marketing support for products across all lines

Requirements from BU heads
- Greater collaboration across business units to meet customers' total needs

Source: Srivastava, Rajendra K., Tasaddug A. Shervani, and Liam Fahey, "Marketing, Business Processes, and Shareholder Value," *Journal of Marketing* 63 (Special Issue, 1999): 168–179; CEB research.

CHAPTER 32: "MINEFIELD" LAYOUT

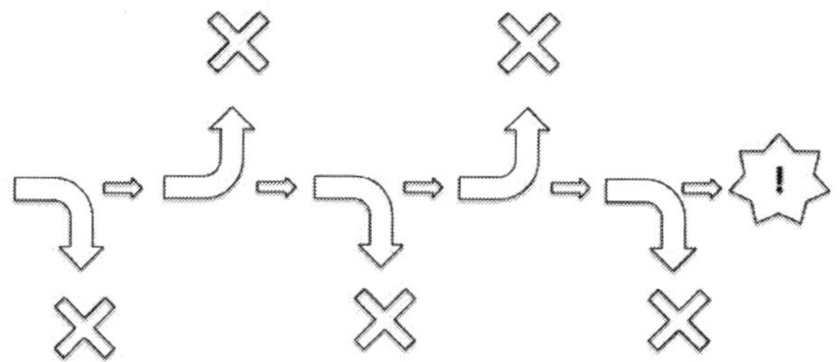

The Minefield layout can be very powerful when the presenter needs to show the audience the pitfalls to be avoided on a path to achieving a goal. The flow of the slide takes the audience through a number of stages toward a desired goal or end-state. Along the way, a number of challenges or detours are spelled out in text and negative icons, such as the skull-and-crossbones or an "X." The main message of this layout is that the desired goal can be achieved only by avoiding all of these challenges.

Slide: "Managing Interfaces and Uncertainty"

This example of the Minefield layout flows from box 1 on the left—the starting situation, in which multiple project requests are received—through the minefield to the star on the right: successful project delivery management. In the left to right journey there are four main pitfalls that could kill the process, each symbolized by a skull-and-crossbones icon, a detour from the critical path, and textual treatment that describes the problem, its result, and its root cause.

The visual impact of the Minefield layout immediately communicates to the audience that the process under discussion entails a sequence of challenges that a successful project must overcome one by one. For example, once the multiple project requests have been received, the projects must be prioritized objectively. But objective prioritization is not enough: each project's requirements must also be accurately scoped in order to avoid the next misstep, and so on. Each step must be followed successfully if the overall project is to succeed.

Managing Interfaces and Uncertainty

Outsourcing magnifies the coordination complexity of project execution, increasing the risk of delivery failure

Obstacles on the Path to Successful Project Delivery

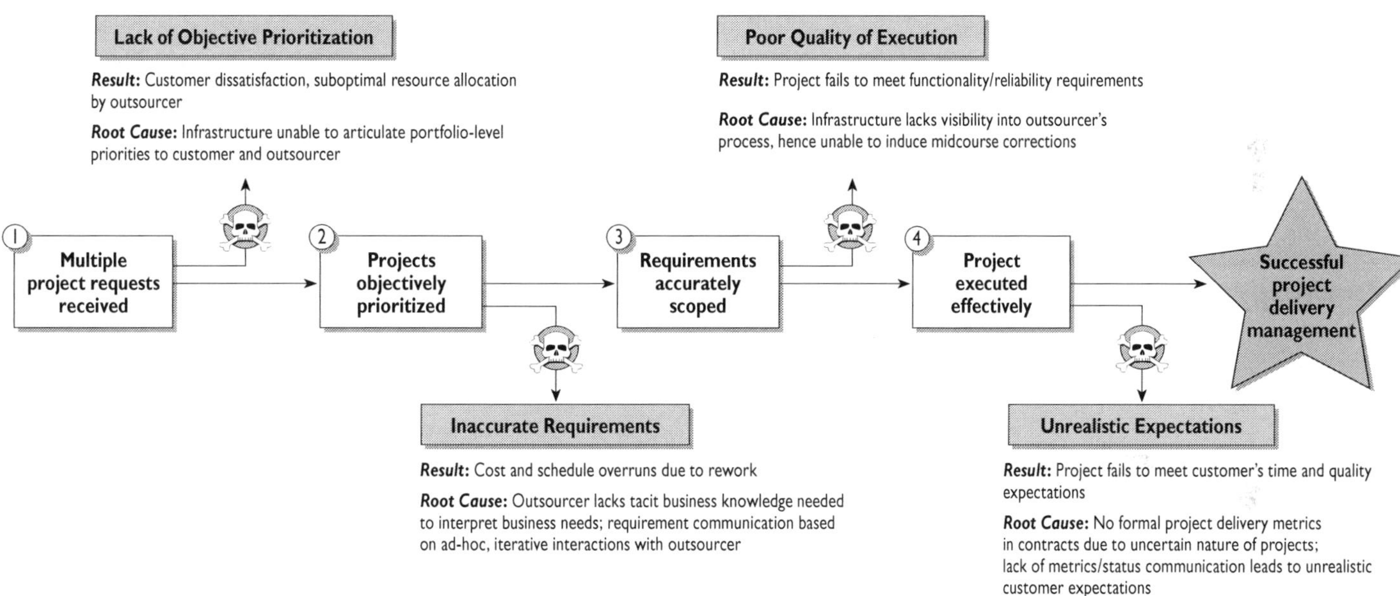

Source: CEB research.

Slide: "Getting Through the Minefield"

This version of the Minefield layout describes the dangers that market researchers face when trying to understand their client's business decisions. In addition to showing how the researcher-constituent conversation can evolve and improve (compare the "conversation" graphic on the left side of the slide to the one on the right), each stage along the process also includes questions to help the audience navigate successfully. Whereas the previous slide summarized each pitfall and described its root causes, each detour in this layout includes practical questions that arm the audience with the very tools needed for success at that stage. These questions help the audience to ensure first Relevance, then Completeness, then Validity, and finally Alignment for the decisions to be discussed in the final conversation. The layout itself provides the tools to reach the goal successfully.

Getting Through the Minefield

Focused Questioning Overcomes Obstacles to Effective Decision Refinement

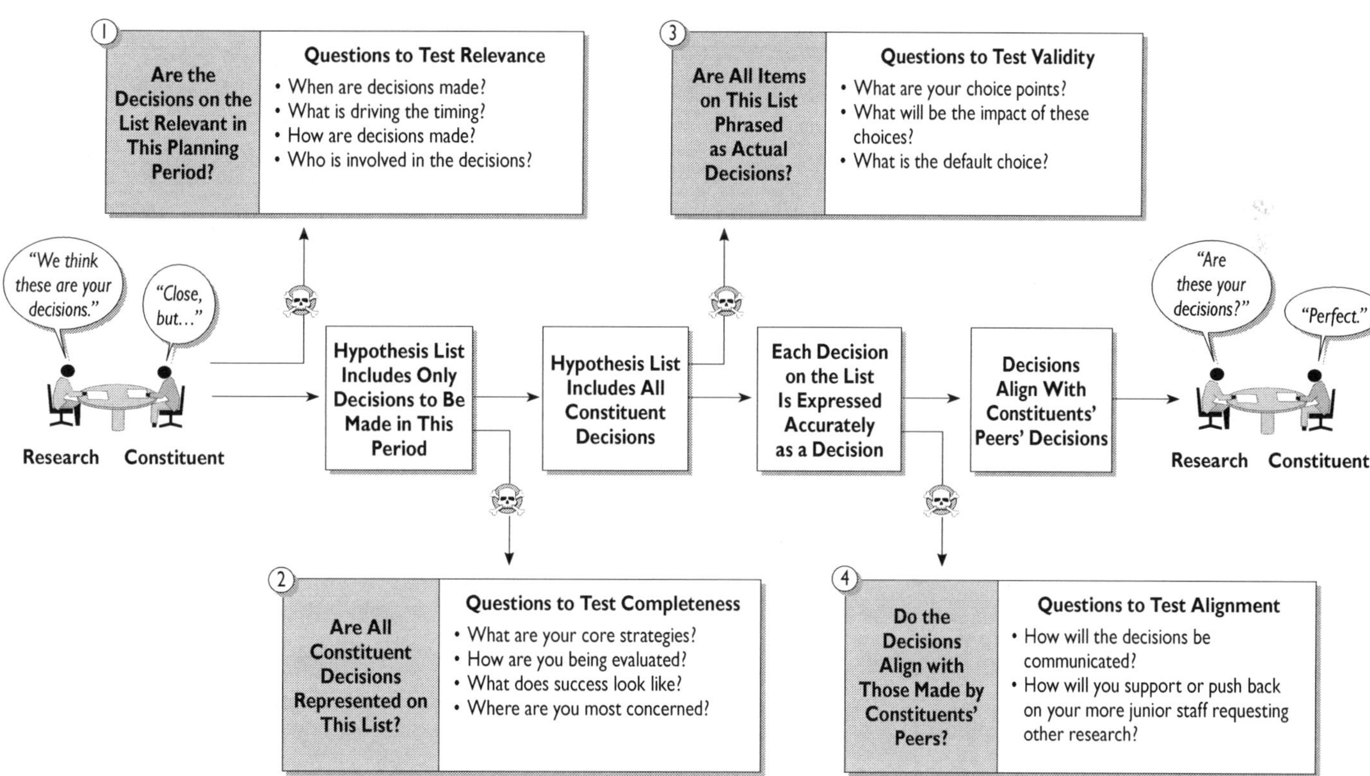

Source: CEB research.

"Minefield" Layout

Slide: "Seven Sourcing Sins"

This alternative version of the Minefield layout borrows the lethal icon of the skull-and-crossbones to portray simply how seven key mistakes combine to diminish net value of an outsourcing contract. The slide flows from the upper left to the lower right: the net value on the vertical axis starts high, but deteriorates to almost nothing as time proceeds in the lifecycle depicted by the horizontal axis across the bottom. The seven deadly sins of sourcing—key failure points in strategy and tactics—appear in various places on the path, contributing to the destruction of value.

Seven Sourcing Sins

Across the outsourcing lifecycle, strategic and execution risks threaten to erode the value provided by outsourcing contracts

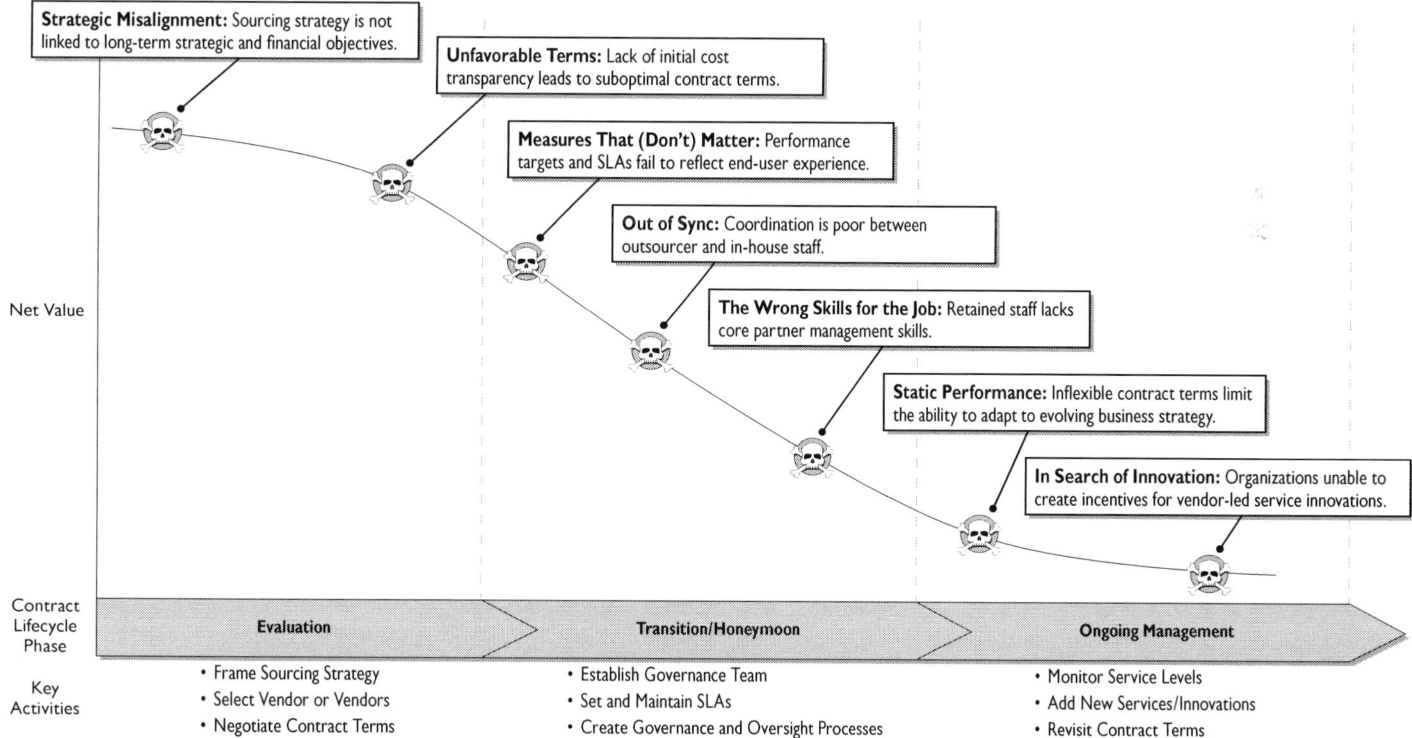

Source: CEB research.

Slide: "Making Your Way Through the Minefield"

In this example, the pitfalls to achieving organization-wide impact from market research are identified in a vertical rather than horizontal layout. What is also distinctive about this example of the Minefield is that each pitfall is illustrated with a quote from someone who faced this pitfall, making that pitfall more vivid and concrete. And by drawing from five different industries, the presenter illustrates how widespread these pitfalls are.

Five pitfalls are identified, any one of which can thwart a successful mission: research portfolio doesn't address the full range of business issues; the research team is unable to say "No" to low-value research requests (and so they spend time working on such requests instead of more strategic questions); the research staff focuses on delivering their research projects, not on providing broader solutions to business challenges; the research department ends their involvement with their clients once they hand over their findings; and the research team is unable to break through to a senior audience.

Making Your Way Through the Minefield

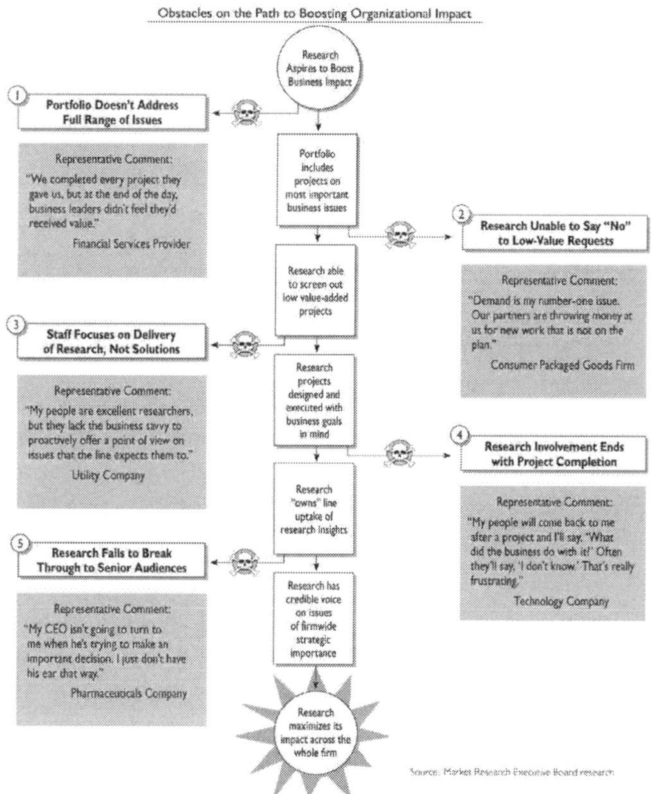

Source: MRC, *From Insight to Action: Boosting the Impact of Research on Business Partners and the Firm*, Washington D.C.: Corporate Executive Board 2006, p. 11.

CHAPTER 33: "ORG CHART" LAYOUT

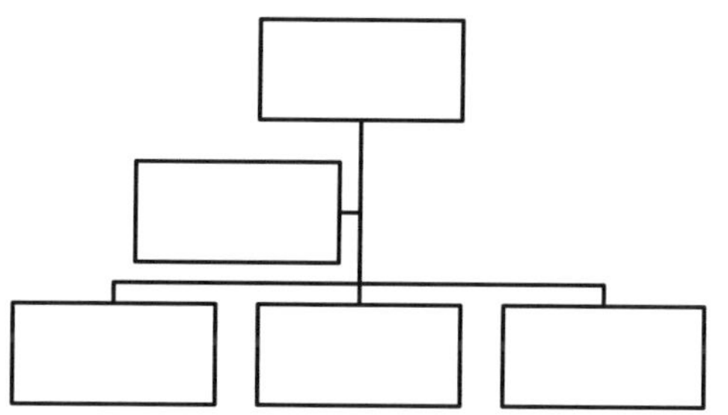

The Organization Chart layout is immediately recognizable as a visual description of an organization; the individual rectangles represent positions in the organization, and the connecting lines show the positions' hierarchical relationships to one another. The use of the layout in explaining organizational development and recommending organizational change is widespread, as the examples in this chapter show.

How to draw the "Org Chart" Layout

Charteo

www.Charteo.com
Concept Charts, Org Charts, Org Chart Horizontal 40

Diagrammer

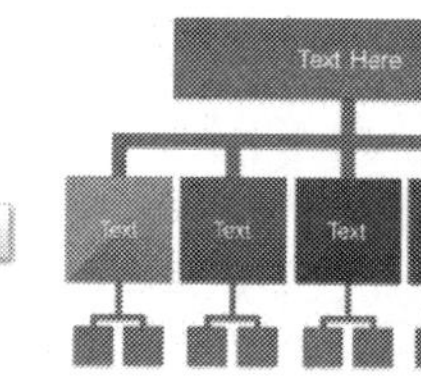

www.Diagrammer.com
Network, Flare, 5 Nodes, 2D Angled, Network Flare 38

PowerFrameworks

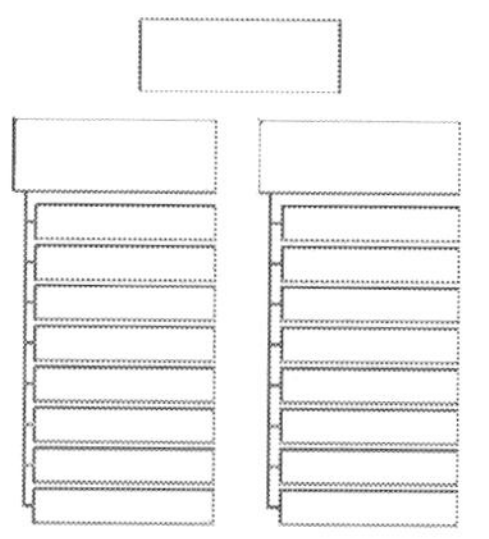

www.PowerFrameworks.com
Keyword Search "HI004", HI004-0203

SmartArt

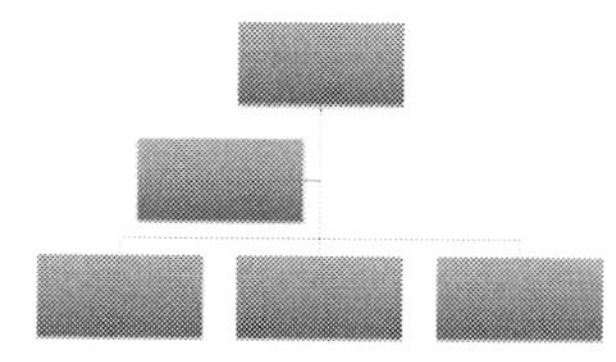

PowerPoint SmartArt
Hierarchy/Organization Chart

Slide: "A Necessary Evil"

This Organization Chart layout lists seven major functions that report to the CEO, and then delves deeper into the workings of one of those functions: Technology and Operations. This chart shows how the Technology group and the Operations group report separately to the Technology and Operations executive, emphasizing the Operations group (in the middle left of the chart) by means of the shaded boxes, which add a visual weight that draws the audience's attention.

In addition to the customary direct or primary reporting relationships, which are indicated by solid lines, the dotted lines show secondary reporting relationships. Within Operations, for example, the Asset Management group reports secondarily to the Asset Management executive, and the Program Management Office within the Technology group reports secondarily to the head of Operations.

This slide itself describes some of the Organization Chart layout's strengths in depicting organizational design; for example, the gray double-headed arrows along the right and the bottom of the chart emphasize the authority and hierarchical relationships shown on the vertical dimension, and the division of work into specialized functions or jobs shown on the horizontal dimension. The box in the lower right corner lists some of the limitations of using an Organization Chart: although it reflects the formal structure of a company, it doesn't reflect the informal structure or diagonal interactions as well (or at all).

A Necessary Evil

Structure is a necessary, but not sufficient, element of organizational design

Characteristics of Organization Structure

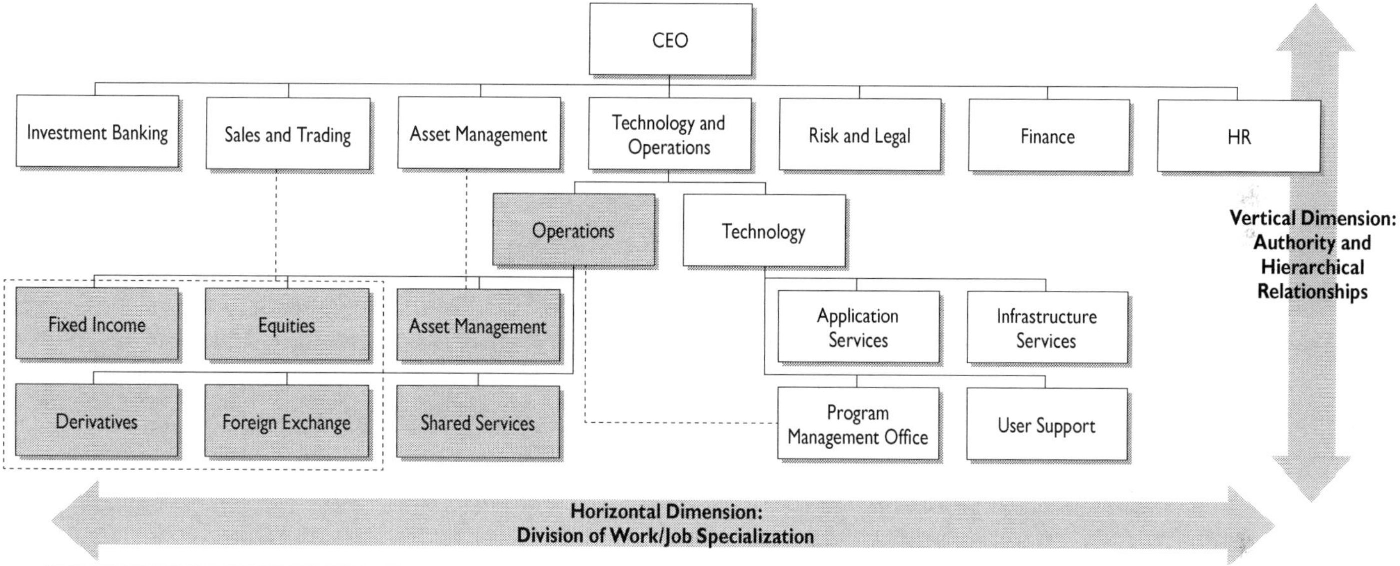

CEO

Investment Banking | Sales and Trading | Asset Management | Technology and Operations | Risk and Legal | Finance | HR

Operations | Technology

Fixed Income | Equities | Asset Management

Derivatives | Foreign Exchange | Shared Services

Application Services | Infrastructure Services

Program Management Office | User Support

Vertical Dimension: Authority and Hierarchical Relationships

Horizontal Dimension: Division of Work/Job Specialization

Key Strengths

- Depicts flow of authority and degree of role specialization
- Acts as a change catalyst
  - Builds vision for the future
  - Provides skeletal structure for all organizational decisions
- Emphasizes importance of strategic business units and functions

Limitations

- Does not reflect "informal structure"—the vertical, horizontal, and diagonal interactions outside formal lines of authority
- Significant activities and realities of how work is performed are not reflected on organization charts
- Can cause staff and managers to adopt an overly narrow view of the required duties and interests of their positions

Source: Maurer, John G., Judith M. Nixon, and Terrance W. Peck, *Organization Charts: Structures of 200 Businesses and Nonprofit Organizations*, Detroit, Mich.: Gale Research, 1996; CEB research.

Slide: "Link Critical Executive Decisions to Top Talent through a Rigorous Review"

In this example the individual rectangles symbolizing positions are divided diagonally into two, communicating position importance in the upper left triangle, and employee rating in the lower right triangle. The shading communicates the degree of importance of the position (highly critical, critical, noncritical) and the favorability of the rating (gold standard, good performance, deficient performance).

This color-coding allows the audience to identify quickly the mismatches between position importance and employee rating. A light shaded (highly critical) upper left triangle along with a dark shaded (deficient performance) lower right triangle indicates a serious talent problem for an important position. (The reverse is also relevant: gold standard employees in noncritical positions may indicate a suboptimal allocation of resources.) The mismatched positions that are higher up in the hierarchy, and therefore presumably more critical, are further highlighted by an encircling oval, indicating that they are priorities for action.

Link Critical Executive Positions to Top Talent Through a Rigorous Review

EXAMPLE

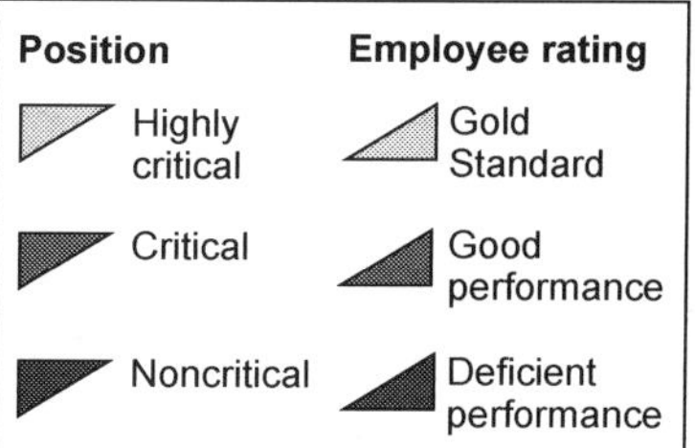

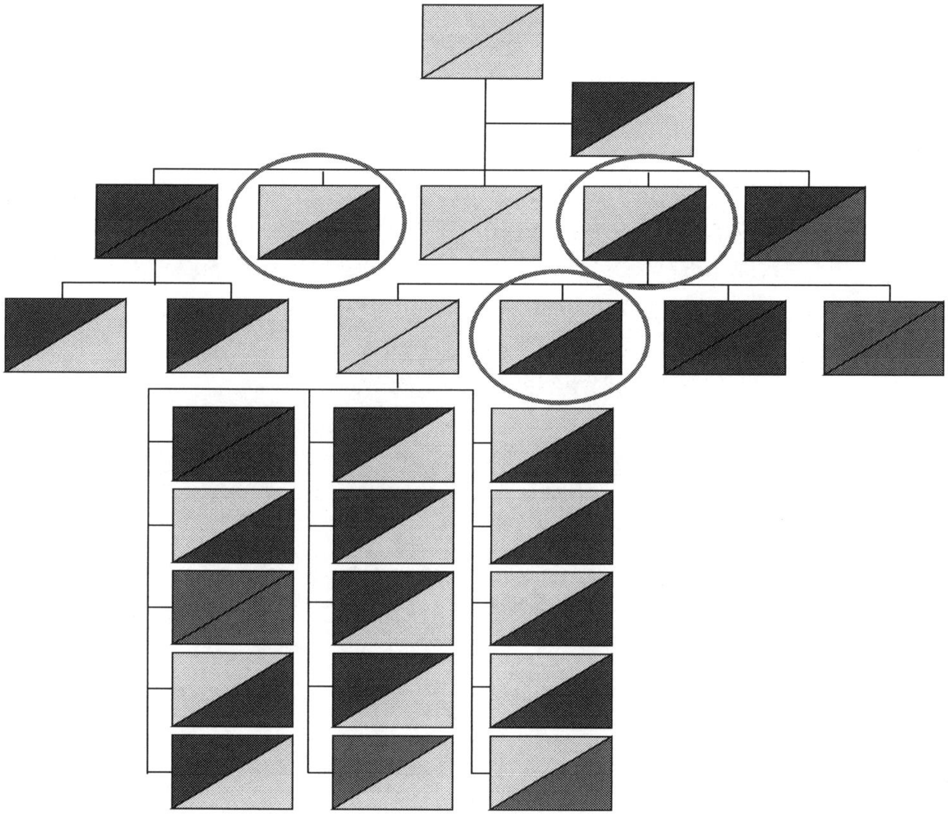

Filling high-profile roles with high-potential leaders means

- Identifying key positions and the performance potential of managers
- Addressing mismatches through skill building and recruitment
- Accelerating the advancement of talented players by moving out low performers

Slide: "A Changing Profile"

The Organization Chart layout is also useful for explaining relationships among different positions and/or functions. In this example, the core functions of a firm are laid out as an Organization Chart, and a series of call-out boxes identifies the important relationships between the marketing function (on the chart's left) and selected other functions. The marketing function's core activities are presented in a white call-out box, while the additional, cross-functional relationship activities (such as assisting Human Resources with employee selection, or helping Operations to manage complexity and experience) are in gray boxes. The bottom of the slide presents a boxed quotation summarizing the main point of the slide.

A Changing Profile

Marketing Executives Must Increasingly Coordinate the Firm's Collective Efforts

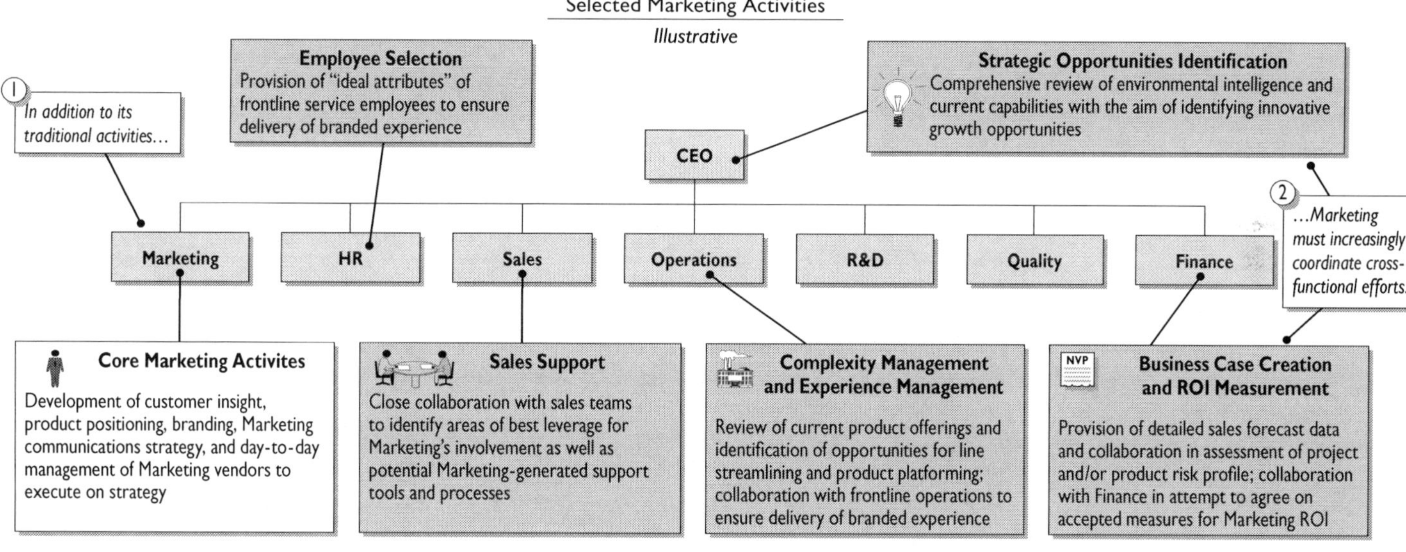

The Emerging Marketing Leader

"Instead of looking for people skilled in dealing with ad agencies, media channels, and trade and consumer promotion programs, [two leading Fortune 500 firms]…wanted people who could both rethink the conventions of brand management and partner with senior executives across functions in the organization to develop and execute marketing plans that achieve business goals."

Partner

Source: Silver, Steve, "Bring in the Super CMO," *Strategy & Business* (Issue 31); CEB research.

Slide: "Payors Should Consider Which Organizational Design Options ..."

It is not necessary to be limited to one organization chart per slide. In this example four different organization charts are presented, illustrating four alternative organizational approaches for supporting a particular line of business. The chevron on the left provides reasons for considering alternative organizational forms.

Speaking Their Language

CMOs need to show peers "what's in it for them" to generate and sustain support

The Internal Exchange for Securing Buy-In to Customer-Focused Investments

Benefits to CEO

- New avenues for company growth
- Differentiation of company's proposition

Requirements from CEO

- Executive support for customer initiatives
- Approval of resource reallocation

Benefits to CFO

- Reduced volatility of cash flows (due to increased customer loyalty)
- Sustained premium pricing (due to differentiation)
- Greater leverage in marketing investments through concentration on key segments

Requirements from CFO

- Funding for customer-focused investments
- Collaboration with marketing to model and prioritize most promising investments
- Sensitivity to adverse customer (and ultimately cash-flow) impact of cost-cutting measures

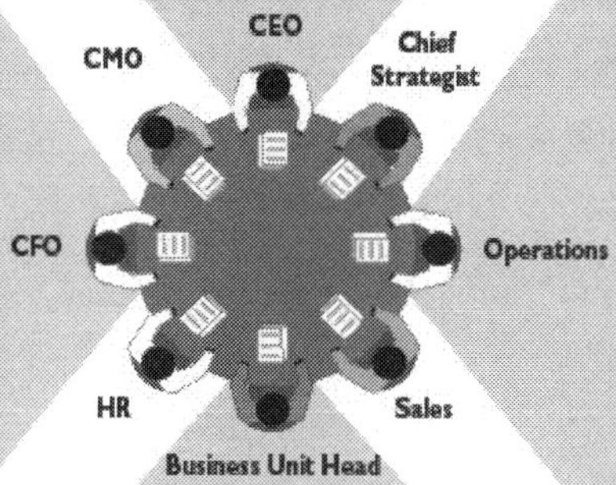

CMO

CEO

Chief Strategist

CFO

Operations

HR

Sales

Business Unit Head

Benefits to Operations

- Clarity of executable priorities based on customer values
- Principled SKU reduction (through better understanding of consumer preferences)

Requirements from Operations

- Consistent frontline execution in keeping with customer values
- Support for investments in physical plant to improve the customer experience
- Tolerance for changes in processes to accommodate customer needs

Benefits to BU heads

- Identification of new sales growth opportunities
- Shared marketing support for products across all lines

Requirements from BU heads

- Greater collaboration across business units to meet customers' total needs

Source: Srivastava, Rajendra K., Tasaddug A. Shervani, and Liam Fahey, "Marketing, Business Processes, and Shareholder Value," *Journal of Marketing* 63 (Special Issue, 1999): 168–179; CEB research.

CHAPTER 34: "PUZZLE PIECES" LAYOUT

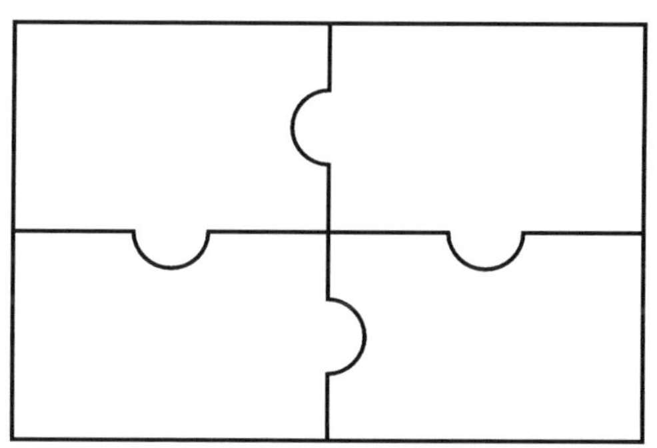

The Puzzle Pieces framework is used to communicate multiple factors that are interconnected. The metaphor is universally understood: if one of these pieces is missing, then the picture is noticeably and significantly incomplete.

How to draw the "Puzzle Pieces" Layout

Charteo

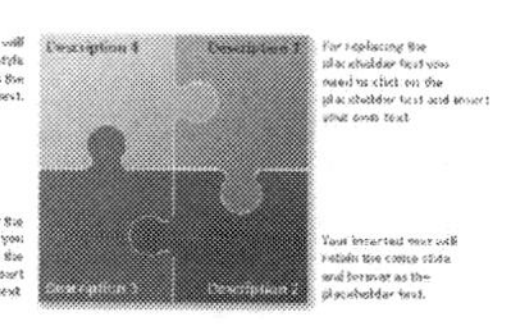

www.Charteo.com
Concept charts, Puzzles/Jigsaws, Puzzle Chart 9

Diagrammer

www.Diagrammer.com
Join, Hook, 3 Nodes, 2D Angled, Join Hook 134

PowerFrameworks

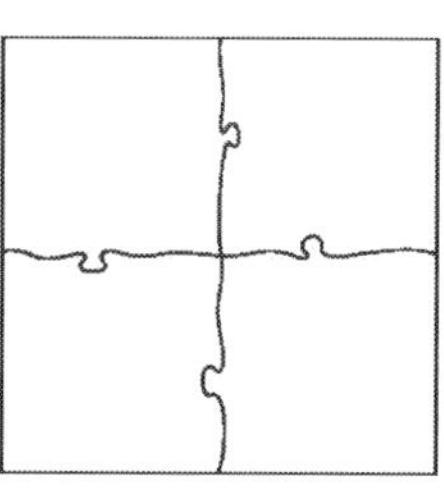

www.PowerFrameworks.com
Keyword Search "SG001", SG001-0400

Slide: "Change Model: The way we lead change at Company X ..."

This "Change Model" slide communicates the interconnected elements that are required for a change management effort to stick. Four puzzle pieces name the necessary elements: role-modeling, fostering understanding and conviction, developing talent and skills, and reinforcing with formal mechanisms.

In a nice touch, each element is illustrated with an attitudinal statement (e.g. for role-modeling, "I see superiors, peers and subordinates behaving in a new way") that clarifies the mindset that accompanies it, and provides an indication that it has been achieved. Additional detail about each element is provided in the call-outs on the left and right sides of the slide.

Finally, the loose arrangement of the 'almost-but-not-yet-connected' puzzle pieces employs a subtle visual cue to help elicit from the audience a desire that the puzzle be completed – and perhaps a desire that the presenter's company should be hired to lead the process.

Change model

The way we lead change at Company X—and make it stick

Role-modeling
"I see superiors, peers and subordinates behaving in the new way"

- We are personally passionate and committed to leading the change
- We are working together to make trade-offs and solve problems
- We ground our performance discussions in operational metrics

Fostering understanding and conviction
"I know what is expected of me – I agree with it, and it is meaningful"

- We always give our people the 'why', not just the 'what'
- We set clear roles and expectations for each level in the organisation
- We train our people to understand the whole company—not just their part

Developing talent and skills
"I have the skills and competencies to behave in the new way"

- We always test if our people have the tools and capabilities to deliver what we expect of them
- Our talent is rotated through different parts of our company to deepen system thinking

Reinforcing with formal mechanisms
"The structures, processes and systems reinforce the change in behavior I am being asked to make"

- We always ensure that what we ask people to do is backed by the structures, processes and metrics

Slide: "Components of a Successful Retention Program"

The standard Puzzle Pieces layout is here enhanced by dividing the pieces into different categories. The slide presents components of an employee retention program. These are divided into organization-wide components at the top and bottom, and skill- or individual-specific components in the middle. Finally, the darker gray at the bottom draws the audience's attention to that puzzle piece, for emphasis during discussion.

Components of a Successful Retention Program

Targeting
- Focuses the program on the right individuals
  - Segments personnel by skills and performance
  - Classifies skills according to local labor market conditions and criticality to the organization

Organization-wide

Non-financial incentives
- Communications
  - Organization-wide communications
  - Targeted communications with customized message to critical personnel
- Training

Financial incentives
- Cash bonus for retention commitment
- Other forms of financial incentives

Skill- or individual-specific

Tracking
- Feedback mechanisms
- Attrition monitoring and reporting tools
- Program adjustment

Organization-wide

Slide: "Ensuring Strategic Clarity"

This slide shows a five-piece puzzle layout on the left. The puzzle communicates the five essential elements of an effective brand growth strategy. The most important of the five, "Single-Minded Growth Idea," is highlighted by being placed in the center of the puzzle and shaded gray: as the most essential element, it holds all the other pieces together.

Each of the five elements is identified with an icon. These icons are then repeated in the "Case in Point" box on the right, which uses one organization's bleach brand to show how the five elements play out in a particular case.

Ensuring Strategic Clarity

Series of HighFlyer Outputs Supports the Brand's Chosen Growth Strategy and Facilitates Execution

HighFlyer Outputs

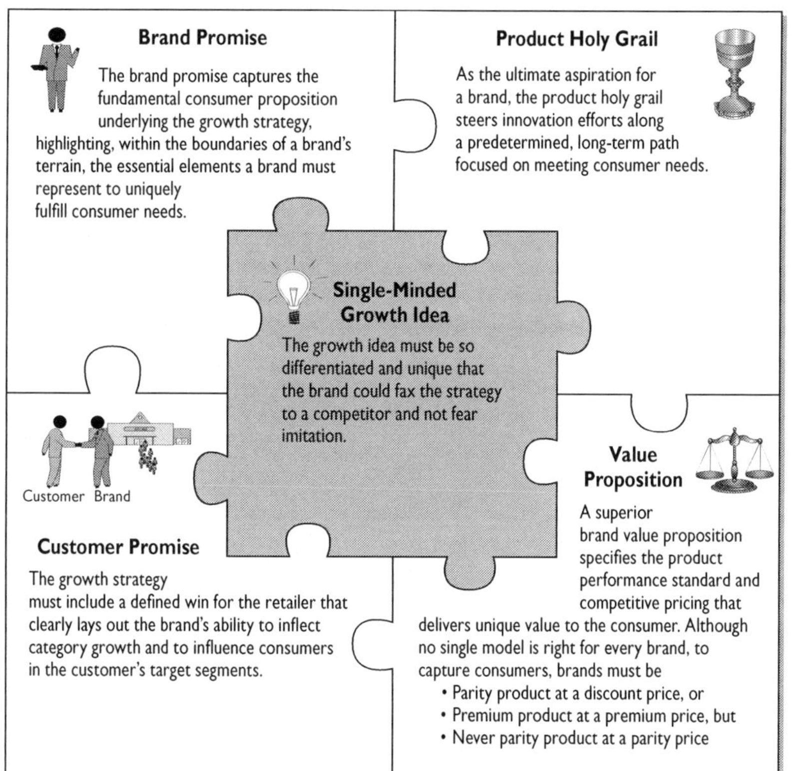

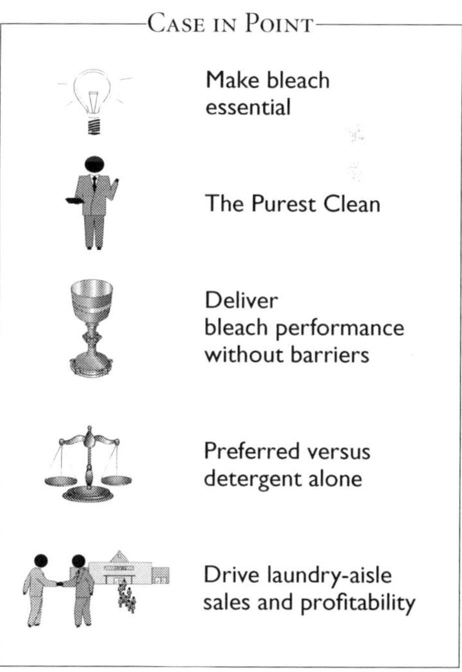

Source: CEB research.

CHAPTER 35: "PYRAMID LIST" LAYOUT

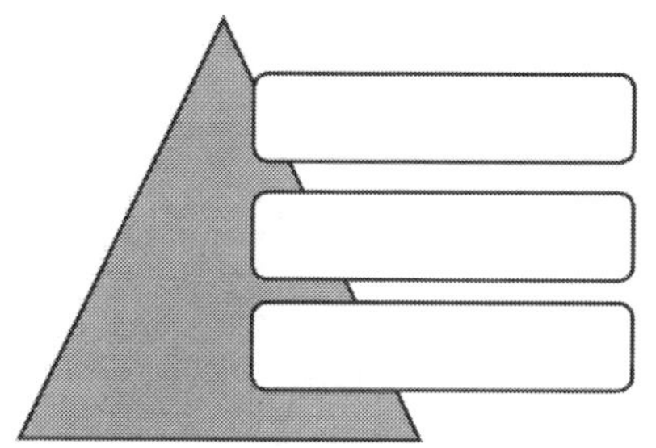

The Pyramid List layout is used to communicate change in quantity within a hierarchical structure, with the rising, narrowing shape of the pyramid suggesting decreases in quantity as one moves up the hierarchy.

How to draw the "Pyramid List" Layout

Charteo

www.Charteo.com
Concept Charts, Pyramids, 2D Pyramid 12

Diagrammer

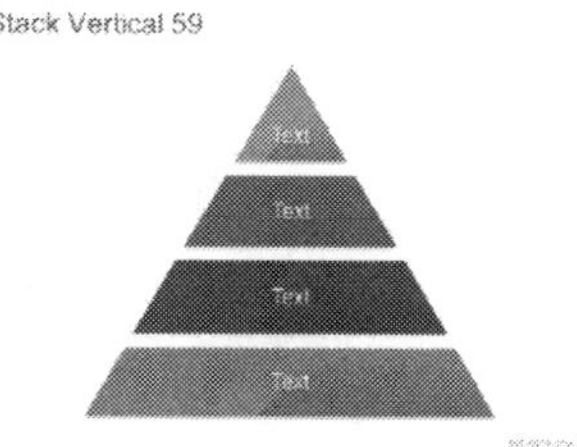

www.Diagrammer.com
Stack, Vertical, 4 Nodes, 2D Angled, Stack Vertical 59

PowerFrameworks

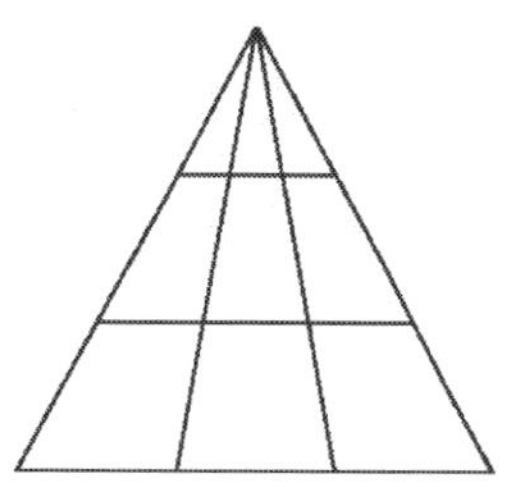

www.PowerFrameworks.com
Keyword Search "HI008", HI008-0303

SmartArt

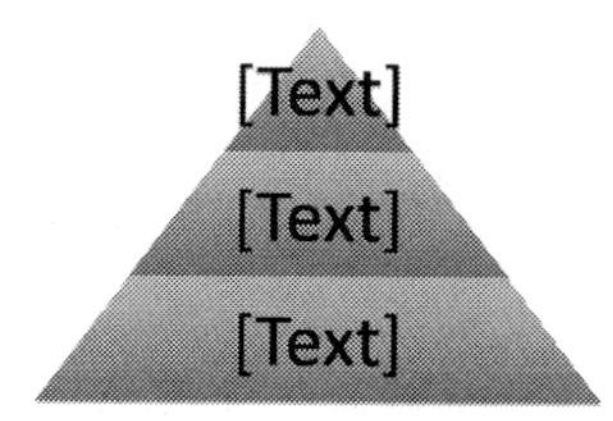

PowerPoint SmartArt
Pyramid, Basic Pyramid

Slide: "Driven to Tiers"

The Pyramid List is commonly used to present levels or tiers—in this case, tiers of customers. The pyramid structure shows five tiers of customers, from the least valuable and most numerous on the bottom, to the most valuable and least numerous at the top.

The characteristics of each tier are described to the right of the pyramid. A presenter using this layout should avoid the temptation to force all the relevant details into the pyramid itself. Aligning them alongside is perfectly acceptable, especially when the groups of details are delineated by lines cutting across from the pyramid's divisions, as in this case.

The arrows that push upward from each pyramid level into the level above reinforce the point in the callout box at the top of the pyramid: namely, that the company's strategy is to migrate customers upwards in the pyramid. The table at the bottom of the slide gives an example from the scoring exercise which is used to determine in which tier to place each individual customer.

It is worth remembering here that a title should describe the slide's main point. Occasionally the presenter is inspired with a particularly apposite pun, which, as in the case of this slide, could drive an audience to tears, either of humor or pain ....

Driven to Tiers

Segment strategic customers into value-based tiers...

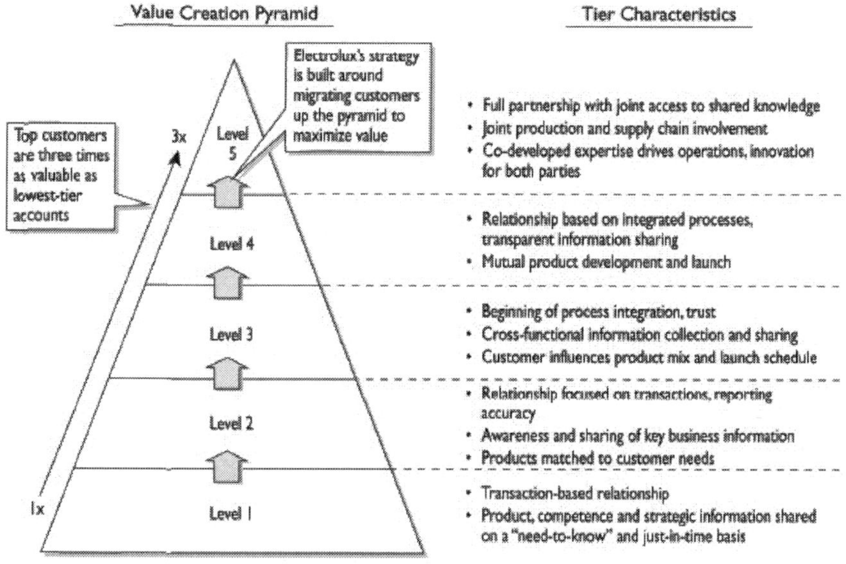

...as determined by a rigorous cost-to-serve scoring exercise

Illustrative Scoring Exercise

Customer: Athena, Inc.

Dimension	Weighting	Score
Supply Chain	10%	76
Value Creation	22%	81
Strategic Value	12%	94
Relationship Depth	18%	62
Brand Strength	16%	92
Profitability	20%	85
	Weighted Average	*80*

Six dimensions of customer and relationship potential are weighted and assessed to drive tier assignment

Source: CEB research.

Slide: "Responsibility for Medical Expenses with an HSA Plan"

The Pyramid List is used here to explain sharing of medical costs between employer and employee. The employee's share of the costs is shaded in gray, as indicated by the key in the upper right. Motion up the pyramid signifies higher medical expenses—a fact which is emphasized by the arrow at the left of the page. The pyramid shape, with its wide base and narrow peak, reinforces the fact that the higher the cost, the lower the likelihood of its being incurred.

Details for each layer in the pyramid are again listed on the pyramid's right, this time in two columns. The first column (immediately to the right of the pyramid) lists the key feature of each layer of insurance, and the second column shows the dollar amounts that are typical of each kind of insurance. Details about the specific potential scenario presented are included at the bottom of the slide. In this example, notice that the shading both shows the cost shared by employee and employer at the bottom of the pyramid, and also neatly indicates how the employee's co-insurance cost is limited in the top tier of the pyramid, should a catastrophe occur.

RESPONSIBILITY FOR MEDICAL EXPENSES WITH HSA PLAN

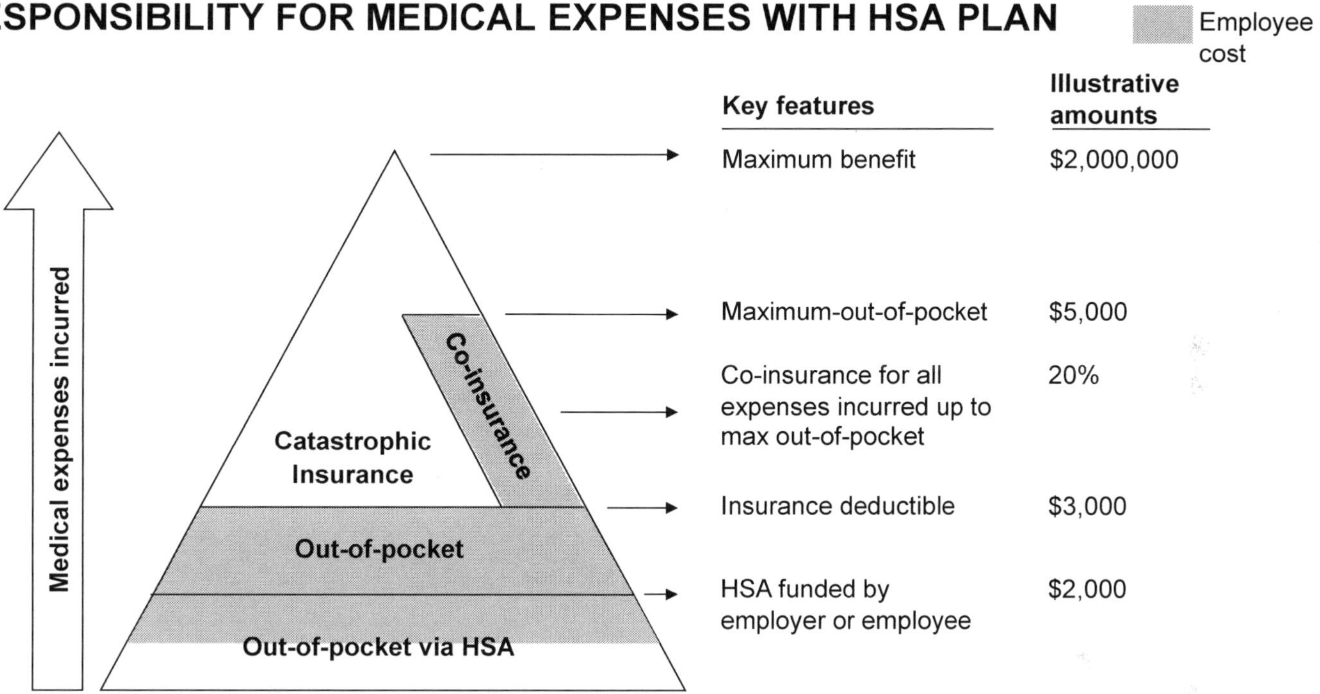

Key features	Illustrative amounts
Maximum benefit	$2,000,000
Maximum-out-of-pocket	$5,000
Co-insurance for all expenses incurred up to max out-of-pocket	20%
Insurance deductible	$3,000
HSA funded by employer or employee	$2,000

Potential scenario:

- Employer provides an HSA and “catastrophic” health plan with a $3,000 deductible and 80/20 co-insurance
- Employer and employee each contribute $1,000 to HSA tax-free (i.e., total initial HSA funding of $2,000)

Coverage liability

- First $2,000 of qualified medical expenses are paid out of the HSA tax-free
- Next $1,000 of expenses paid by employee with post-tax dollars (unless HSA has accumulated assets)
- Employee pays co-insurance for additional medical expenses up to out-of-pocket cap
- Insurance covers additional medical expense up to maximum lifetime benefits
- All HSA funds not spent remain in account and accrue interest/investment earnings until withdrawn

CHAPTER 36: "QUOTES" LAYOUT

In the absence of hard, quantitative evidence, a collection of quotes can form the basis for an effective slide. In the Quotes layout, several quotations are arranged across the slide, with or without speech balloons. The source names provided for each quotation convey the impression that many authorities have been consulted. In its simplest form, the Quotes layout is a straightforward collection of quotations; but visual variations of the layout can allow the presenter to depict additional nuances, as our examples show.

How to draw the "Quotes" Layout

Charteo

www.Charteo.com
Text Slides, Quote Slides, Quotes 2

Slide: "There is Limited Consensus and a Lack of Rigorous Quantification …"

This first example presents seven different quotes about expectations for growth of what was at the time a new product. A layer of interpretation is added by visually dividing the quotes into two groups, so that quotations projecting dramatic growth are placed on the left side of the page, while quotations that make more modest claims are on the right. Placing the pointers or "tails" of the speech balloons in random positions further emphasizes the fact that there are many voices and many sources, but little consensus.

There is Limited Consensus and a Lack of Rigorous Quantification Around HSA Growth Projections

Some are predicting revolution…

"We expect more than 40 million HSA accounts to be established over the next decade. "

— Congressional analysts

"Health Savings Accounts Will Revolutionize American Health Care"

— National Center for Policy Analysis January, 2004

"I predict you will see a very rapid expansion in the use of catastrophic insurance."

— Milton Friedman, Economics Nobel Prize winner

"Beyond revolutionizing health-care benefits, defined-contribution plans will create 50 million-100 million new individual investment accounts [by 2010]."

— Booz Allen, 1/2004

… while others expect evolutionary impact, if any at all

"We believe HSAs should be a niche product and early adoption rates should be modest… We expect HSAs to appeal mostly to small employers and individuals that need low-cost options."

— UBS December, 2003

"I don't see there being any difference [from today]…You may have a few more people moving over to higher deductible policies, but that's typically what's being sold in the individual marketplace now."

— Kris Haltmeyer, director of policy for the BlueCross BlueShield Assn. in Washington, D.C.

"How popular they will become remains to be seen… Some think this will revolutionize the health market. That sounds to me like a bit of marketing hype. It will be some time before we know, until we have some solid data."

— Dallas Salisbury CEO Employee Benefit Research Institute.

Slide: "Remember Me?"

In this example of the Quotes layout the speech balloons are omitted; the idea that these are quotations is conveyed by scattering them around the page and placing them at a variety of angles. In this case the quotations are, more specifically, definitions; the purpose of the slide is to convey an actionable definition of "insight."

The triangle in the middle interprets the scattered quotations, providing a consensus definition of "insight." This definition is created through the identification of three aspects of insight, each of which is found in several (though not all) of the definitions on the page. At the center of the page the word "INSIGHT," with its phonetic pronunciation immediately below, reinforces that idea that the slide is about the definition of a word.

(The title "Remember Me?" refers to the fact that this slide had been previously presented to the audience, and was being repeated here because of its importance.)

Remember Me?

Members' Understanding of Insight Coalesces Around Three Essential Characteristics

Market Research Executive Board Synthesis of Members' Insight Definitions

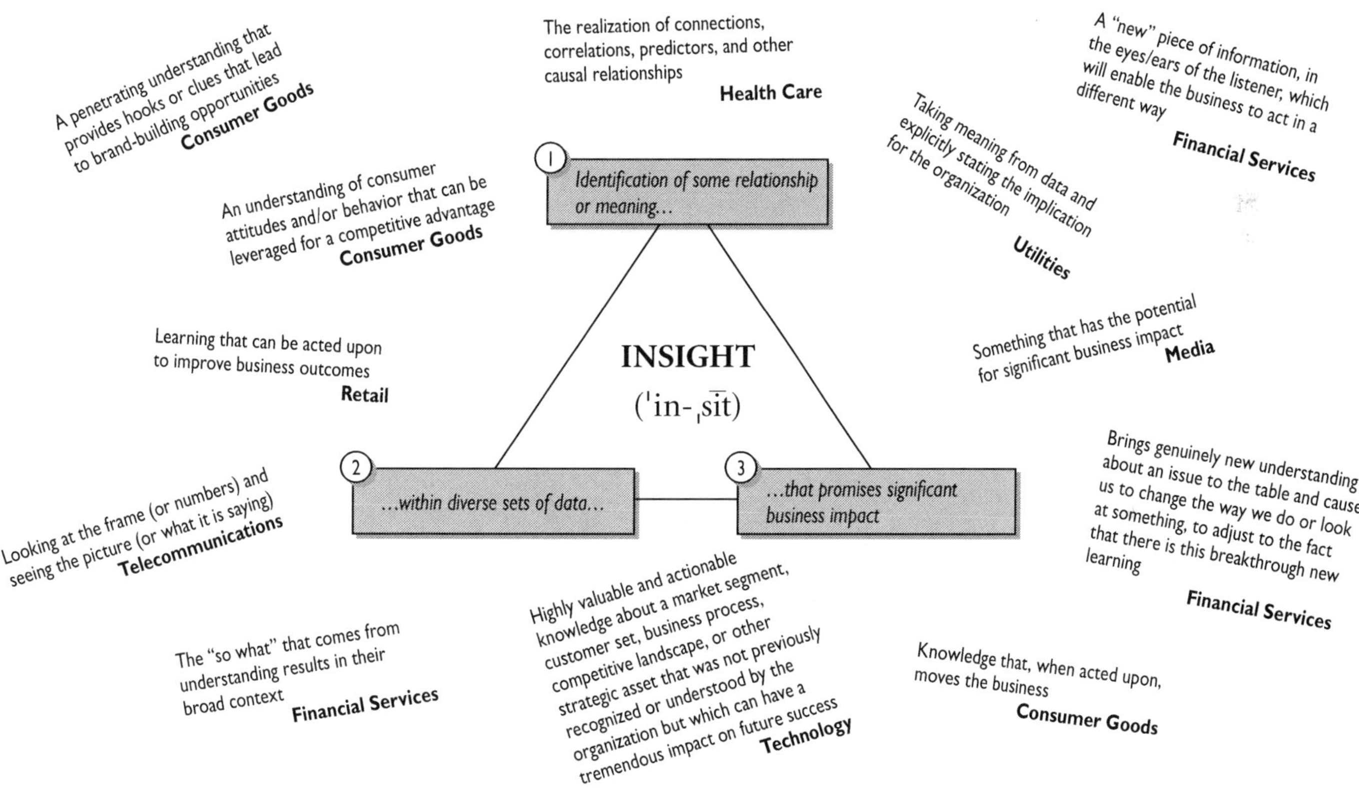

Source: CEB research.

CHAPTER 37: "RASCI" LAYOUT

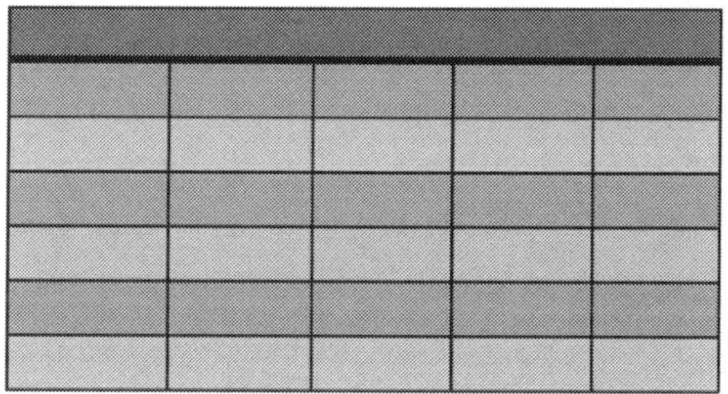

The RASCI layout enables the presenter to communicate a lot of information about a project by showing what type of responsibility each party has for each of the project's tasks. RASCI is an acronym for Responsible, Accountable, Supportive, Consulted, and Informed—a list of the types of participation by which the parties help execute tasks. The various tasks and roles are listed down the slide's left, and the people or groups involved in the project are listed across the top; then each row lists the letters R, A, S, C, and I in the column underneath the person or group that fulfills each role.

Slide: "Task Responsibility Guidelines"

This example of the RASCI layout acts as a project management tool to communicate the precise roles of everyone involved. The roles and tasks are listed down the left-hand column of the chart, and the three people involved are listed across the top. Then, at the intersection of the rows and columns, the way in which each relevant person participates in each role or task is listed. For example, in the fifth row the task is project-level Presentation Creation and Delivery; reading along the row the audience can see that the Research Manager is Responsible for executing this task, while the Consultant and the Insights Manager are Consulted regarding the task.

Some people do not participate in certain tasks, and for some tasks certain people participate in more than one way. We also see some variation in what the letters mean: A, for example, which stands for Accountable in other versions of the layout, here means Approval or Attend. The particular choice of words or letters is not important; what is important is the clear definition of who participates in what way.

TASK RESPONSIBILITY GUIDELINES

Roles/Tasks	Research Manager	Consultant	Insights Manager
Agency Selection—Local/Regional Fieldwork/Moderators	Responsible		
Internal Kickoff	Responsible	Attend	Attend
Fieldwork Attendance	Responsible (of Determining Who Should Be Present)	Attend, If Necessary; Ad Hoc—Attend First Market	Attend, If Necessary; Ad Hoc—Attend First Market
Regional/Country Alert on Schedule/Scope Changes	Responsible		
Presentation Creation and Delivery and Follow-Up—Project Level, If Required	Responsible	Consulted	Consulted
Presentation Creation and Delivery and Follow-Up—Topic Level	Consulted	Consulted	Responsible
Presentation Creation and Delivery and Follow-Up—Internal Business Partner Level	Consulted	Responsible	Consulted
Internal Business Partner Communication	Inform	Responsible	Inform, Relevant
Changes (After Pilot/In Field)	Responsible	Inform	
Business Objectives Identification		Responsible	Consulted
Research Objectives Identification	Consulted and Approval	Responsible	Consulted
Methodology Proposal (Including Sample Size)	Responsible (Consultant for Ad Hoc)	Consulted and Approval	
Market Selection Proposal	Responsible (Consultant for Ad Hoc)	Consulted and Approval	
Agencies to Bid	Responsible (Consultant for Ad Hoc)	Consulted and Approval	
Agency Selection—Multi-Country	Responsible		
Stimuli Selection	Responsible	Consulted	
Research Instrument Design and/or Modifications	Responsible	Consulted	Consulted
Fieldwork Oversight	Responsible		
Fieldwork Changes/Adjustments	Responsible, Approve	Consulted	Consulted
Project Report (Document)	Responsible	Consulted	Consulted

CHAPTER 38: "RELATIONSHIP" LAYOUT

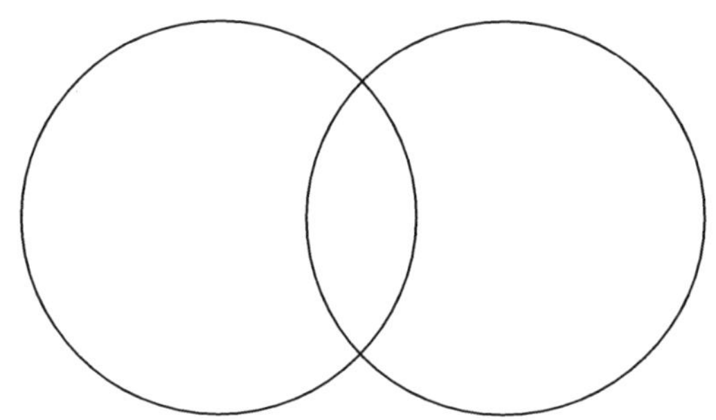

The Relationship layout uses a Venn diagram to show that two or more ideas or entities are related through overlapping aspects or concerns. This simple yet powerful layout enables the presenter to show quickly which aspects or elements are shared – in the regions that are overlapping – and also to show which aspects are not shared.

How to draw the "Relationship" Layout

Charteo

Diagrammer

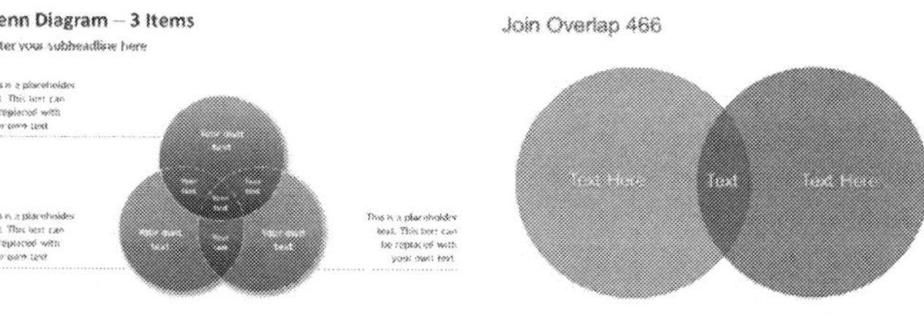

www.Charteo.com
Concept Charts, Venn Diagrams, Venn Diagram 12

www.Diagrammer.com
Join, Overlap, 2 Nodes, 2D Curved, Join Overlap 466

PowerFrameworks

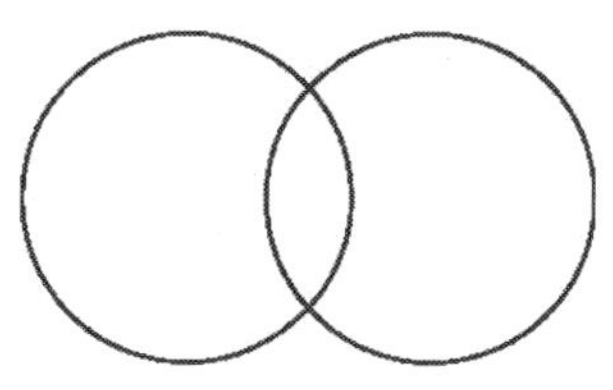

www.PowerFrameworks.com
Keyword Search "RE002", RE002-0200

SmartArt

PowerPoint SmartArt
Relationship, Basic Venn

Slide: "Step #4: Coopting Business Units for Service Model Definition"

This Relationship layout exhibits a three-circle Venn diagram on the right side, where the circles represent the location of responsibilities with respect to the business or organization: Central, Local, or External. The text embedded in the circles shows that the Central group has some exclusive responsibilities and the Local group has others, while the External group holds no portion of responsibility exclusively. The overlapping areas of the circles show that the Central and the Local groups share Cross-Divisional Committees, the Central and the External groups share Infrastructure responsibilities, and the Local and the External groups share Code and Test tasks.

On the left of the slide, the IT Steering Committee works together to determine the optimal organizational approach and service model, and supports the hybrid model depicted on the right in the Venn diagram.

Step #4: Coopting Business Units for Service Model Definition

CIO-selected IT Steering Committee reviews proposed approach and objectives...

IT Steering Committee

- Evaluate merits of organizational approach, management objectives
- Decide endstate service model
- Set broad IT strategy and manage performance to goal

...and supports resulting hybrid service model

Proposed Approach, Objectives, and Organizational Location

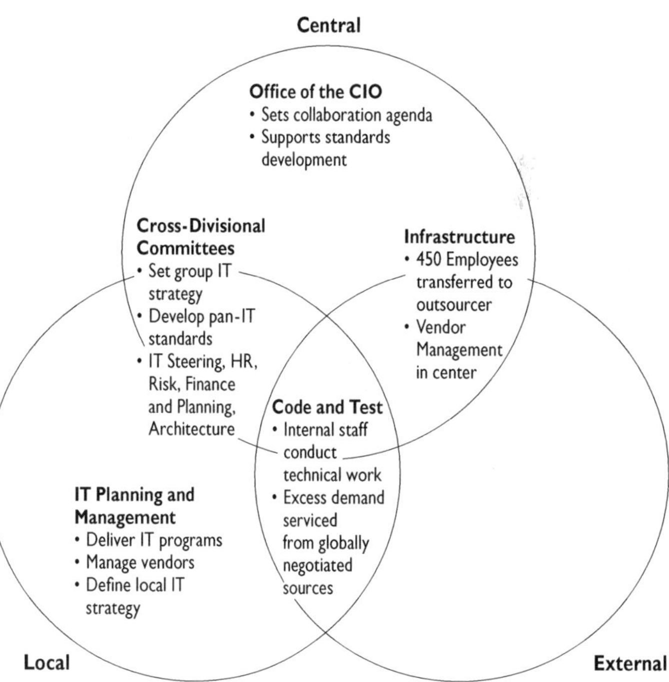

Source: CEB research.

Slide: "Everybody Wants Some: Many Companies Witnessing a Convergence Around Critical Skills"

The purpose of this slide is to show how different corporate functions—sales, marketing, operations, and administration—are all looking for staff who share a common subset of skills. The Relationship layout is an ideal choice to communicate this fact. Four partially overlapping ovals represent the four corporate functions; and the common skills are listed in the center of the slide, where all the ovals converge. The remaining skills, which are unique to each function, are listed in the non-overlapping part of each oval.

Everybody Wants Some

Many Companies Witnessing a Convergence Around Critical Skills

Skill Set Overlap for Various Corporate Functions

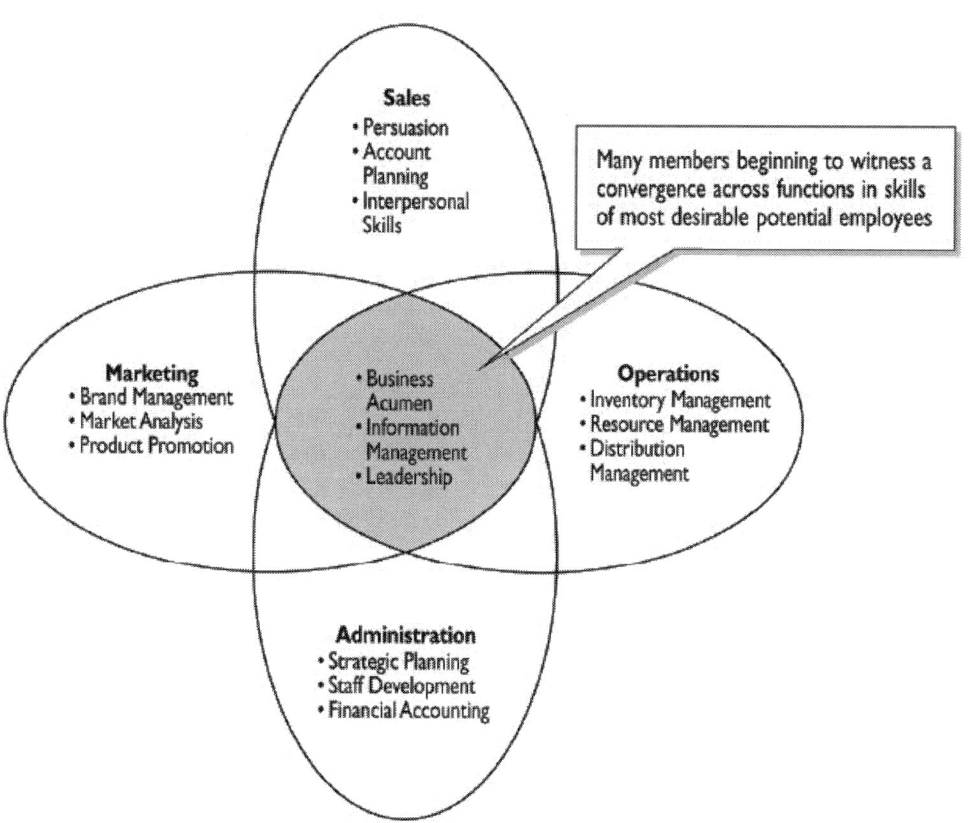

Source: CEB research.

Slide: "A New Synthesis of Employee Potential"

This slide is conceptually similar to the previous one, but adds a helpful nuance. Whereas in the previous slide the main focus lies on the area where all four ovals overlap in the middle—an area which is consequently shaded—here there are three levels of shading. Each circle is shaded, and the center overlap of all three is of course shaded the darkest; but there is also a middle shade of gray that occurs where only two circles overlap. In the previous slide, the overlap of only two ovals was not relevant, since the purpose of the slide was to show what everyone had in common. Here, however, intermediary overlap is relevant: an employee might have high Aspiration and high Ability, but not have high Engagement; and the implication is that leaders need to motivate or reward that kind of employee differently from an employee in the very center, who has all three attributes.

Each of the three circles has an accompanying textbox that describes fully what is meant by the circled term. A callout box highlights those few, High-Potential employees in the darkest middle region of the diagram who combine the ability, aspiration, and engagement to succeed in more senior, more critical positions. The presenter can move the circles closer together, making that central, overlapping region relatively large, if there is a large number of employees in that group, or slide the circles further away from the center to make that middle region rather small, as needed.

A New Synthesis of Employee Potential

The Corporate Executive Board's Model of Employee Potential

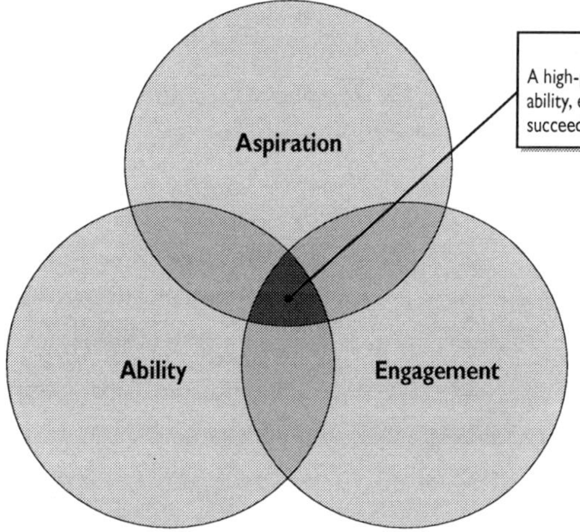

The High-Potential Employee
A high-potential employee is someone with the ability, engagement, and aspiration to rise to and succeed in more senior, more critical positions.

Ability

Ability is measured by a combination of the innate characteristics and learned skills that an employee uses to carry out his/her day-to-day work:

Learned Skills

- **Technical/functional** skills
- **Interpersonal** skills

Innate Characteristics

- **Mental/cognitive** agility
- **Emotional** intelligence

Engagement

Engagement consists of four elements:

- **Emotional Commitment**—The extent to which employees value, enjoy, and believe in their organizations
- **Rational Commitment**—The extent to which employees believe that staying with their organizations is in their self-interest
- **Discretionary Effort**—Employee willingness to go "above and beyond" the call of duty
- **Intent to Stay**—Employee desire to stay with the organization

Aspiration

Aspiration involves the extent to which an employee wants or desires the following components:

- **Prestige** and **recognition** in the organization
- **Advancement** and **influence**
- **Financial rewards**
- **Work–life balance trade-offs**
- Overall **job enjoyment**

CI017R64BL

Source: CEB 2005 High-Potential Employee Database; CEB research.

Slide: "(Profitably) Reaching the Low End"

This variation of the Relationship layout eschews the overlapping circles of a typical Venn diagram, and instead uses a shaded graphic that resembles an hourglass tipped on its side to show overlapping assets. The left side of the graphic shows the details of the company's full-service offering for a high-end brand, and the right side shows the corresponding details for the company's alternative sub-brand, which is a no-frills model. Although the details on the right and the left effectively contrast the two sub-brands, the middle of the slide—accentuated by the overlap of the left and right gray sections, which form an oval—shows the assets that the two brands share: products, research and development resources, and manufacturing.

The callout box at the bottom highlights the key to success in this scenario: the incumbent company can offer a low-end brand by sharing components of the cost structure already supporting the high-end brand.

(Profitably) Reaching the Low End

Dow Corning's No-Frills Xiameter Brand Enables a Truly Price-Seeker Position by Sharing Critical Assets with a Higher-End "Full-Service" Model

Strategic Choices	Unique to Dow Corning Brand *Full-Service Model* DOW CORNING	Shared Assets	Unique to Xiameter Brand *No-Frills Model* XIAMETER
Value Added-Services	Technical support Research support		No services offered
Distribution Model	Flexible shipping options No restrictions on size Shipped through warehouse		Standardized sizes Shipped directly from plant to customer
Product Breadth	7,000	Same (but limited) products are offered.	400
R&D Intensity	Owns research activities	Products shift from Dow Corning to Xiameter after testing.	No research required
Product Manufacturing	Flexible	Off-peak manufacturing supports Xiameter.	Predetermined manufacturing lead times
Sales Model	Telephone, fax, EDI, E-mail, post		Fully automated Web portal
Sales Support	Included in pricing	Incumbent advantage through shared components of cost structure	$250 extra charge for phone/fax/e-mail communication
Pricing	Competitive market prices		Average price below Dow Corning's price

Source: http://www.hoovers.com; Gary, Loren, "Dow Corning's Push for Organic Growth," *Strategy & Innovation* (December 2004); Kumar, Nirmalya, "Strategies to Fight Low-Cost Rivals," *Harvard Business Review* (December 2006): 104–112; "Online Business Model Energizes Company, Provides Customer Choices," *Chemical Week* (2007); CEB research.

CSB18MMM5H

CHAPTER 39: "SCREENING ALTERNATIVES" LAYOUT

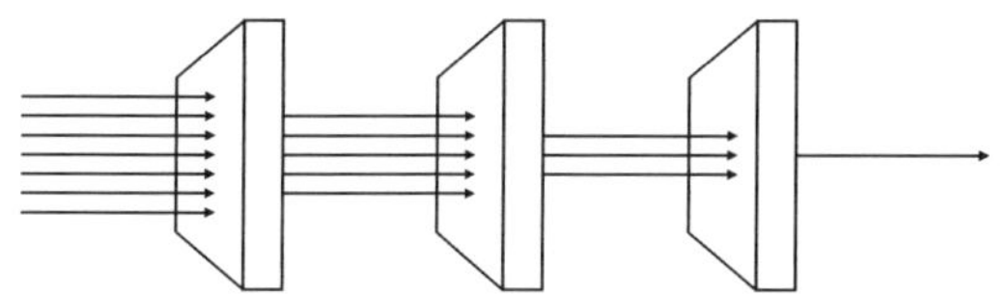

The purpose of the Screening Alternatives framework is to show how a number of items—such as prospects, product ideas, or solutions to problems—pass through a series of screens, with some items being filtered out at each stage of screening, and others proceeding through to the next stage.

There are many ways to draw Screening Alternatives. The generic form shows screens with arrows in between them. Other versions omit the arrows; and some even omit the screens, communicating the filtering effect with the image of a funnel, or by showing (visually or numerically) a process flowing from left to right in which item quantity decreases.

How to draw the "Screening Alternatives" Layout

Charteo

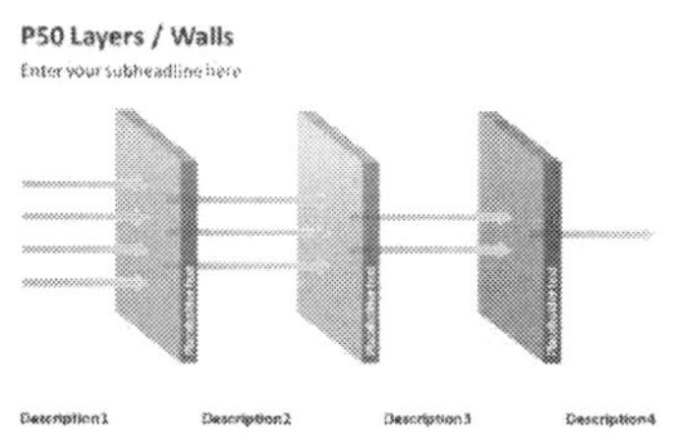

www.Charteo.com
Text Slides, Text Boxes, Text Box 35

SmartArt

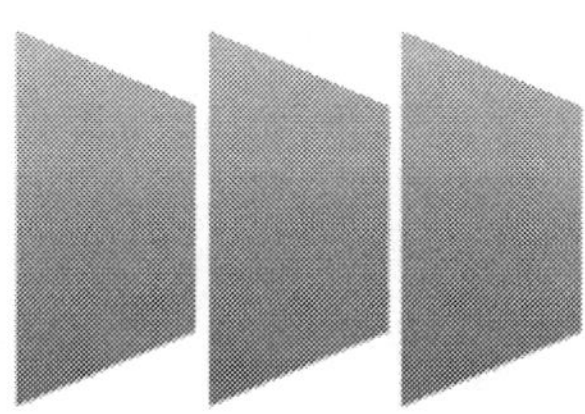

PowerPoint SmartArt
List, Group List

Slide: "Picking a Future that Fits"

This slide shows how a list of insights about world-class marketing is screened in order to create a vision for "next generation" marketing. The slide uses the image of a funnel running from left to right to convey the screening, with trap doors representing the expulsion of the items rejected at each stage.

The left side of the page lists the specific attributes that are inputs in the filtering process. Three screens are identified: frequency of occurrence, support of corporate objectives, and resource intensity. The scope of each type of screening is clarified by the type of items which that screen rejects. The "resource intensity" screen, for example, rejects items that give insufficient return on investment: they are identified below that screen's trap door (from which they "fall out"). Screen #1 rejects attributes that are mentioned infrequently by interview participants; screen #2 removes any attributes that are misaligned with company strategy.

At the end of the funnel, on the right of the page, the attributes that have made it through all the screens are combined into the future marketing vision. The combination of the final elements is reinforced by the use of a building metaphor with the integral elements representing pillars in the structure. (For more examples of this, see Metaphor chapter.)

Picking a Future That Fits

From numerous insights generated through interviews...

World-Class Marketing Attributes

From Survey Results

- Marketing Program Profitability Focus
- Leadership Development Skills
- Marketing-Influenced Strategy Development Process
- Customer Insight—Value Creation Processes
- Customer Needs-Based Targeting and Positioning Competencies
- Collaborative New Product Development Process
- Brand Management Orientation
- Integrated Marketing Communications Skills
- Integrated CRM Process
- Creativity and Innovation Skills
- e-Business Marketing Capabilities

Key Takeaways

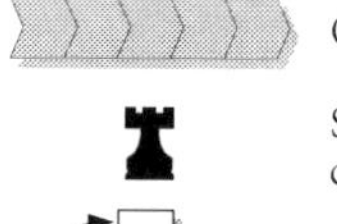

Cross-functional process focus

Strategic orientation (at both the corporate and business unit levels)

Structured career paths and mentoring programs

...screen ideas for value and applicability...

...to create a marketing vision of the future

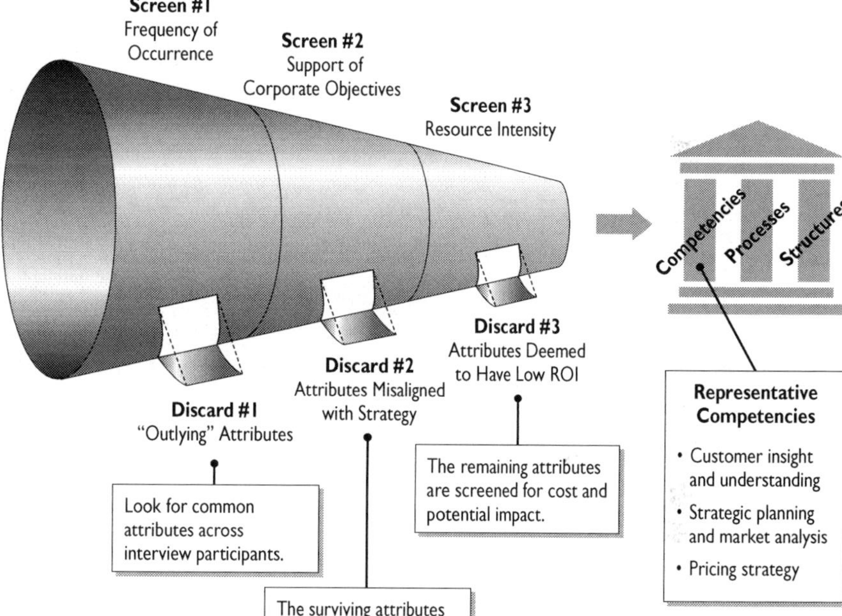

Source: CEB research.

Slide: "Analysis Along the Recruiting Funnel Reveals Strengths and Weaknesses"

In this example, the screening effect is signaled visually by the declining size of the chevrons as they move from left to right, and numerically by the declining amount of the "funnel stage value" or percent of the original inputs—the target group—that is still in the funnel at a given stage.

The purpose of the slide is to identify problems in recruiting by showing the losses from a target pool, the gray box or "base" at the left of the slide, as the applicants proceed through the stages of awareness, familiarity, consideration, and intention to apply, to the point where they decide that the particular company is their employer of choice.

This example is an interesting case, inasmuch as the screens are not "good"—they are not filtering out something undesirable. Quite the opposite: the desire here is for the "conversion rate" from one stage of recruiting to the next to be as high as possible. The company would like 100% of the attractive candidates ("the target group") to consider it their employer of choice, rather than only 4% of them. The looping arrows underneath the chevrons indicate that a certain percentage of the previous group "make it in" to the next group – and the conversion rate related to each arrow appears beneath it, in a gray oval.

Analysis Along the Recruiting Funnel Reveals Strengths and Weaknesses

Detailed funnel for employer A

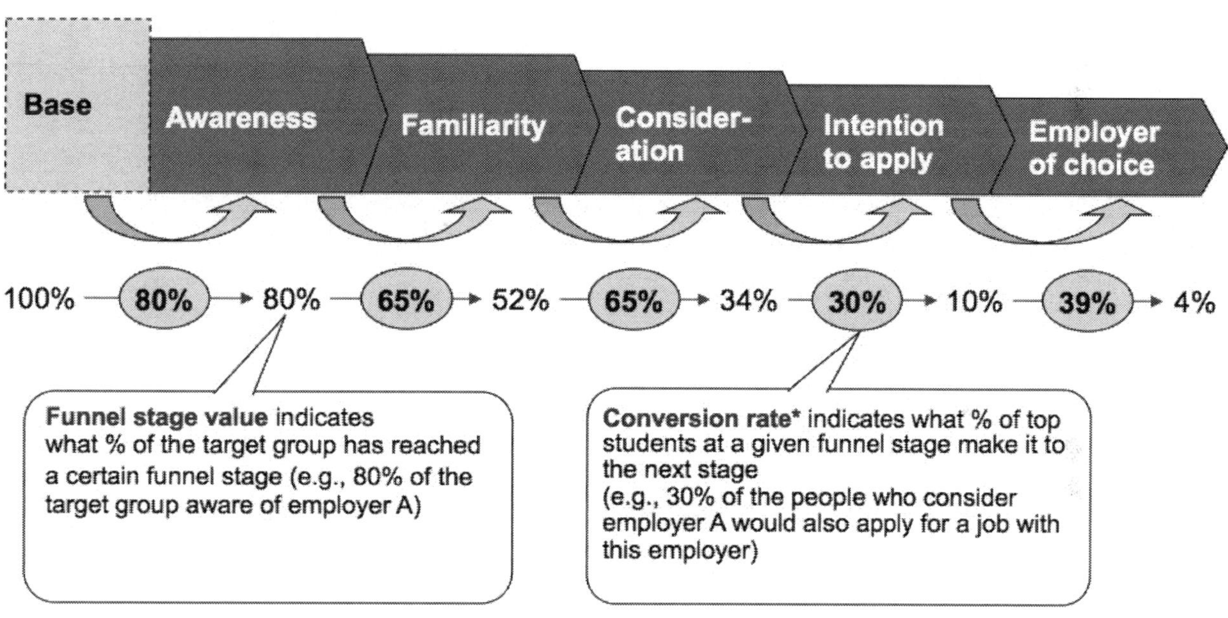

* Sometimes also referred to as "loss rate": a conversion rate of 59% is a loss rate of 41%

Slide: "Getting to What Really Matters"

This slide presents a screening process for deciding which elements to include in a solutions bundle. In typical fashion, the process flows from left to right. The initial elements are customer-stated priorities and action items that have arisen in past sales calls, combining into a total of 150 elements.

The first filter, which is drawn as a sideways sieve, screens elements for how often they are demanded and how highly their importance is rated. Only the most frequent and important elements pass through, yielding a total of 23. In the second filter, something unusual happens. Here the incoming elements are analyzed to determine how much differentiation they provide; they are augmented, divided, and added to, so more elements come out of this "filter" than went into it—a total of 30—which is physically impossible when filtering with inanimate objects, but perfectly plausible when creative human beings are involved. The filter is accordingly depicted as a funnel with the larger end facing to the right, since the process at this stage has increased the total number of elements.

In the final screen, elements are filtered according to their perceived value versus cost, and the customer's willingness to pay, leaving 17 elements at the end of the filtering process. A final stage, shown on the right of the slide, highlights that not all 17 solutions elements are of equal relevance to all customers; they are therefore combined into different subsets of solutions elements for different customer profiles.

To offer further context, the text at the bottom of the slide summarizes aspects of the three components of the filtering process: customer priorities (Filters I and II); market value (Filter III); and predictive solutions (the final stage).

Getting to What Really Matters

Screening Process Limits Solutions Elements to the Small Subset That Truly Adds Value

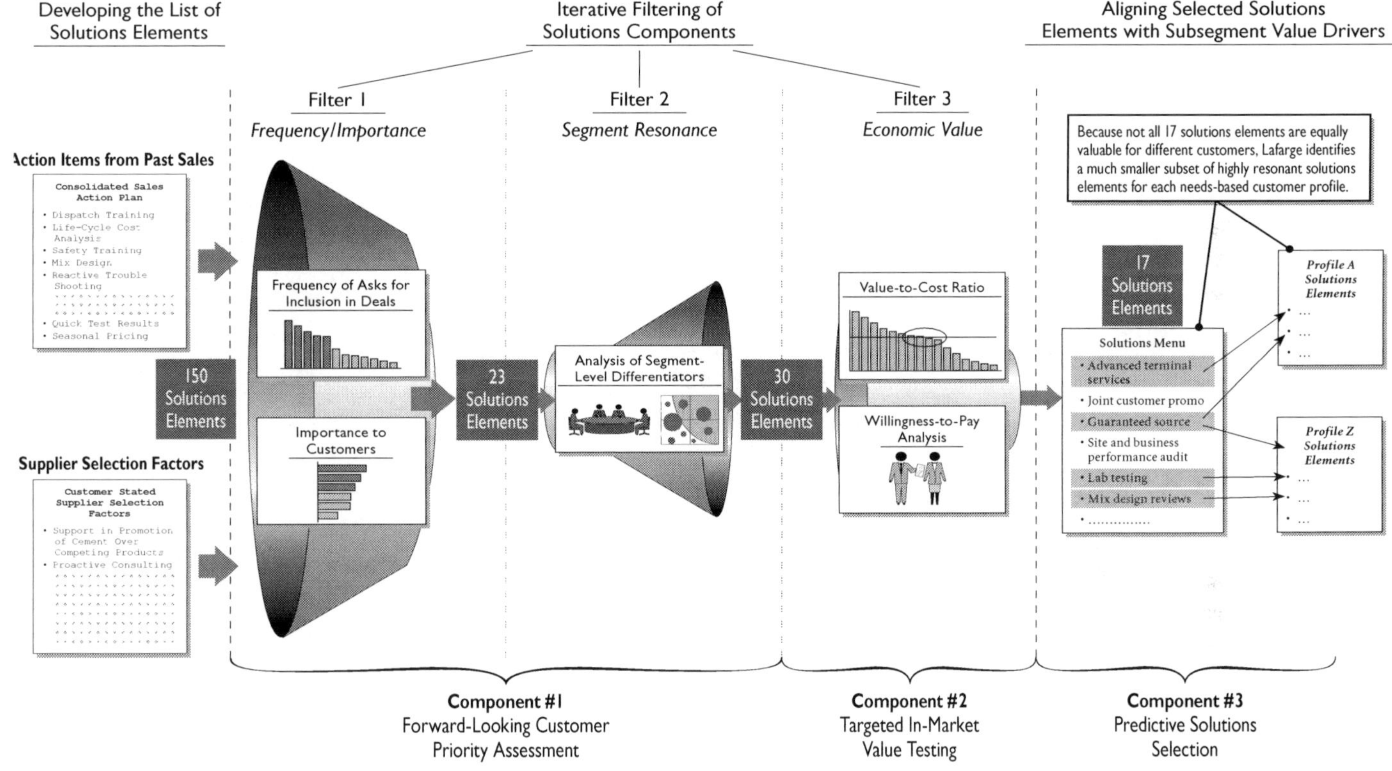

Source: CEB research.

MLC1A5CSPB

CHAPTER 40: "TENSION" LAYOUT

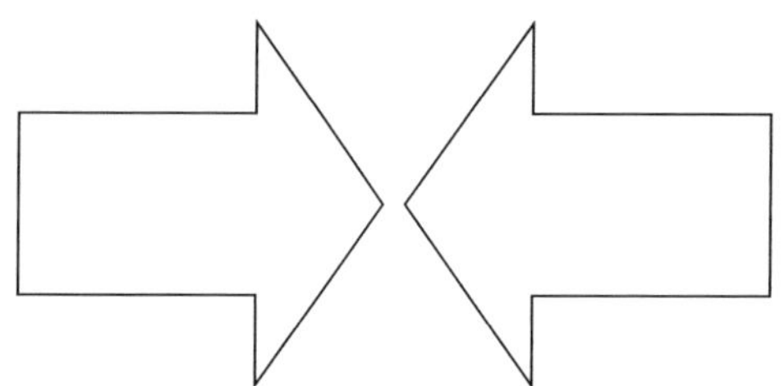

The Tension layout shows two or more forces or ideas in conflict—most often through visually depicting two arrows opposing each other. This layout can be used effectively to demonstrate that the source of a certain problem or challenge is a disagreement between competing sides.

How to draw the "Tension" Layout

Charteo

Diagrammer

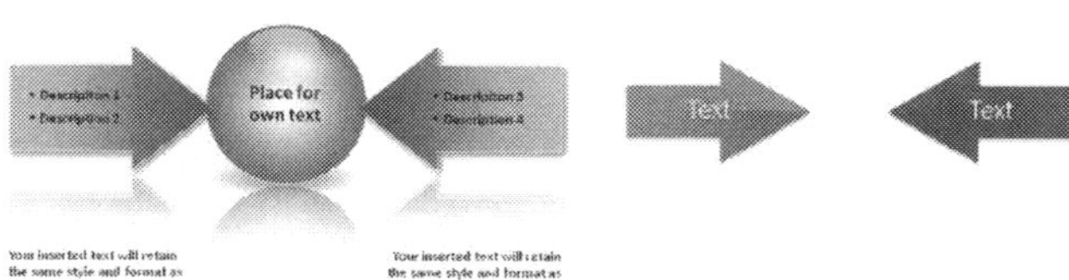

www.Charteo.com
Concept Charts, Arrows, 2D Arrows 29

www.Diagrammer.com
Flow, Merge/Divide, 2 Nodes, 2D Angled, Flow Merge and Divide 456

PowerFrameworks

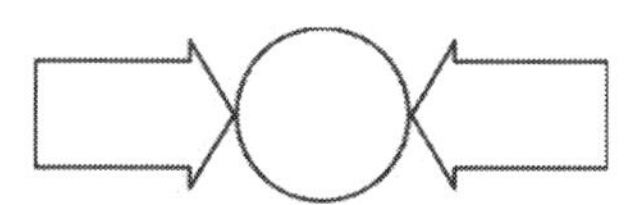

www.PowerFrameworks.com
Keyword Search "FR004", "FR004-0200"

SmartArt

PowerPoint SmartArt
Relationship, Converging Arrows

Slide: "Squeeze Play"

The Tension layout here shows two competing forces on either side of the slide, with arrows pointing from each towards the company at the center. From the left the company is feeling pressure to lower Administration and Recordkeeping Costs, while from the right it is feeling pressure to lower Investment Costs. These two forces squeeze the company's revenues, an unfortunate effect that is reinforced visually by the compression of the building at the center.

Squeeze Play

Defined Contribution Revenue Pressures

Illustrative

Pressure to Lower Administration and Recordkeeping Costs

Under significant pressure to reduce benefits costs, plan sponsors are pressuring providers to lower overall fees.

Plan Provider

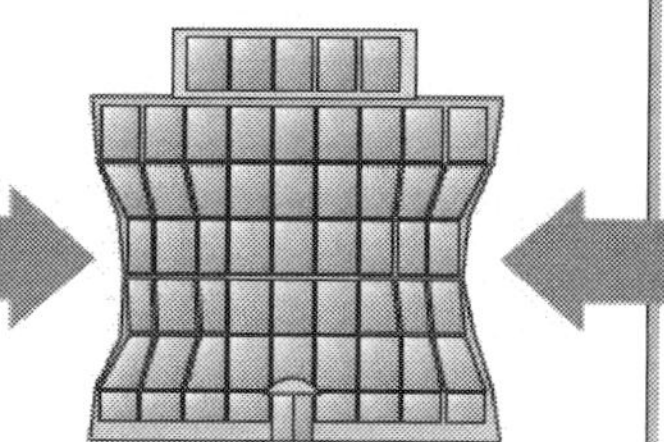

Continued pressure on providers' revenue threatens many firms' viability.

Pressure to Lower Investment Costs

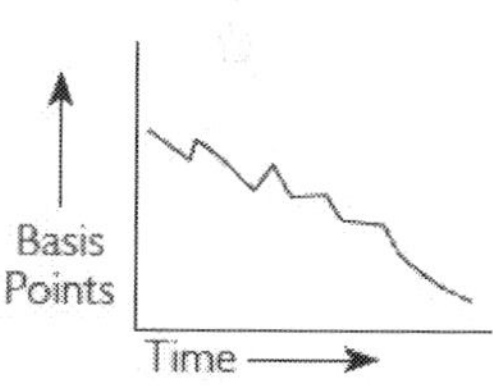

With plan participants often bearing a large portion of plan fees, plan sponsors feel an obligation to ensure that investment-related fees are "fair."

Source: Retirement Services Roundtable research.

Slide: "The New Global Research Model"

This version of the Tension layout plays on the opposition of two forces—the requirements for Global Support vs. the requirements for Local Support. The five requirements for Global Support on the left of the slide are countered by five requirements for Local Support on the right. Each requirement points an arrow to the center, where—in a neat twist on the standard layout—the demands from both sides emerge as unified imperatives in the middle. If these imperatives are not ready solutions to the tensions depicted, they at least provide vision and guidance towards the process for resolving them. The pressures here yield a positive result.

The New Global Research Model

The Characteristics of a Global Research Function Capable of Aligning Its Support with Global Requirements, While Still Meeting Those of the Local Business, Are Beginning to Emerge

Imperatives for Global Research Functions and Related Support Requirements

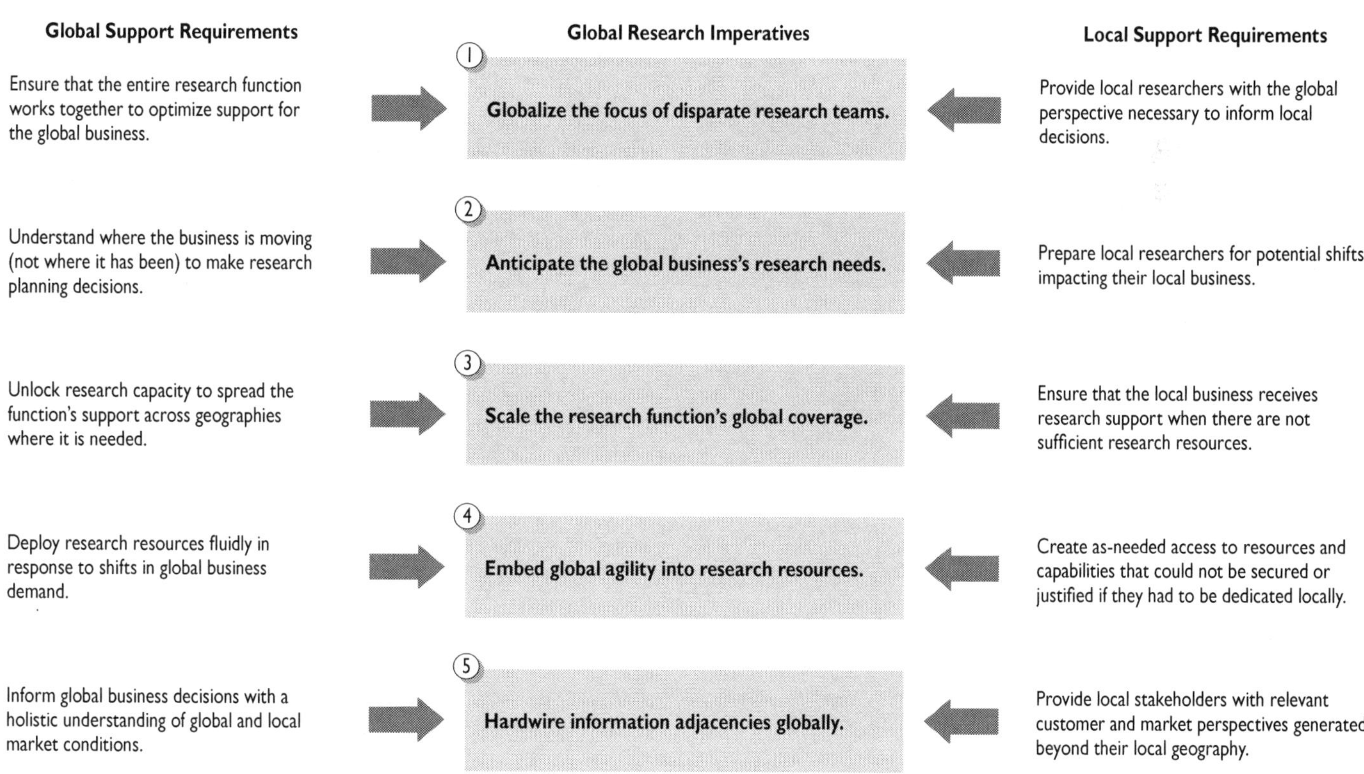

Source: CEB research.

Slide: "Breaking the Compromise"

This version of the Tension layout counters the demands of one group on the left with the realities of another group on the right. Here, instead of pointing or pushing toward the center, each side is pulling away as in a game of tug of war. This version of the layout also builds into the center of the slide the resolution of the tension, listing four specific approaches that companies can use to prove the value of their plans, thereby breaking the impasse.

Breaking the Compromise

Tension Between Sponsor Demands and Provider Economics

Illustrative

Plan Sponsor Demands

- Lower recordkeeping and administrative fees
- Less-expensive investment options

Proving Value

- Highlight service offerings and usage
- Compare plan performance to industry benchmarks
- Assists with investment selection and monitoring
- Proactively recommend plan improvements

Plan Provider Realities

- Difficult business economics
- Reliance on revenue sharing
- Limited budget for expenditures

Source: CEB research.

Slide: "Built for Another Purpose"

This version of the Tension layout shows the difficulties faced by certain research teams that are pulled in more than one direction—a pressure which here metaphorically tortures the person who is required to do too much. (While the torture analogy may be overdone, some people in the audience may also be able to commiserate.) Rather than resolving the opposing forces in the middle, as other versions of this layout do, this slide tells a story that flows from left to right. The left side shows that many efforts have been deployed to resolve the tension, while the right side's depiction of immense continuing pressure to the team indicates that the problem has yet to be solved. (For related examples of the map on the left, see the Map layout chapter.)

Built for Another Purpose

To meet emerging global support expectations, many research organizations are pursuing greater coordination across their localized operations...

Common Research Approaches to Cross-Geography Coordination

Global Research Team

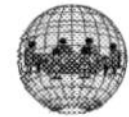

Team established in headquarters coordinates development of methodological standards.

Rolling Research Forums

Periodic research forums occur sequentially by region to stage-gate discussions on global issues.

Global Research Blogs

Research blogs allow disparate researchers to discuss broadly relevant issues in real time.

Global Research Calendar

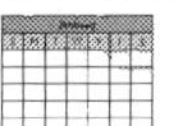

Online calendar of global research projects allows local teams to adjust their project plans accordingly.

...yet these efforts ultimately fall short because they are rooted in a localized model that prioritizes local responsibilities

Tension Resulting from Conflicting Global and Local Support Requirements

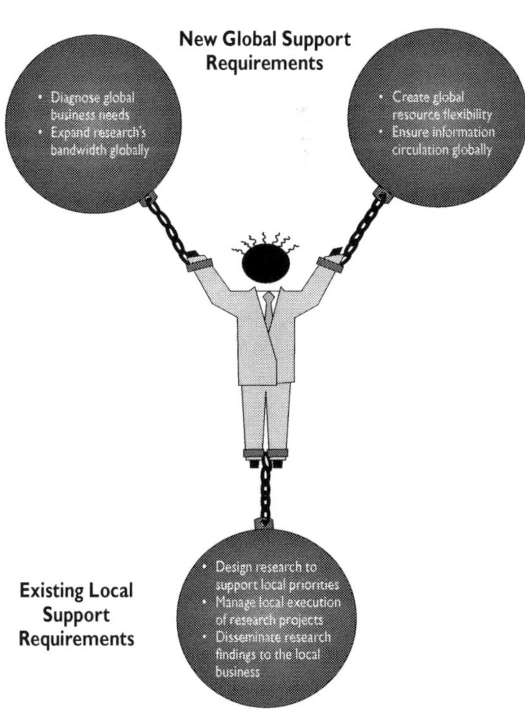

Source: CEB research.

CHAPTER 41: "TIMELINE" LAYOUT

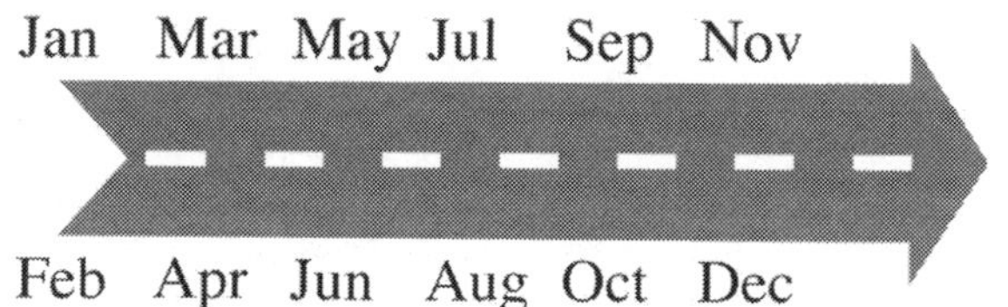

The Timeline Layout works well when the presenter needs to show a sequence of events in chronological order. The organization of the layout across time frames gives context to the information—it shows the relationship of the events to each other, as well as to any relevant historical events. The chronological order inherent to the layout provides a background structure for the audience, and also frees the presenter to embed a significant amount of detail, as the examples on the following pages show.

How to draw the "Timeline" Layout

Charteo

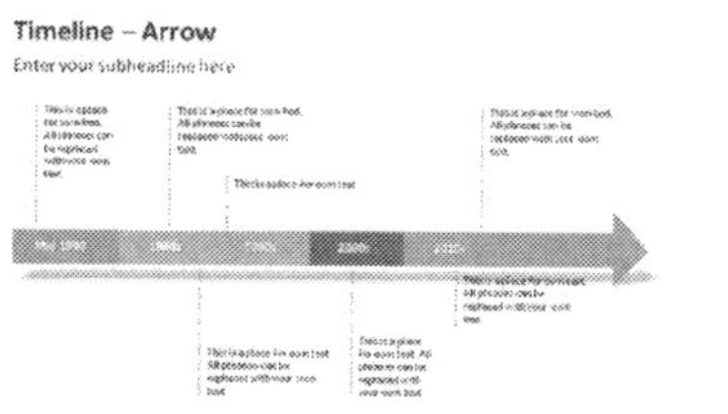

www.Charteo.com
Time/Planning, Timelines, Timeline 35

PowerFrameworks

www.PowerFrameworks.com
Keyword Search "TI002", TI002-0800

Slide: "529 Plans and Educational Savings Accounts Are Relatively Recent ..."

This Timeline packs considerable detail along the historical spectrum, highlighting eight specific events that established and developed two financial instruments for college savings. The legend in the upper right tells the audience that seven of the eight events described pertain to 529 Plans, and one to Coverdell ESAs. This timeline spans 20 years; and the broken scale between the first event in 1986 and the year 1996 represents a 10-year gap—further emphasizing a key point of the slide, namely, that (at the time the slide was presented) these instruments were relatively recent additions to the financial landscape.

529 PLANS AND EDUCATIONAL SAVINGS ACCOUNTS ARE RELATIVELY RECENT ADDITIONS TO THE FINANCIAL LANDSCAPE

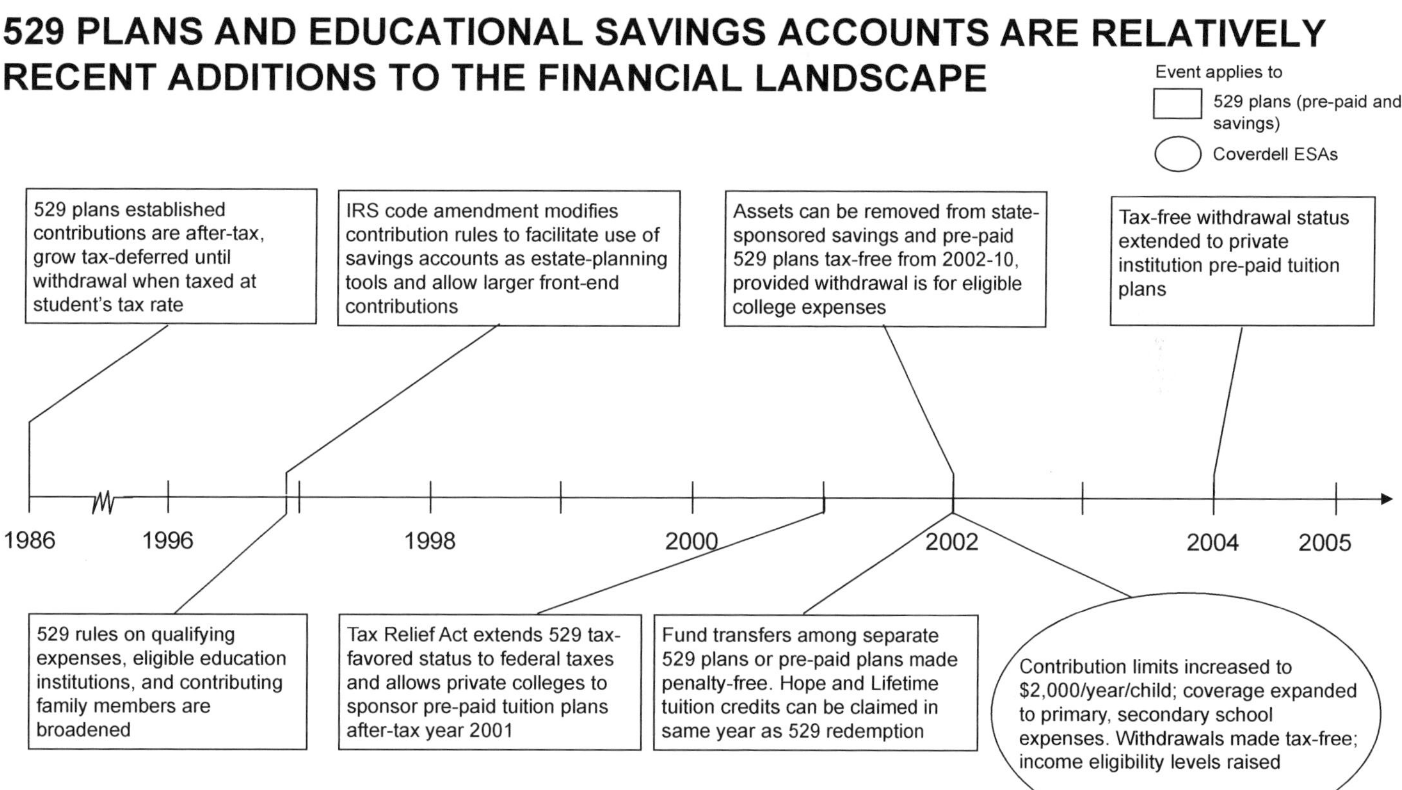

Source: Literature searches

Slide: "Be Nimble, Be Quick"

This eight-event Timeline layout provides the structure for a case study. Above the case example sits an attention-seizing chart, encouraging the audience to wonder how the company could have achieved such incredible growth so quickly. The case example answers that question by showing how in a brief five-month span a sales group was able to adjust quickly and decisively to a customer's emerging need. The drama begins on January 17, when an account manager overhears that the customer is considering outsourcing 100% of its manufacturing business. The layout separates the unfolding events into account activity (above the timeline) and the group's own actions (beneath the timeline). This clever technique allows the audience to see clearly that the events do not happen randomly over five months, but actually occur in pairs; providing the dates allows the presenter to emphasize how each of the sales group's quick actions take place between three and ten days after the corresponding customer activity.

The chart in the lower left, beneath the timeline, shows the financial results: the group not only retained at-risk revenue, but tripled business with this customer. The quotation in the lower right further illustrates the urgency conveyed by the timeline, and how important the team's intense focus was in taking advantage of the rapid change in the customer's business.

Be Nimble, Be Quick

Agile Response to Customer Change Enables Company to Retain "At-Risk" Business and Capitalize on New Opportunities

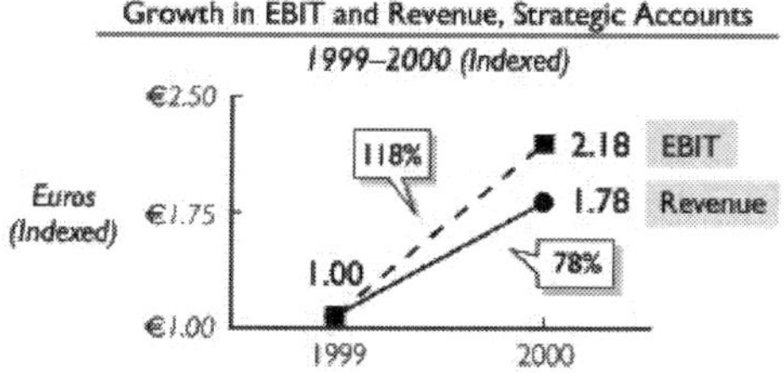

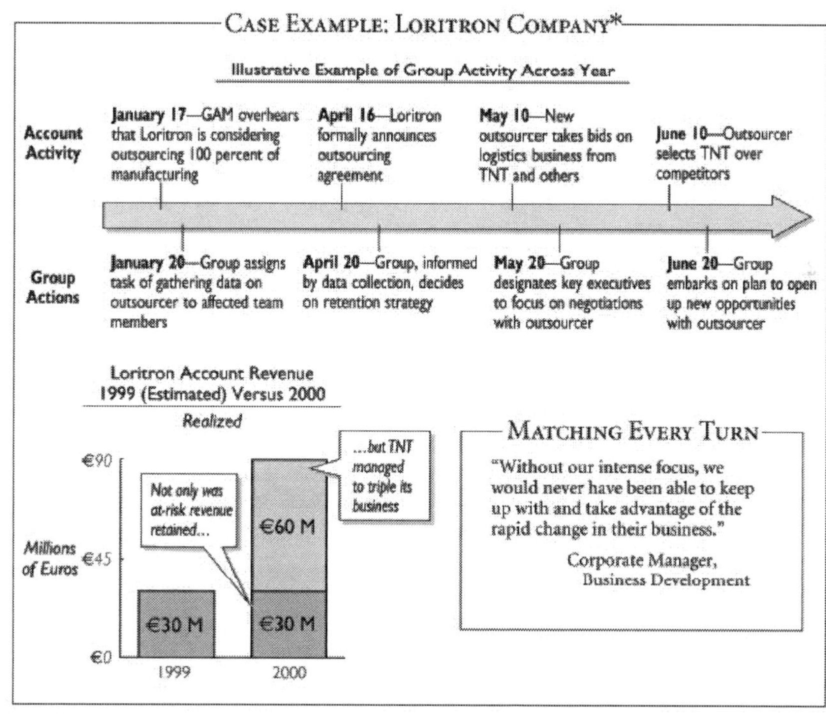

*Pseudonym

Source: CEB research.

Slide: "Competence 'Reality Check' Averts a Major Misstep"

This version of the Timeline layout adds some additional complexity of detail, while maintaining overall simplicity of design. The 21-month timeline spans four stages of a company's strategy planning assessment. Below the timeline, each stage is described through a text header, an image or graphic portraying what happened during that stage, and detailed text explaining the steps the company took. Even without reading the text, simply following the images across from left to right gives the audience the sense that the company began by having meetings, after which different people championed different competencies; this stage was followed by some rigorous analysis, finally leading the company to take one main path. The box above the timeline on the left provides a small case study as an overview; the box in the upper right gives an example of one Vice President's experience of the whole process.

Although this slide was originally laid out across two vertically oriented pages, as indicated by the gutter down the middle, it can work effectively as a single slide.

Competence "Reality Check" Averts a Major Misstep

Coble learns that its internally identified core competencies...

Case in Point: Coble Company*

- Coble Company generates $2 billion in annual revenue in the utilities industry
- In response to the 1992 National Energy Policy Act, which accelerates federal and state deregulation of utilities, Coble begins consideration of strategy alternatives including global expansion, new product and service offerings, various acquisition opportunities to be based on company core competencies
- Initial assessment of company's core competencies—achieved through brainstorming workshop—found to be gross overstatement through external benchmarking; company pulls back from expansion plans to build current capabilities

...are grossly overstated, and company retrenches to build its capabilities

Reality Check

"After we identified our core competencies, we had people carrying banners in a variety of directions, but our CEO was concerned that we might be heading off in the wrong direction. He was right. After the benchmarking study hit people's desks, we had a lot fewer banner carriers. We are no longer moving in nearly as many directions. We are spending time retrenching around a smaller set of competencies. We are investing to build competencies rather than thinking about them as an expansion tool in the near term."

Vice President, Strategic Planning
Coble Company

Four Stages of Coble's Journey to Self-Realization

1994: September October November December
1995: January February March April May June July August September October November December
1996: January February March April May

Stage 1: Fall–Winter 1994

Initial Core Competence Identification

Coble Company conducts internal assessment of core competencies; identifies six areas that are to serve as cornerstones of future strategy.

- Billing and collection
- Customer/field service
- Distribution system management

Stage 2: Early 1995

Billing and collection outsourcing

Expanded service opportunities

Utility acquisition strategies

Competing Interests

After initial core competence study completed, Coble senior managers begin building fiefdoms around competing competencies in an attempt to attract investment dollars. Potential competence-based strategies include:

- **Billing and collection outsourcing**—Coble plans to sell meter-reading, billing and collection services to local water authorities
- **Customer/field service**—Coble plans to provide physical asset management services to large industrial electricity consumers

Stage 3: Late 1995

Coble Area of Competence: Customer/Field Service

Cost Advantage (Index)

Value Advantage (Index)

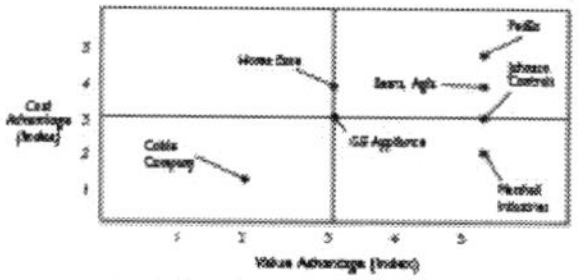

Core Competence Benchmarking Study

Concerned about perceived competencies, Coble's CEO commissions benchmarking study. Findings reveal Coble trails other companies in several of its internally identified competence areas.

Stage 4: 1996

Core Competence Development Strategies

Retrenchment

Coble cancels plans to start billing and collection outsourcing service and physical asset management business, focuses instead on building current capabilities.

Source: Corporate Leadership Council, *Heart of the Enterprise: Core Competencies and the Renaissance of the Large Corporation*, Washington: The Advisory Board Company, 1996, pp.132–133.

* Pseudonym.

CHAPTER 42: "TIP OF THE ICEBERG" LAYOUT

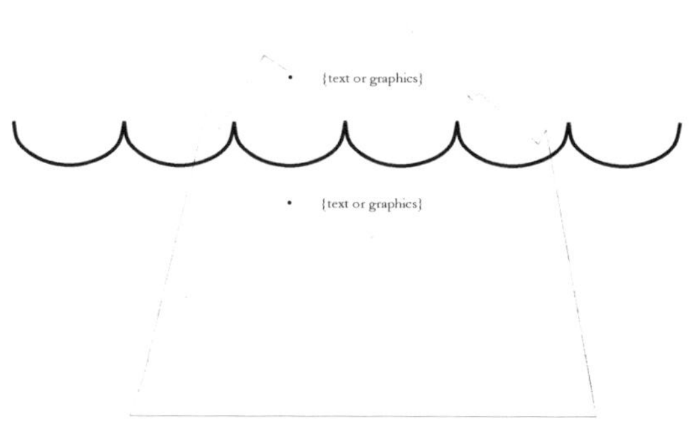

The Tip of the Iceberg layout helps the presenter to show a situation where that which is visible and apparent to the audience turns out to be only a small portion of the overall story, like the 9% of an iceberg that protrudes above the waterline. As in nature, it is oftentimes the rest of the picture, the part hidden under the surface, that presents the bigger problem—or opportunity. This layout enables the presenter to help the audience recognize a complex situation as having more about it than meets the eye.

How to draw the "Tip of the Iceberg" Layout

Charteo

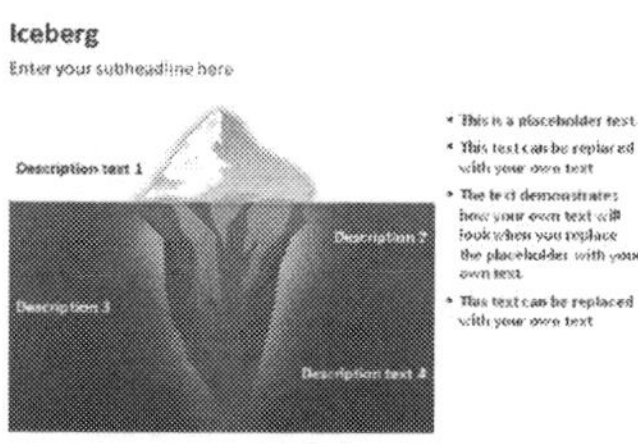

www.Charteo.com
Graphics and Metaphors, Iceberg, Iceberg 1

Slide: "Just the Tip of the Iceberg"

This Tip of the Iceberg layout separates the obvious, traditionally recognized sources of poor quality (above the waterline) from the "hidden" nontraditional sources of poor quality (below the water line). The depiction of the iceberg on the left is reflected on the right by relevant examples of familiar impediments to quality—which account for only 5-10% of revenue—and examples of nontraditional impediments to quality—which account for 10-20% of revenue. This layout reveals to the audience that what they see as the causes of poor quality have only a relatively small effect on the overall situation.

Just the Tip of the Iceberg

The Nontraditional Sources of Poor Quality That Lie Under the Surface Can Be a Larger Drain on the Organization Than More Traditional Sources

The Sources of Poor Quality

Illustrative

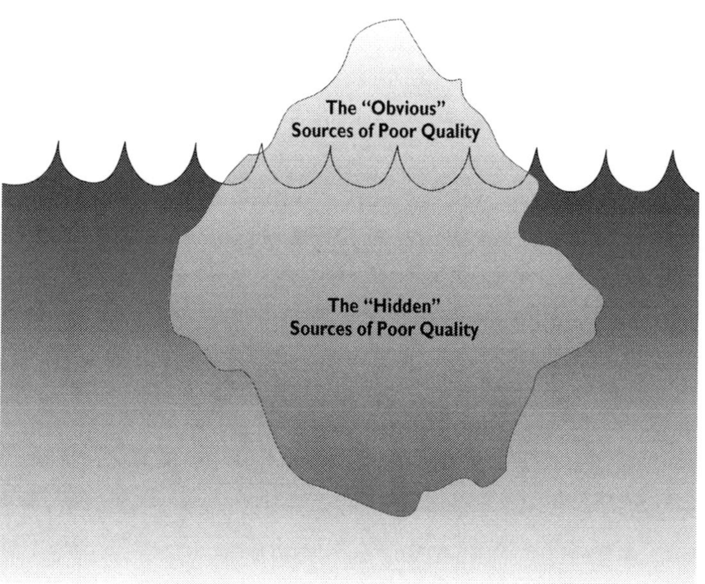

Traditional Sources of Poor Quality (5–10% of Revenue)

Relevant Examples

Scrap

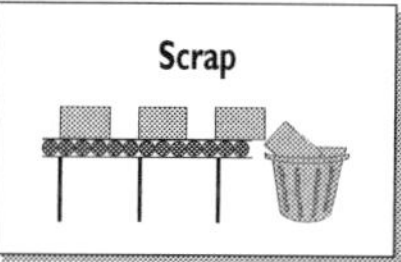

Rework

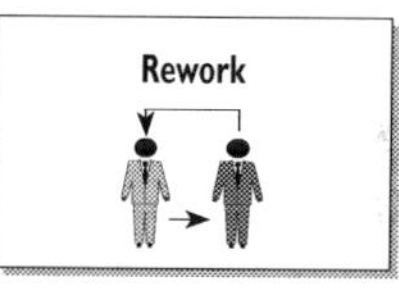

Warranty Costs

Nontraditional Sources of Poor Quality (10–20% of Revenue)

Relevant Examples

Lost Sales

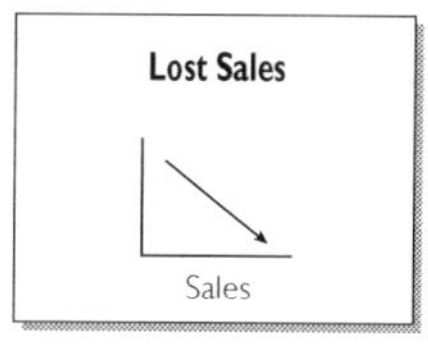

Legal Fees

Inefficient Product Development Processes

Source: CEB research.

QEB18HTPUH

Slide: "Depth Charge"

In this variation of the Tip of the Iceberg layout, the aquatic theme is taken to warmer waters, where the contrast is between the limited vision of a snorkeler and the deeper vision of a scuba diver. When it comes to recognizing solutions opportunities, what is visible "from the surface" is not enough. An account manager has a tactical focus on transactions and the current relationship; but there is a need to go deeper for the customer's benefit, into the waters that are home to emerging industry trends and new-to-world solutions—which is the work of "forward-deployed segment experts" (see the box in the lower right). This dichotomy is delineated by the checked boxes near the water's surface that show what the account manager does, while the unchecked boxes in deeper water show the unmet opportunities involving work that the account manager cannot do—thus revealing the need to change—to use this new kind of expert.

On the right side of the slide, the icons and text detail the key areas where the company has been investing to achieve that change: realigning territories, upskilling the sales force, and aligning around industry verticals. The gray-back box in the lower right contains text (reinforced by the chevrons and runner icon) explaining how the new forward-deployed segment experts impact the company. Callout boxes at the upper left of the slide help to accentuate the differences between the two approaches, and the quotation at the bottom left offers anecdotal testimony about the previous approach's limitations.

Depth Charge

With solutions opportunity recognition requiring much deeper segment knowledge than is viable for most sellers...

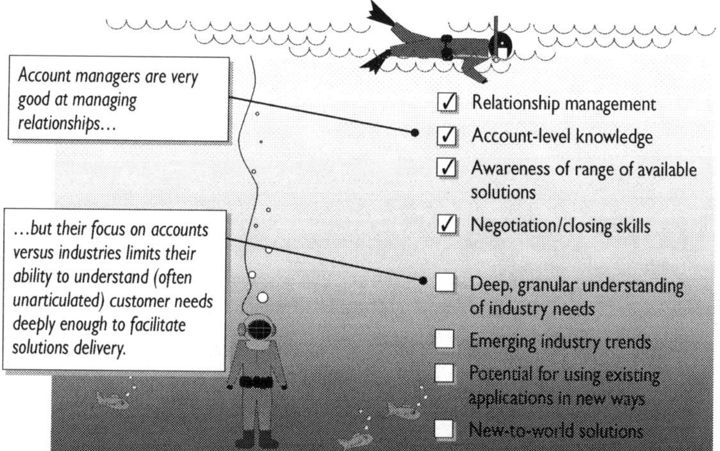

...Company A makes big investments to gain a deeper understanding of customer needs

Key Areas of Investment

Territory Realignment
Reps given smaller, more clearly defined pool of accounts to manage and/or pursue

Sales Force Upskilling
Entire sales force reviewed and recertified

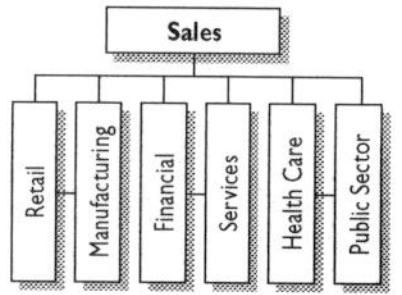

Industry Verticals
Sales force realigned around six business segments and Global 1,000 accounts

Forward-Deployed Segment Experts
Pre-sales specialist carved out of Marketing and Sales to boost needs sensing and leverage market-level insights at the segment level

Reaching Their Limits

"Printers were getting commoditized fast. Five to ten percent faster printing wasn't going to convince someone to shift their installed base to a new system. We had to really improve our ability to create demand by getting deeper into customer segments."

Vice President and General Manager
North American Printing Solutions
and Services

Source: CEB research.

Looking for Additional Resources to Make Your Presentations More Effective?

⇨ **Tools and Templates:** on our Blog – Find more tools and templates to help you save time while designing your next presentation: http://extremepresentation.typepad.com/blog/tools.html. Also find practical guidance on current topics as well as ongoing discussions.

⇨ **The Workshop:** Bring the Extreme Presentation™ Method to your organization: Find out more about how your team can learn to design presentations that are impactful, elegant, and *brief*.

⇨ **The Website:** Visit www.ExtremePresentation.com to learn more about the workshop and the Extreme Presentation™ Method, and to practice designing your next presentation.

Other books in the Extreme Presentation™ Series:

#1: *Advanced Presentations by Design: Creating Communication That Drives Action*
Practical and evidence-based, this book shows you how to turn your content into a story, and how to design persuasive yet comprehensible visual layouts.

#2: *The Presentation: A Story about Communicating Effectively Using Very Few Slides*
Follow the story of David who, with the help of his boss, Barbara and the enigmatic Professor Edwards, is preparing for the most important presentation of his life.

? What other resources would be helpful? Please let us know what your needs are, and if there are other layouts you would like to see examples of, or if you have some helpful layouts that you would like to include in the next edition of the *Encyclopedia of Slide Layouts*.